to the memory of my mother, Maria R. Gutierrez,

and

my stepfather, Ignacio Gutierrez.

— WORLD WAR II TO THE JET AGE —

PILOTO

Migrant Worker to Jet Pilot

Lt. Col. Henry Cervantes, USAF (Ret.)

Piloto: Migrant Worker to Jet Pilot
© 2002 by Henry Cervantes
Original paperback edition published in 2003 by Hellgate Press
Republished in paperback in 2007 by the author Henry Cervantes

All rights reserved. No part of this publication may be reproduced or used in any form or by any means, graphic, electronic, or mechanical, including photocopying, recording, or information storage and retrieval systems without permission of the author.

Editor: Harley Patrick
Book designer & compositor: Constance C. Dickinson
Cover designer: Mark Hannah

Library of Congress Cataloging-in-Publication Data

Cervantes, Henry, 1923–
    Piloto : migrant worker to jet pilot / Henry Cervantes. — 2st ed.
    p. cm.
    ISBN 1-55571-628-8 (paper)
    1. Cervantes, Henry, 1923– 2. United States. Air Force—Officers—Biography.
    3. World War, 1939–1945—Personal narratives, American.
    4. Bomber pilots—United States—Biography.
    5. Test pilots—United States—Biography.
    6. World War, 1939–1945—Aerial operations, American.
    7. World War, 1939–1945—Campaigns—Europe. I. Title.

UG626.2.C4 A3 2002
358.4'0092—dc21
[B]
    2002068738

Printed in the United States of America
First edition   10 9 8 7 6 5 4

 Printed on recycled paper when available.

Contents

Preface   vii
Acknowledgments   ix

Chapter 1: *La Familia* (1913–1941)   1
        (Here They Come)
    Mexican!

Chapter 2: I Wanted Wings (1942–1944)   31
    We Don't Take Filipinos, Spics, or Niggers
    I Won't Serve Him, He's Indian
    Graduation Day
    So Long, It's Been Good to Know You

Chapter 3: Aerial Combat (1945)   57
    The "Bloody 100th" Bomb Group
    Jet! Jet! Jet! What's That? I Dunno
    Rammed at 15,000 Feet
    Louisa, the Bar Room Contortionist

Chapter 4: Post War Years (1945–1950)   109
    America, Land of the Big PX
    "This Flag Is Presented to You"
    "Given That You're Mexican …"

Chapter 4: Post War Years (1945–1950) continued
    The Great Schnozzola
    Wolf, the Pilot's Seeing-Eye Dog
    General Ike and Mrs. Eisenhower

Chapter 5: The Jet Age (1951–1955)   137
    Wichita, Air Capital of the World
    Fiesta Time!
    Jet Jockey
    Chuck Yeager
    Thelma
    Flight Testing
    Julie
    California, Here I Come

Chapter 6: Strategic Air Command (1956–1960)   179
    Peace Is Our Profession
    Never Ride Shotgun for a Hothead
    Going Hollywood
    Help Keep Greenland Green
    Miss Kansas

Chapter 7: The B-58 Hustler (1961–1965)   215
    Willing, Able, Ready
    Greased Lightning!
    Cats and Dogs
            (Health, Money, Love)
    Shove in Your Clutch

Epilogue   251

Preface

Author Franz Kafka once wrote, "A book is the ax for the frozen sea within us." True to his words, for a variety of reasons, parts of this book have been painful for me to write.

My original intent was to model my account on books written by other wartime pilots. However, after many stops and starts, it became obvious that try as I might, my book would not parallel theirs. My virtual singularity as a Mexican-American in the close-knit fraternity of Caucasian military pilots was inescapable. To give my story heart, I would have to reveal parts of my life that were so private that I had lied and cheated rather than discuss them with strangers. Two topics were the most troubling to overcome.

The son of proud, albeit destitute parents, my Latino culture has always been entrenched in the deepest part of me. Yet, like many children born in the United States of mixed Spanish and Indian blood, constant badgering during my early childhood implanted identity issues in my mind. I eventually learned to cope with them outwardly. However, when subjected to bigotry, regardless of how veiled it might have been, sensitive antennas picked it up, and I became even more reserved and judgmental about discussing my ancestral roots with all but close friends.

Second, my vision of becoming a pilot began as an eight-year old when I sat in the cockpit of an ancient crop-duster in Fresno, California. Twelve years later, I learned that mastering a military plane is difficult. Many hours were required to absorb a whole constellation of new facts and skills. Pilot training called for excellent perception, decision-making, and psychomotor abilities, with intellectual capacity being the most important of the human characteristics involved. Suffice to say that people below average in this respect are not normally found in the ranks of aviators. Accordingly, the day silver wings were pinned on my chest was the proudest moment of my life. For the insignia certified that I was among the best mental and physical specimens this nation had to offer.

Paradoxically, while flying school instructors were honing these attributes in us, unbeknownst to me my mother—like her father before her—was descending into the vice-like grip of Schizophrenia, a chronic and disabling brain disease. Within days of my becoming an officer, she was committed to a mental hospital. Thus began a dilemma that would haunt me during my entire military career. Ensuring that her family history of mental illness would not taint my professional career or private life became a secret obsession. Whatever was necessary, I did it. Moreover, my first inclination was to not reveal it in these pages either. However, until I went into the military, Mother had been my Rock of Gibraltar. To idealize my life without acknowledging that she had shaped it would be impossible. Consequently, discussing her illness and its impact on me was the most emotionally difficult facet of this work. Still and all, it would have been deceptive and self-serving had I not and this required me to become more personal than I ever imagined.

In fact, nothing I have written was intended to hurt anyone. On the contrary, I hope that my story and insights will serve as a road map to help young men and women, particularly those from distressed backgrounds, realize the American dream as I have known it. To them I say that the uniform of a United States Air Force pilot will enable you to enjoy pride of skill, instant social acceptance, and a life that few have experienced. My journey from looking like a rag pile discarded in a vegetable field to streaking across the skies in a swept-wing speedster took place years ago. Yet, the passage of time has not diminished the relevance of the events recounted here. If, like me, you are interested in unparalleled adventure, I invite you to follow my footsteps. If I could succeed back in a time when racial intolerance was a way of life, civil rights laws were a decade away, and affirmative action had yet to be conceived, you can do it today. You will never regret it.

In many ways, my small slice of personal history is a harbinger of a much broader story—that of an exploding Latino population, the overwhelming numbers of which are of Mexican descent. The handwriting is on the wall and the facts are staggering: The Latino segment of the population is growing six times faster than the overall populace; 39 percent are twenty or younger. Even more noteworthy, it is reliably estimated that by the year 2020, they will account for more than 16 percent of the population and by 2050, the figure will hit an astounding 24.5 percent. This change means that Latinos are poised to play a pivotal role in reshaping every aspect of our societal, governmental, and economic infrastructures, as we know them today.

It also means that in the future Latinos will play a much more important role in America's military forces, and both must prepare now for that eventuality. The services must do a better job of recruiting Latinos; Latinos must ready themselves mentally and physically to pursue the rewarding military careers that await.

Finally, this book is about a journey that is currently nearing the end of its eighth decade. Surely, I am not the only Latino who has trod this path, but there aren't many others. I thank God that it was accessible to me.

Acknowledgments

This book would not have been possible without the help and guidance of several talented people and I would like to acknowledge their contributions. Among those whose encouragement and advice were essential are my editor and publicist at Hellgate Press, Harley B. Patrick; retired Air Force Colonel Walter J. Boyne, former director of the National Air and Space Museum in Washington and author of 38 books, the most recent of which is *Aces in Command*; James S. Corum Ph.D., author of 12 books, his latest being *The Luftwaffe*; and Harry H. Crosby Ph.D., author of *A Wing and A Prayer*.

For the opportunity to check my memories and records: *The Los Angeles Times*, the Los Angeles City Library, USAF Biography of Leaders, The Mighty Eighth Air Force Heritage Center, The Hundredth Bomb Group Association, and William E. Thompson Colonel USAF (Retired). Also, in the United Kingdom I express appreciation to Richard Le Strange, the Committee of the Hundredth Bomb Group Memorial Museum, and to Adrian Weir, author of *The Last Flight of The Luftwaffe*. In Germany, special thanks to former Luftwaffe *Rammkommando Elbe* pilot Werner Zell.

I want to reaffirm my gratitude and affection for the crew I flew with during World War II. Some are no longer with us but I remain close to their families and will until the end. Were it not for Joe Carl Martin, Antonio Picone, William Dudecz, Norman E. Larsen, Ralph E. Spada, Celeste Rossi,

Alfred E. Collins, Matthew Schipper, and Paul R. Gerling, I would not be here. I also have a special place in my heart for former Master Sergeant Alfred T. Conte, the crew chief of our B-17 bomber *E-Z Goin'*, as well as a host of other largely unheralded aircraft maintenance specialists with whom I served. To all of you a heartfelt thank you.

I also owe a debt of gratitude to the many men and women whose bits of history aided to the content of this book. In some instances I have changed their names or where prudent have changed the names of other individuals who should also remain anonymous. I trust my readers will understand.

In particular I would like to acknowledge the fine officers who were willing to overlook my weaknesses in order to bring out the best in me: Lt. Gen. James W. Wilson, Maj. Gen. Warren R. Carter, Maj. Gen. Henry "Russ" Spicer and Maj. Gen. William R. Hayes—thank you one and all. If I have misrepresented any incident, conversation, or impression of you, please attribute it to my faulty memory and the cobwebs of time.

Lastly I want to express my love for my siblings Gus, Evelyn, Aurora, Jennie, Ruben, and Steve. They also had full, productive, successful careers and I am enormously proud of each of them and their families. Collectively, we are the product of parents who invested their hearts, ethics, and hard labor in their children, and not one of us ever failed them.

Chapter 1

La Familia
(1913–1941)

Ay Vienen (Here They Come)

Dawn, May 1, 1965

Drivers had begun to turn off their lights when I turned west from the main gate at Offutt Air Force Base, Nebraska. As the Omaha skyline faded in the rearview mirror, Father Flanagan's Boys Town came into view. During four years at the nearby Strategic Air Command Headquarters, I often stopped to watch the boys go about their chores. I empathized with them for like me, most were from disadvantaged homes and like them, my mother also dwelled in an institution. I stopped again, perhaps for the last time, and after a minute of reflection my eyes closed, and I said a prayer: "Lord, You made my dreams come true. Help them to dream the impossible. Open doors for them as you did me. And please watch over my mother, I love her so much. I know that I've asked for a lot in the past but please grant me this prayer." The Thunderbird's rear wheels spun gravel, and I returned to the white line that would lead me back to "the coast" where it all began. The blacktop stretched straight to the horizon and with endless miles of wheat gliding by, I became introspective.

Only yesterday, a general had handed me a retirement order along with a medal "For being instrumental in making the B-58, the first supersonic bomber in the Strategic Air Command (SAC)." Given that during twenty-two years in the Air Force I only met one Latino military pilot, it might have been as meaningful if he had cited me "For being one of the few

Mexican-Americans to ever fly a SAC aircraft." Nonetheless, my career as a "rare bird" had ended. Today was start of a new life, and my mind backtracked to where it all began.

Guanajuato, Mexico, is an old colonial town that seems to have been dumped into a narrow river gorge. Rich in history, the area is noted for its remnants of grand haciendas, once majestic buildings, subterranean roadways, and cobblestone streets that twist and turn up steep mountainsides. Its grandiose past is owed to a nearby mine, once renown as the richest silver lode in the world, La Valenciana.

Afternoon, August 1913
Slat-ribbed mongrels yawned, stretched, and fell asleep in the street on a hot, listless summer day. Pottery and serape vendors at El Mercado struggled to stay awake. Even the ghoulish gapes and vacant stares of *las momias* (the mummies) at *el panteon* (the cemetery) seemed to be silent pleas for air.

Crack! "*Ay vienen.*" (They are coming.) From an outpost high above the town, a rifle shot and a lookout's familiar cry reverberated between the canyon walls. At the height of the Mexican Revolution, the warning had but one meaning, another band of revolutionaries, rogues, or outlaws had been spotted galloping hell-bent toward the ravine.

The townspeople reacted quickly. Those who could locked their doors. Shops closed, vendors disappeared, and everyone scurried off to long-established hiding places.

Near the stately Teatro Juarez, Juan Guevara's daughter Mariquita "Quita" was in the family-owned silver shop dusting displays, rearranging doo-dads and anxiously waiting siesta-time. The gorgeous teenager planned to close a bit early and sashay by the saddle shop next door in hopes of seeing the owner's son, the handsome Francisco "Pancho" Rincon. The Guevara and Rincon families were friends and she had grown up with Pancho and his younger siblings Enrique and Maria. But things were different now. Almost overnight, Quita had blossomed into a sensuous young woman and she felt quirky inside whenever nineteen-year-old Pancho passed by astride his horse, looking magnificent in his white shirt and tight-fitting pants.

Gumaro, the Rincon family patriarch, was descended from Don Antonio Rincon de Guemes, a Spaniard who came to Mexico in 1535. Tall and fragile, Gumaro had an aquiline face, a shock of prematurely gray hair, a luxurious goatee, and wore pince-nez eyeglasses. His father, who was also a saddle-maker, had taught him well. For whether a saddle was to be of simple natural leather or heavily embossed with silver, Gumaro crafted them one at a time, each designed precisely for the rider's needs.

A decade earlier, the highbred and well-educated Gumaro had caused tongues to wag by marrying Hermelinda "Linda" Arvides, a five-foot tall firebrand from nearby San Luis Potosi. Their love had outlasted many of their critics, yet for more years than she cared to remember, his birthday present to her had been a fancy leather wallet. Awl in hand, he sat at his workbench skillfully etching intricate designs into this year's gift. Being more creative than observant, it mattered little to him that the billfold would soon join thirteen mates of assorted sizes and shapes in a special section of Linda's *petaquilla* (trunk).

Fearful, Quita shuttered the store and as she hurried by Gumaro's open doorway, looked in and shouted, "*Apurese Señor Rincon, que ay vienen.*" (Hurry, they are coming.) But Gumaro knew that the ore smelters along the river were the prime targets; he had time, he continued working.

Suddenly the clatter of hooves on cobblestones shattered his concentration. He ran to bar the door but failed by a step. Several bandits stormed in, threatened him, and demanded that three saddles be ready by the following day. Gumaro pleaded that it was an impossible task and offered one that he had on hand. But the leader was in no mood to listen and growled, "*Si no estan listas, me la vas a pagar.*" (If they are not ready, you will pay for it.)

Gumaro only knew one way to do the job and when the gang returned and found a half-made saddle, they brutally pistol-whipped Gumaro to the floor. The shop fronted the family's large adobe and upon hearing the commotion, Linda rushed to the scene. Bloodied and battered, Gumaro lay in a fetal position with a bandit's pistol pointed at his head. Linda threw herself at the leader's feet, showered his boots with kisses, and begged for her husband's life. Without so much as a glance, the thug callously kicked her aside and joined his friends rummaging through the shop's tools and equipment. Seething with hatred, Linda stood protectively over her husband and waited for expected death. The leader returned and apparently impressed by Linda's fearlessness, patted her on the head and in a fatherly voice said, "*Ya no me frieges mijita; llevatelo.*" (Don't bother me my child; take him). She helped him home and the men continued to loot the shop.

Spurred by the assault, Gumaro and Linda made plans to join the scores of Mexicans streaming toward *El Norte* (the north; United States). Enrique,

Pancho's younger brother, learned English while working as a paymaster for an American mining company in the area. Therefore, to avoid an uncertain arrival, Enrique went ahead to establish a beachhead in El Paso, Texas. At Quita's insistence, the Guevara's joined the Rincon family and together they prepared for a stealthy departure. Trusted employees helped them secret valuables in and about the houses, and the remainder was buried in the central patios for later retrieval. In return for guarding them, the employees were awarded deeds to the properties. When Enrique signaled that all was ready, the families only took what would not invite unwarranted attention and rode atop a railway boxcar to the border. Many arriving refugees were detained at Fort Bliss. Enrique's bilingual ability, however, spared them that indignity and they worked in the post laundry washing soldiers' uniforms.

Once they were settled, Enrique and Pancho returned to Guanajuato for the first of several trips to retrieve the hidden reserves. They found the employees gone and armed strangers camped in the houses and shops. Back in El Paso, the news was accepted with typical stoicism. Destitute, the clan set out on the well-worn California trail that Mexican immigrants had followed for years. They harvested whatever needed picking in the Imperial Valley, Bakersfield, Porterville, and Selma, then settled in Malaga, a hamlet south of Fresno. Pancho and Quita married and soon thereafter, Enrique married Quita's teenage half-sister, Concha (Chita) Galvan. Enrique and Chita differed so greatly in age that not even a thirty-year marriage and five children could break her habit of addressing Enrique as "Señor Rincon," or referring to him as "El Señor Rincon."

The Rincon brothers were sharp and became *contratistas* (farm labor contractors) while their sister, Maria, worked as a nanny for the Hildreth's, a family noted in the San Joaquin Valley for having invented the pruning shear. Along the way, Maria fell in love with a tall, handsome, thirty-year-old railroad worker, Pedro Cervantes. Proud and unbending, her family made it clear that they disliked the unschooled *traquero* (railroad worker), but Maria was as headstrong as they were rigid. Deeply ingrained with the need to respect decorum, she waited until she turned twenty-one, then eloped. The couple married in Sacramento, honeymooned aboard a ferryboat to San Francisco, and returned to their first home: Santa Fe Boxcar #5, Calwa Siding, Fresno, California. The bumpy marriage produced two sons, Gustavo Ulysses (Gus) born in February 1922 and me, Enrique Rincon, born in October 1923. Within days of my birth, my father, Pedro, found himself facing two angry brothers who accused Pedro of assaulting

Maria, my mother. My uncles knocked Pedro about, and Maria fled to the family home from where she filed for divorce. That same year, *Abuelito* (Grandfather) Gumaro died in the Stockton State Mental Hospital. The cause of death: general paralysis of the insane.

Mother had a stereotypical Mexican mother's appearance—attractive symmetrical features and long black hair that she wore in a *chongo* (chignon). Her penmanship was beautiful; straight up and down, with no unnecessary beginning strokes and connected, stick-like capital Ls with no loops or flourishes. The kind of script that a graphologist might describe as characterizing a person predominantly ruled by the head not the heart, independent, practical, energetic, and intelligent. She was all business but I do not fault her for that, poverty is a full-time occupation. Although she did not make over us as much as we might have liked, we never lacked attention; we got plenty of that.

Mother, Maria R. Gutierrez

"Mama, where is our father?" my brother Gus would ask. (I can still hear the insistence in his voice.)

"Why do you want to know *mijo* (my child)?"

"Because. What was his name?"

"Pedro."

"What was he like?"

"You don't need to know that now."

"Doesn't he like us?"

"That's not important because I'm here and I love you."

"Where is he?"

"I don't know."

"Will he come to see us?"

"I don't think so."

Our feelings of rejection continued into adulthood and although she never spoke against him, Mother never gave in to our persistent questions.

In later years, older cousins Connie (Consuelo) and Angie (Amparo) Rincon judged that Gus inherited Pedro's physical characteristics: tall, light-skinned, bold, mischievous, and handsome even as a little boy. I favored Mother. Picture a shy Mexican *muchachito* (little boy) nicknamed Chacho, average height, *moreno* (tanned) skin, and thick, black every-which-way hair that Mother governed with gobs of Vaseline.

1926, Delano, California. Henry and his older brother Gus. Their front yard was a corn patch

I idolized Gus. He began the first grade at the nearby grammar school and I wandered into his classroom so often that the teacher assigned me the desk behind his.

Some scoff at the idea that a four-year-old can learn anything in that setting, but I did. The teacher taught me to say, "We do not speak Spanish here," and "My name is not Enrique, it's Henry." I can still see the hurt in Mother's eyes when Gus ran to tell her that I had a new name. She defiantly pursed her lips then sighed, nodded, and remained silent. The following year I was officially admitted into the first grade.

Whatever divorce may be today, back then it was scandalous. Ashamed to admit that I did not have a dad, I claimed that Pedro was a border guard killed by smugglers. Many years would pass before I realized that Mexicans are far less critical of divorce than they are of *La Migra* (the INS).

Mother began seeing a truck driver who worked for my uncles. He was good to Gus and me, so in 1929, shortly after her divorce became final, Mother again defied her family's wishes that she not marry "beneath her class" and wed Ignacio Gutierrez. Nicknamed "Nacho," my stepfather stood about 5'8" with black wavy hair, deep brown eyes, and bronze skin.

Together with a well-muscled body and a slightly lanterned jaw that angled a bit, he resembled a middleweight fighter that had taken one-too-many right crosses.

Perhaps due to his lack of formal education, Mother made it clear that we were her children. For although he was a kind, gentle, courteous man, she never instructed us to call him father, he never held us or corrected us, and we never sought his arms for comfort. We eventually grew to love him dearly, but the emotional distance Mother created between us at the start remained fixed until the end. Nevertheless, I considered him my father, not my stepfather.

Stepfather, Ignacio Gutierrez

We lived in a tiny white cottage across the street from Columbia Grammar School in Fresno. While there, a schoolmate gave me a homemade model airplane that I treasured. Despite my begging, Mother refused to buy me an imitation-leather pilot's helmet and goggles to go with it; such extravagance was out of the question. To soothe my disappointment she often took us to nearby Chandler Airport to watch open-seated biplanes practice landings and take-offs. The sound of the grumbling engines and spinning propellers was music to my ears.

In February 1930, my sister Evelyn was born. That summer, we joined Tio (Uncle) Pancho's labor gang, and like gypsies, we chased crops throughout the area, Madera, Mendota, Clovis, and Firebaugh. Father picked and Mother cooked for the crew. We lived in a dirt-floored tent. A hole in the ground with a grate over it served as a stove, a kerosene lamp provided illumination, and our mattresses were scratchy burlap sacks stuffed with cornhusks. At bedtime, burning horse manure shooed away the mosquitoes and we were lulled to sleep by *braceros* (migrant workers) sitting around a campfire singing sad songs like "La Paloma," "Las Golondrinas," and "El Rancho Grande."

When the last raisin tray had been stacked, we returned to Fresno where a large agribusiness, Mosesian Brothers, hired Father to care for an apricot orchard that eventually gave way to the Internal Revenue Service's area office. Nearby, the brothers Paul and Mose, owned a weathered old farmhouse that we shared with a young Armenian couple. A high-pressure Jacuzzi water pump and a weed-choked irrigation ditch defined our front yard. An outhouse, a pigsty, and a swayback barn marked the far reaches of the back area, and the entire expanse served as a parking lot for yellow farm machinery of all types. The Mosesian's were fighting rooster aficionados and we maintained a flock of their fiercest veterans, carefully restored to life to sire new generations. The cocks preened, strutted, and fought territorial battles among themselves. But if one attacked us, as they were prone to do, the family had a Sunday chicken dinner, scars and all.

Our parents took a team approach to raising us. Father trained us to farm and care for livestock, and Mother taught us to cook, wash, iron, and mend our clothes. She had a standard answer when we complained about the never-ending chores, "I'm not going to be here to take care of you forever. You have to learn to take care of yourselves. I don't want you to ever go hungry or have to ask anyone for money." Farm kids learn about the finality of death at an early age and I winced whenever she said it. I was a mama's boy and the thought of losing her was more than I could bear.

One frosty January morning, we awakened to the sound of strumming guitars and singing. Father opened the door and the house filled with family friends all shivery and calling for Mother. Gus and I were mystified when told that it was her birthday, it had not occurred to us that parents had them. But that hardly compared to our surprise when Father borrowed a guitar and expertly tuned it. In fine voice, he led everyone in serenading Mother with the Mexican birthday song, "Las Mananitas":

Estas son las mananitas que cantaba El Rey David
A las muchachas bonitas,
Y por ser tu dia de santo,
Te las cantamos a ti.
Dispierta mi amor, dispierta.
Mira que ya amanesio.
Pajaritos estan cantando,
Y la luna se metio.

Teary-eyed, Mother lovingly scolded him for having withheld knowledge of his musical talent. Then someone turned off the lights and Tia

(Aunt) Chita brought in a huge snow-white cake sprinkled with shredded coconut and topped with big red strawberries and flickering candles. Mother gathered us to her side, made a silent wish, and did the honors. Outside of pictures, Gus and I had never seen a real cake before and we oohed and aahed over its splendor. Why it was so big that it barely fit on the lid of a twenty-five pound can of lard! We reminisced about the size of that cake for years. Then we saw a like-size can in a Mexican grocery store. It downsized our image of the pastry but not the memory of the only time I can recall seeing Mother enjoying her birthday.

Mexican!

The word was spat at us with all the hate and scorn only kids can muster. No one had to tell us we were different, we just couldn't understand why they were so mad about it.

Unable to speak English, Mother taught us to read and write in Spanish. If she heard us speak Spanglish, she would scold, "Stop that, others will consider you ignorant." Her reproaches still ring in my ears. She bought a *Collier's World Atlas* and a dictionary "on time" and required that we read our homework aloud. If we stumbled over a word, out came the book and together we would sound it out. Her often-faulty tutoring continued even after Gus bragged that I had won a fight at school.

We often mispronounced words as she had taught us to say them and a chubby little bully named Billy Campbell led the mimicking. Billy had a ski nose that required him to frequently readjust his coke-bottle glasses in order to see and he teased me once too often. Furious because he was mocking my mother, I waited for the perfect moment then jumped him. Holding on to him like a leach, I snatched the bifocals and flung them away. It wasn't much of a fight; without the glasses poor Billy was probably certifiably blind.

Our arrivals at school were the most painful. All the students but Gus and I aligned their colorful metal lunch boxes in a long row on an anteroom shelf, while we did our best to conceal our flat packets of bean tacos under the discards and lost-and-founds at the far end of the shelf. Mother wrapped the tacos in old issues of the *La Opinion* newspaper and the beans emitted a hearty fragrance that we enjoyed. Our classmates, however, claimed that the stink made their ham sandwiches taste funny and it became habit to find the packets on the floor or in a wastebasket. Too proud to complain or endure their smirks, we switched to hiding the lunches in the branches of the apricot grove we crossed on our way to school. That didn't work either; by the time we hiked back for lunch, black ants had infested the beans and we often went hungry. Later when the trees were leafless, the parcels stood out like abandoned bird's nests and Father found them. He brought a few home once and questioned us; then never did again.

My third grade teacher, Miss Neilmeyer, was not into social promotions. Nearing the end of the year she kept me after-school and said, "Henry, because you speak Spanish at home is no excuse for you not to learn to speak English. You will repeat the third grade until you do." My tears were mostly make-believe, for I loved her honey-blond beauty and gentle hands that guided me whenever I failed to understand. Her wise decision had another payoff that did not become apparent to me until I went out for sports in high school. She enabled me to compete against athletes my own age. On my eighth birthday, Miss Neilmeyer gave me a card on which she had written:

"Dream your dreams upon a star.
Dream them high and dream them far.
For the dreams we dream in youth,
Make us what we are."

I thought it had to do with flying—"high, stars, far"—and that led me to read Charles Lindbergh's book, *We*. The few parts of it that I understood conveyed visions of fluffy white clouds, golden sunsets, and comets streaking across starry skies. I yearned to leave the world behind and go there to escape the shame I felt for being Mexican, brown, and poor.

In June 1931, Mother returned from the hospital with our second baby sister, Aurora. A few days later, she took the baby in her arms and me by the hand, and went around the house to the Armenian couple's kitchen window. I was so proud, she wanted me to help her show-off the baby. But I was about to learn that when hurt, Mother was not one to shed a tear and stalk off with a quivering lip. Mother called the woman to the window and accused her of promoting an affair with Father. The screaming match began in English and quickly deteriorated into an incomprehensible babble as each reverted to her native tongue. Terrified by Mother's fury, I pulled free, ran home, and hid, hoping the nightmare would go away.

Despite all, the ranch was an ideal place for two youngsters to grow up. Free, unafraid, and barefoot nine months of the year, we roamed the serene countryside for miles. We learned to swim, build forts, fricassee pollywogs, and dissect everything that crept, crawled, slithered, or flew.

One season to the next, our surroundings provided new adventures on the two-mile hike to school. In winter, when dense tule fog blanketed the valley, we imagined the fruit trees were an impenetrable jungle and we were Tarzans bravely trekking to rescue Jane. Above the gray muffled silence, the skies were clogged with migrating geese and to us their raucous honking came from spooky animals stalking us from behind every tree. Undaunted, we bravely beat our chests and challenged our foes with flimsy versions of Tarzan's fierce cry of defiance: "Aahahhhheeeeeaaaah."

Overnight, spring transformed the orchard from shades of brown to long canopies of pink and white blossoms where we strolled from carpet to carpet of fragrant flower petals. Across the street we blazed a path through a broad field of green waist-high alfalfa, where blizzards of yellow butterflies swirled, cottontail bunnies scurried, brilliant ring-necked pheasants sprang into flight when we neared, and distant quails softly cooed their mating calls. On our return, we would swim among the pollywogs in a ditch then lay down on the macadam road in a futile effort to dry our overalls before we got home. We seldom succeeded in hiding our misdeeds from Mother, but it hardly bothered me, for as a matter of course she usually lectured Gus while I smirked at him from behind her back. This not withstanding, I secretly worried that because he was older, lighter, and better looking, that she loved him more than me. Whether perceived or real, this pushed me to prove that I was just as good.

The Mexican National Symphony Orchestra came to town one year and Mother insisted that Gus and I be exposed to this rare exhibition of Mexican culture. Father worked every day, so Mother obtained tickets for her, Gus, and me to attend a Saturday afternoon performance. God only knows where she got the money or the courage, but on the only time I ever saw Mother drive a car, she wobbled us to the city auditorium at five miles an hour. The performance was a lavish blend of orchestral music, mariachi singers, and shimmering costumed dancers twirling and swinging through intricate routines. At the first strains of the grand finale, Mother nudged us to our feet, fiercely gripped us to her, and joined the crowd in singing the stirring Mexican National Anthem, "Mexicanos al grito de Guerra . . ." (Mexicans, a call to arms . . .). Gus complained, "*Duele mamà*" (It hurts). Rather than acknowledge him, she held us tighter and continued singing. I looked up to add my objection but her voice was so compelling that all I could do was gaze at her, knowing that I had the best mother in the whole world.

* *. * *

Only the calendar differentiated between summer and fall until the day that a distant metallic sound broke the unending silence. Flat and slow, the noise sounded like the bell atop Fresno Chinatown's Buddhist Temple when it summoned the faithful to a funeral: Clonk; Clonk; Clonk. Far up the road, undulating like a dirty wool blanket on a waterbed, came an unending flock of sheep. An emaciated donkey draped with a cow bell led the snail-paced parade, while two blue-eyed sheep dogs kept the laggards moving and two Basque herders brought up the rear. Sheep scattered in all directions as we raced through the advancing horde to throw ourselves at the two flush-faced men. They held us up to eye-level, admired how much we had grown since the last time, and gave us crushing *abrazos* (embraces). Then, with windmilling arms and guttural half-shouts of *coño* (hell, damn) this and *coño* that, they scolded us for having disturbed the sheep.

Weeks earlier, the band had left the foothill pastures of the Sierra Nevada to winter in an alfalfa field behind a barn. The men settled the flock, gave the dogs, Dempsey and Tunney, whistled commands to patrol the perimeter, and maliciously ordered us to stable Silver. (The donkey wasn't really named Silver. We called him that after cowboy star Buck Jones' horse.) Silver remained rigidly immobile until he realized that we intended to remove the bell. He resisted in every way possible until defeated, then woeful braying let half the world know of his unhappiness.

The herders' menu never varied. Our mouths watered as they wolfed down huge juicy roasted mutton sandwiches made with hot crusty homemade bread spiced with raw onions and garlic cloves. Every other bite was washed down with a long swig of dark red wine from a *bota* (wineskin). Swinging the *bota* on to a forearm, they would squeeze a stream high into the air, unerringly hitting their mouths. We were mesmerized by their skill and one evening, after a lot of begging, they allowed us one try apiece. Mother spotted our stained overalls the moment we walked in the door. Her *palote* (tortilla-making rolling pin) clattered to the floor as she grasped an ear in each hand and quick-stepped us out the door. Upon seeing three fast-approaching dust-plumes, the men quickly retreated into their tent. But Mother didn't miss a beat. She released us, slapped the tent-flap aside, and held a short one-sided conference. She marched out, again taking us each by the ear, and danced us home. Once there, she made us bathe, brush our teeth, and gargle with salt-water, then sent us to bed without dinner.

We learned the facts of life during lambing season. Far into the night, Gus and I held kerosene lanterns high while Father and the herders helped ewes through difficult births. Occasionally one would deliver a stillborn baby. The men immediately skinned the dead lamb, reversed the hide, clipped it loosely around an orphan, and offered it to a lamb-less mother. After sniffing at it a bit, the mother would often allow the foundling to suckle her.

Hundreds of cuddly lambs perfumed with the delicate scent of new babies became our playmates. One of our games had to do with giving our little sisters "horsy rides" on the backs of adult sheep. The lambs gazed at us like puzzled spectators until it dawned on them that we were having fun. Then they'd rush forward, rub against our legs like cats, nuzzle us, and plaintively bleat, "I'm next, I'm next." Wherever we went, they pranced around us like jumping jacks with springs under their hooves. If we tried to

September 1927, Fresno, California. Gus (far left) and Henry (2nd from right) rode the church float in the Mexican Independence Day parade

chase them home, they stubbornly stood their ground and acted dumb. But let Dempsey or Tunney come by and they scattered like teenagers caught out after curfew.

By spring, the lambs had gained the strength necessary for the trek back to the foothills. The tent came down, the bleating became more discordant, the lambs stayed by their mothers, and Silver shook his bell mightily to announce his return to leadership. As wave upon wave of sheep passed by the house, the herders would stop to exchange hugs all around and give us an orphaned lamb. Then off they went with the dogs dashing about, the lambs bounding like four-legged pogo sticks and the flock methodically paving the roadway with clumps of black jellybeans. Dejected by our loss, we sat on the baking asphalt road and watched them until two squiggly mirage-like figures blended into distant heat waves. With that, tranquil solitude returned broken only by the sound of buzzing horse flies and gnats.

* * * *

One Christmas, *Tios* Pancho and Enrique brought their families over for the holidays. Typically, they arrived unannounced. Since Mother was their baby sister and Father had once worked for them, they treated us in a paternalistic manner. Although Father was at work, they took it upon themselves to slaughter a huge pig we kept in the sty. Lacking a gun, they got two axes. Round and round the pen they went, chasing the shrieking animal and swinging the axes like baseball bats. The pig died with its intestine partially out of its body, one eyeball popped out, and his head split open. They then turned their attention to one of our pet sheep. I was afraid of them but Gus let out a howl that brought Mother running. She chilled that idea so they prevailed upon the herders to donate a sheep. They hung the ewe by her hind legs, put a white enamel wash pan underneath her head, and slit her throat. Crimson blood gushed into the pan with every heartbeat then slowly ebbed to gurgling froth and stopped. She never uttered a sound, just stared at us with huge frightened eyes until she died. Her silence shocked us more than the death of the pig. Our nightmares kept Mother at our side most of the night and the next morning Gus lashed out at our uncles for having killed the pig. We tearfully refused to eat breakfast and with that the let's-have-a-party atmosphere went downhill. They left and took the meat with them.

For us, Christmas revolved around our annual visit to Gottschalk's Department Store on Tulare Street, whose window displays were visible from a block away. Pressing our noses against the cold glass, we would admire the ornaments, wave back at the fat little mechanical Santa, wonder aloud what the brightly wrapped boxes held, and point out gleaming red toys to Mother as a choo-choo train continuously circled an oval track. On our way home, we crouched on the rear floor of our old Model T Ford for warmth and loudly debated why Santa Claus did not seem to know where we lived.

* * * *

Early on, the family uncharacteristically converted from Catholicism and became charter members of Fresno's First Mexican Baptist Church. Mother insisted on strict adherence to the church rules. This meant no swearing, smoking, drinking, dancing, or makeup; in our house, the code was law.

Pastor Edwardo Madrigal was our spiritual leader. A barrel-chested bear of a man, he had a rumbling voice, bushy black hair, and a fierce handlebar mustache. Regardless of the weather, he always wore a black suit, white shirt, and black tie, vest included. On Sunday evening during the hot summer months, the congregation assembled in front of the church on E Street. Promptly at 6:30 P.M., he would launch into the Spanish version of "Onward Christian Soldiers" and, waving a museum-size black leather bound Bible, move through the crowd urging everyone to join in. We repeatedly sang the hymn with increasing fervor until he had us ready to take on the lions in the Coliseum. At that point, thrusting the Bible into the air like a saber, he would resolutely lead us to a nearby pool hall frequented by *braceros* (farmworkers) in the area to work the summer crops. We would form a semi-circle in the litter-strewn gutter as he sounded a tinny "A" on a little harmonica, opening the service with a hymn. He followed the hymn with a prolonged prayer that included shouted invitations for the men inside to "leave this den of iniquity, come out, and be saved." If not devoutly Catholic, the *braceros* were almost to a man from Catholic families, and we were as welcome as the bubonic plague. The loiterers and drunks laughed at us, whistled at the women, questioned the men's manhood, and generally did their best to be obnoxious. Undaunted, the pastor would turn the other cheek with a hymn, then invite converts to come forward and deliver their heartfelt testimonials.

With the preliminaries aside, the reverend took center stage. He opened the coat wide, hitched up his pants so high that you could see everything he had, then dramatically plopped the Good Book open with a flourish. He took a couple of swipes to re-align any errant mustache hairs, stuck his tongue way out, wet his thumb, and turned the pages individually as if flipping tortillas. This was our cue to lean forward from behind Mother's skirt and count the scraps of paper sticking out from the Bible. They marked the verses he intended to quote and were reliable indicators of the time remaining for us to be under her eagle eye.

Gus could make me laugh whenever he wished and delighted in doing so when she had us on a short leash. Every time a bookmark fluttered away, Gus would roll his eyes and heave a huge sigh of relief. Then while I struggled to contain my laughter and hip-hopped to keep from peeing in my pants, Gus would tug at Mother's skirt and point at me. But Mother knew everything and usually applied her three-strike disciplinary system. The first offense drew a glare and the second a discreetly pinched ear. Capitol punishment was a finger-wagging lecture once we got home.

1931, Fresno, California. Henry's sisters, Evelyn (L) and Aurora (R), with a pet lamb

Mother admired the reverend deeply and refused to believe that he had been caught in the baptismal doing something bad with one of the choir girls. Even we kids knew about it. But mindful of her concern, we listened to the level of piety in the undertone of "Amens" and "Hallelujahs" that backed the pastor's stem-winders. Anyone who did not sound convincing, we reported to Mother as a possible source of the rumor that the pastor was more interested in saving his job than sinners.

At the onset of the service, the more courteous *braceros* acted penitent-like school kids trapped under a teacher's tirade. But contrition melts quickly in stifling heat and by the time the last "Amen" rolled around most of them, even the converts, were back in the bar sucking *cervezas* (beers). Few were ever persuaded to convert and fewer yet donated when a tambourine was passed among them for contributions. Disappointed again, the congregation straggled back to the church looking like lost nomads seeking an oasis in the night. Whatever penalty Father paid to miss those embarrassing evenings was worth it.

Tragically, Pastor Madrigal died in a car accident and his wake was held at the church. Mother wanted to be among the first to pay her respects, so we arrived early. A mustachioed mortician wheeled in the coffin and everyone was so impatient to see the remains that he opened the lid before he had finished assembling the permanent base. Gus and I were staring at our first corpse when the fellow said, "*Muy bien, firme*," (Very well, it's firm) and gave the foundation a final reassuring shake. The body shuddered and we bolted for the door. Father stayed with us in the car while Mother attended the service. He didn't impress me as being too upset about missing the service. Poor Pastor Madrigal replaced *La Llorona* (weeping woman) as our *El Cucuy* (bogeyman).

* * * *

One evening, we returned from church to find a bug-splattered cropduster plane parked in the cropped alfalfa field. Gus and I ran to it and pushed and pulled at things until Gus became bored and left. Once alone, I undid a canvas cover on the open cockpit and climbed in. An hour later Mother came for me and I shouted, "*Mama, mama, mira yo soy piloto*" (Mother, look I'm a pilot). Instead of applauding, she took the stance all parents seem born with: hands on hips, legs widespread, and a stern look on her face. As she half-dragged me home, I kept looking back to reassure myself that I had actually sat in a plane.

The next morning she had us up at dawn. A white powder was loaded into the plane and the pilot sprayed an adjoining field of melons. Every time he swooped over us, we reveled in a sticky white mist—I was in heaven.

* * * *

Jennie, my youngest (and she claims my favorite) sister, was born in April 1933. (She does not know that I associate her with the depths of the Great Depression.) At the time, Father's wages were nine cents an hour. He was working sixty hours a week and we were living in abject poverty. Meanwhile, our uncles had moved their families north to Pittsburg, a smokestack town at the confluence of the San Joaquin and Sacramento Rivers. There,

Tio Pancho worked for Dow Chemical and Tio Enrique was laying a foundation for what would be California's first statewide Mexican food distribution firm. They advised that we join them there and so two trips were planned to complete the move.

I stayed home to care for my three- and four-year-old sisters while the rest of the family made the first trip. I was only 11 years old but indigence is a hard taskmaster. Father returned two days later. We hung a canvas water bag off the radiator cap, tied Mother's Singer sewing machine to one fender, a Number 10 galvanized tub that doubled as a bathtub and washtub to the other, and strapped our two mattresses on top of the Model-T. The remainder we loaded into the back seat where I sat holding a death grip on a sack full of angry roosters. Other than skin coloring, the Joads in *The Grapes of Wrath* had nothing on us as we clunked up old Highway 99.

1937. (L–R), Sisters Jennie, Evelyn, and Aurora. A new pair of shoes was a big event in the Gutierrez household

We spent the winter of 1933 in Tio Pancho's cold, dank, cement-lined cellar. I will never forget my Tia Quita. She loved birds so much that she screened-in the front porch and stocked it with a flock of canaries. Their inane chirping, together with the din created by five cousins and we five kids, easily qualified the place as a zoo.

The town was home to several industrial plants all of which spewed plumes of noxious gasses. Their effluvium blended into a sulfuric, garlicky fog that was made all the more intolerable by a rotten fish stink emanating from the F. E. Booth Cannery located three blocks from city hall. Yet, residents only counted it a bad day when the wind shifted and a paper mill in nearby Antioch added its foul odor to the yellowish smog from hell.

Father got shift work at the cannery and to improve his availability, we moved into a ramshackle apartment over an abandoned waterfront bar.

Sardine boats unloaded at all hours and work crews were summoned to the processing lines by means of a powerful air horn. We practically lived under the brute, and the horrendous roar sounded like a jet engine in afterburner when it went off.

One frigid December day in 1934, I came home from school to find Father sitting in drizzling rain with a look of utter despair on his face. Mother put it to me straight. The fish were not running so his job had been changed to part-time shift work, the rent was three months in arrears, La Jalisciense Grocery had cut off our credit, and our infant brother Ruben was ill. Father went on relief. Once a week, with guilt and humiliation written all over his face, he queued-up at a nearby storefront for two large bags of groceries.

I was then in sixth grade and the cardboard soles that I cobbled daily to insert in my shoes refused to stay put any longer. Rather than burden Mother with the problem, I stole a quarter from the Lopez Market across the street and went shopping at the local Salvation Army store. A pair of perforated, black and white wing-tip shoes caught my eye. The clerk brushed the cobwebs away, and I tried them on; they were two sizes too big. We stuffed newspaper in the tips, laced them tight, and I shuffled out into a rainstorm feeling like a real dandy.

At about this time, Richfield Oil started the Jimmie Allen Flying Club. Biweekly, the company's gas stations offered pamphlets that described how pilots perform basic flight maneuvers. Sal, a neighborhood station owner, also loved aviation and we often discussed the lessons at length. Nowadays when in Pittsburg visiting family, my thoughts will stray back to my old friend and our imagined wonders of flight. I wish it were possible to pin pilot wings on his oily coveralls and say to him, "These are for you Sal. You and Jimmie Allen inspired my dream to fly." I'll bet he'd get a real kick out of that.

La Pisca

By the summer of 1934, Gus and I had gone from scavenging discarded soda pop bottles to stealing full ones and Mother knew that we were headed for real trouble. So when the school term ended, the family took what it could, abandoned the rest, and left Pittsburg to follow *la pisca* (the crops).

Our first stop was a migrant labor camp at the Balfour & Guthrie (B&G) ranch in nearby Brentwood. We would follow *la pisca* but we weren't ashamed of it; at least not until we learned the rules. There were two camps: the whites were quartered in shaded, permanent cabins with all the conveniences nearby, and the Mexicans were relegated to a barren, remote tent city.

We paid $5.00 a week to live in two framed tents and we slept on two lumpy mattresses that nightly hemorrhaged cotton. The nearest water faucets were twenty yards away and the outhouses and showers beyond that. Groceries were bought on credit at an overpriced company store and Mother prepared our simple meals in a communal kitchen. Father was assigned to a Mexican work crew picking apricots while Mother, Gus, and I, along with dozens of other families, were also segregated as we cut the fruit for drying. We worked in a large, open-sided, packinghouse rigged with kitchen fans that blew this-way-and-that in a vain attempt to dispel the stifling heat. Our siblings had it no better. They spent their days in a one-room day care center equipped with two playthings, a sandbox and a slide that got hot enough to fry eggs.

Esperanza "Hopey" Aguirre was my first experience with puppy love. Hopey had long black hair, bronze skin, big eyes, and wore a loose shirt that if she inadvertently leaned over just right, enabled me to peek at her budding breasts. We never progressed beyond making goo-goo eyes at each other at work. But cutting apricots with a hooked knife is risky business and when Mother noticed us, she faced me in the opposite direction. This sparked a new affair with a little blond girl who worked just beyond the invisible wall that separated us.

The nectarine season had all but ended when word came that prune pickers were needed in the San Jose area. Quickly, Gus and I tied the mattresses to the top of the car while Mother prioritized our belongings into three categories: useful, everyday, and sentimental. Then everyone but Father climbed in, then he filled the spaces between us with as many items as possible. What didn't fit, didn't go. Three hours later, a procession of jalopies, rattletrap pickups, and battered flatbeds, all overflowing with furniture and sad brown faces, took to the open road.

We were rounding a curve when the mattresses flew off the car. Father pulled over and Gus and I ran back to retrieve our most precious possessions. No one stopped; the competition for jobs was too fierce for that. Father went to find more rope while the rest of us collected cotton wads and re-stuffed the pads.

We rented a room in a broken down motel near Mission San Jose. Out back, half-hidden by sagging lines of laundry, was a malodorous eight-holer. The privy had two doors and each side was equipped with a tattered, dung-streaked Montgomery Ward catalog hanging from a ten-penny nail. Our room was so tiny that nightly we moved the kitchen table and chairs outdoors to accommodate the two mattresses. Other families were not as fortunate. They lived next to a stream in crude huts made of wood scraps, bedsprings, and tree branches.

Our workday began at dawn. After a tortilla and bean breakfast, Mother would wrap our heads to ward off the sun and the entire family reported for work. There, we were assigned a piece of chalk, a row of trees, and several buckets. Pay was fifteen cents a box and our number was marked on the boxes as we filled them. We looked like ragamuffins bowing in prayer toward Mecca as we picked prunes out of hard, sun-baked clods. Ten minutes into it, babies were crying, our cuticles were bleeding, our knees hurt, and backs ached. The sun began its arc across a cloudless sky and by midmorning, triple-digit heat was radiating off the ground into our faces. Sweat ate through our clothes, our shirts stuck to our backs like wet cellophane, and every move provoked clouds of gnats and mosquitoes to rise and land on us like tiny vultures. There were no bathrooms, so when a woman had to go, others would form a circle to hide her. Drinking water came in a five-gallon milk can with a ladle chained to a handle. *El patron* (the boss) refused to add ice to it. "If I do, you'll drink it too fast and that's bad for you," he would say in a thick Oklahoma twang. During lunch, we ingested gnats like condiments on the tacos then sprawled in the shade for a short siesta before tackling the most torturous part of the day. We were reeling and groggy by the time the sky dimmed.

One day, three blue-and-yellow military biplanes flew by and I stood up to admire them. Mother saw me and I pointed in the direction they disappeared over the treetops; she smiled, she knew. But dreams are nebulous and poverty is real. Mother pointed at me to get back to work. Other families were standing by waiting to replace any clan that lagged too far behind. Every day was reinvented based upon what we earned the previous day and our hand-to-mouth existence was based on solid priorities: rent, gas, food.

A steel-linked fence that surrounded an isolated complex of low-slung Spanish-style buildings flanked one side of the orchard. The place had a secretive air about it, people were seldom seen, few cars came and went, and those that did were inspected at a well-guarded gate. Everyone speculated about what went on there but no one knew for sure. Our family would eventually discover its mission in a most distressing manner.

Jobs in the area tapered off and we made our way back toward Brentwood by begging for scraps of work along the way. Five miles from there, we were passing through a dusty little farm town named Oakley when we saw a four-room clapboard "barrio basic" that appeared vacant. We stopped to examine it. The shanty had faded asphalt roof tiles, a lop-sided front porch, rusted window screens that flapped in a breeze, a paint job blistered with age, and a raw sand yard with a few fruit trees. Its most attractive feature was a window sign that read: "For Rent, $9 A Month." Perfect! We took it.

Mother assumed command. While the others scrubbed the interior, Gus and I were assigned to clean and relocate the outhouse. We hosed it down, easily dug a new hole in the loose soil, and with everyone's help, moved it. Unfortunately, none of us were students of hydrology and made no connection between the privy, the sand, and the town water well fifty feet away. Had we dug a few feet deeper, undoubtedly we would have struck water. No one complained. It's a wonder that Oakley survived.

The interior of the house can best be described as Early American. An old cast-iron stove and a one-faucet sink dominated the kitchen. Our parents and our youngest sibling, Steven, occupied the bedroom. Evelyn, Aurora, Jennie, and Ruben slept on a castoff couch in the living room and Gus and I had a tiny room off the kitchen. A dangling light bulb centered each room, while a table-model Philco radio provided entertainment and a leftover 8×10 lithograph of da Vinci's "Last Supper" satisfied our appreciation for the arts.

Abuelita Linda was blessed with the type of stoic, sun-creased face one sees on Indians in history books. Born in northern Mexico, she must have had Yaqui blood in her background, for she was tough as a boot, had a will of iron, and if crossed, could become fierce-eyed in a second. She thought nothing of shouldering a load or walking five miles, even into her late sixties. Her life centered on her children and she rotated living with them.

When she figured it was our turn, she simply showed up at the front door with her long-suffering, metal-bound trunk. Although she and

Mother together were a handful for Father to handle, we loved her dearly and welcomed her with open arms. Other than a diamond-encrusted wedding band on her glazed left hand, Abuelita's trunk served as a repository for her entire wardrobe, all her keepsakes, and a sweet-scented concoction of camphor, rosemary, and glycerin. She smoked Prince Albert tobacco on the sly and whenever she opened the strongbox, a sweet aromatic fragrance permeated the house. That was our signal to beg to see her mementos.

Abuelita's show-and-tells always had a sense of drama about them. She'd have us fetch the three kitchen chairs and a wooden bench from the dinner table, then sit us down—eldest in back, youngest up front—and examine our hands to assure they were clean. The care with which she extracted each item made it clear we were dealing with precious keepsakes. There were tintypes of bygone relatives dressed in nineteenth century finery, crinkled photographs of her children, exquisite mantillas, and a revered wallet rubbed smooth by long use and engraved "G.R. RINCON." Only after she had retrieved every item would she narrate the incident that drove the family to *El Norte*. No matter how many times we corrected her, she stubbornly refused to call this land Los Estados Unidos. She had good reason. Back in Guanajuato, her map of Mexico included Southwestern United States, and the area was over-printed with the statement: "Land temporarily in the hands of the United States."

Abuelita was into strange, holistic diets long before they became popular here. For breakfast, she preferred a raw egg and honey-sweetened orange-leaf tea. She could skin a *nopalito* (young prickly pear cactus pad) in a second and loved it with scrambled eggs. Sometimes she favored adding *verdolagas* (a ground-hugging plant that grows in the southwest). Her time-tested remedy for gastric problems was *estafiate* (an aromatic weed found on ditchbanks) tea, and her remedy for all pulmonary problems was an odoriferous hot mustard plaster on the chest.

Once, Abuelita found Gus and me fighting over a quarter. Wielding her ever-present broom, she slapped in all directions until we stopped then told us this about our uncles. They too had once fought over money and one pulled a gun on the other. She called the police and as they were being led away, gave them this bit of sage advice: "When a family member gives you money, treat it as a loan. When you loan a family member money, treat it as a gift."

Father didn't discipline us but he did teach us how to work, and stoop labor is all about discipline. We usually worked in the Delta, a rich farmland created by a vast network of levees and dikes that harness the Sacramento River. There, we knelt, stooped, crawled, and climbed to pull, cut, chop, and pick the many crops that grow in the area. Someone once said, "A Mexican is as talented with a pair of grape clippers as Kreisler is with a violin." Relying on the same type of analogy, I claim that Father deserved to be titled, "The Baryshnikov of the fields." Father had an extraordinary capacity for work and the knack of making tasks look easy. If we fell behind or the quality of our work failed to meet his standard, he silently took over and with muscles that bulged and rippled with fluid grace, completed the job properly. Perhaps the highest compliment anyone ever paid Gus and me came from a *bracero*. In a society where the ability to work is the benchmark for the measure of a man, he pointed us out to several others and with admiration clearly evident in his voice said, "*Son los hijos* the *Nacho.*" (They're Nacho's boys.)

Although my shoulders still bear witness to the towering A-frame ladders we used to pick fruit, *el cortito* (short hoe) left the most lasting impression. The instrument of torture had an eighteen-inch handle and was commonly used to cultivate row crops until the seventies when Cesar Chavez led the fight to outlaw it. Chavez deserves to be revered for that act alone. It can come as no surprise that my criterion for true adversity is the indignity of having to do stoop labor under a hot sun.

Nowadays it is not unusual for an insensitive lout seeking an edge, to ask if I ever belonged to a gang. Yes, I did. We didn't use monikers, handsigns, bandannas, or tattoos. Yet when we sauntered by, people turned their heads, mothers gathered their children, and if possible crossed the street to avoid us.

It all began one brutally hot August when a Japanese farmer offered several of us work picking his crop of Bermuda onions. None of us had done it before but the pay was good so we took the job. We pulled, cut the roots and stems, and sacked the odorous bulbs. The acrid fumes accumulated under our sun hats, the caustic juice impregnated our skin, and tears and sniffles free-flowed constantly. One Sunday evening, we went directly from work to the Oakley Theater for the first showing of a "must see" Mexican movie. The hall lacked air-conditioning and it was not long before the rancid odor of onions and stale sweat drifted over the audience like some kind of frontal system. People seated nearby began to whisper and fan their faces, so we also fanned and looked around accusingly. Our efforts to blend in were futile as an increasingly larger number of empty seats formed a telltale ring of guilt around us and finally a man shouted, "*Hechenlos afuera!*" (Throw them out.) A chant arose, "*Afuera! Afuera!*" (Out! Out!) The manager brought up the lights, sniffed his way to us like a bloodhound, and pointed to the entrance. The theater was the heart and soul of the Mexican community and everyone cheered and clapped as he escorted us to the sidewalk. Thoroughly embarrassed, we dubbed ourselves the Sevoia (onion) Gang and went on a spree.

The tire trick was our most successful caper. The approaching war had created a rubber shortage and new tires were tightly rationed. We wrapped an old tire with the brown paper wrapping of a new tire and tied a long rope to it. When darkness came, we went beyond the lumberyard on the edge of town, placed the wrapped "new" tire beside the highway, and hid in an adjoining vineyard holding the other end of the rope. Cars screeched to

1937, Oakley, California. Henry's eighth grade class. Guess which one I am in the third row.

a stop and when the driver reached for the tire, we yanked it out of their grasp, stood up, and yelled, "Sucker." If we mistimed the move, several of us would play tug-of-war with the driver until we got it back. Occasionally two or more cars stopped and while the drivers bickered over who saw it first, we slowly pulled the tire into the vineyard then stood up and asked, "Hey, what are you guys arguing about?" One night a car pulled over and instead of reaching for the tire, Constable Joe Jesse fired two shotgun blasts over our heads. The Sevoia Gang disbanded on the spot.

* * * *

I was sorry that high school would only last four years the day I entered Liberty High in Brentwood. The school had hot and cold showers, flush toilets, and pretty girls—what more could anyone want? Soon after classes began, I was sauntering down the hall trying to look smooth in my hand-me-downs when our cute little home-economics teacher, Miss White, tapped my shoulder. She guided me to a secluded spot and said, "Let me see your left shoe." I tried to pull away but she held on and demanded, "Let me see your shoe." I rested my hand on her shoulder and raised my foot. She got red-eyed and said, "That's what I thought, come with me." We went to the office of the principal, Mr. Nash, where I suffered the most embarrassing moment of my young life. My high-tops were all but sole-less and to keep them from splaying out further, I had tied the sides together with copper wire. The ends were gouging the soles of my feet and I was tracking blood on the floor. They attended to my wounds and had me remove the wire. Then off I went with the tattered ends of my socks trailing behind.

During my sophomore year, our comely English teacher, Miss Dorothy Hansen, came into the classroom humming a popular love song of the day. Rita Luchessi teased her about having a boyfriend and to gain control, Miss Hansen asked, "Can anyone name that tune?" Lori Johnson called out, "All The Things You Are." Miss Hansen followed with, "Who wrote it?"

Barely above a whisper I replied, "Jerome Kern."

Everyone stared and Miss Hansen asked, "How did you know that?"

I had just read it in *Time* magazine but embarrassed by the attention, I shrugged and slouched down. Nevertheless, the fleeting moment of respect had not escaped me and outdated copies of the magazine stamped "Library" became a common item in our house. Sports were my primary interest but lacking other reading material, I generally read the publications cover to cover.

Mother required that we speak Spanish correctly. One incorrect or mispronounced word and she held school on the spot. Primarily to please her, I enrolled in a Spanish I class along with several other Mexican kids. On the first day of the course our teacher, Miss Gasparetti, said, "I know why all you Mexican kids are here. You think you know how to speak Spanish and that this class will be easy. Well, you don't and it won't be. Here you will learn to speak the language correctly because I teach Castilian Spanish."

That night I said to Mother, "Mama the teacher says that I don't know how to speak Spanish right." Mother frowned, pursed her lips and remained silent. But not Abuelita; she said, "What a strange country. In grammar school they punish children for speaking Spanish and in high school the pay teachers to teach them the language."

* * * *

1940, Brentwood, California. Henry (bottom, 2nd from left) played end on the high school football team. Only proud parents and diehard fans had the patience to watch the team's low-scoring games

My love of track and field began as a junior, when I rescued a badly worn pair of track spikes from a trash can—John Giannini, a classmate of mine, had discarded them—and I tried them on. The shoes were too small, but I removed the inner-soles and, although this bared the metal spike-heads, I soaked them overnight and ran in them until they dried. That year, as the team's half-miler, my best effort was 1:58. But I picked up speed during my senior year of competition and won the league championship.

It was Leroy French who made my high school football career possible. Coach Frank Vonder Ahe caught Leroy smoking in the Delta Theater and benched the first-string tackle. Furious, Leroy quit the team and threw his shoes under a row of lockers. The cleats were much too big for me, but I relied on past experience to solve the problem. I was the leading pass receiver on the varsity for two years but would have been much more effective had I not be weighed-down by the over-sized cleats. It is easy to spot me in team photos, I appear to be wearing steel-capped shoes. Given that the entire student body numbered 360 students and that there were only 60 boys in the Junior and Senior classes, even I have to admit that it was no great accomplishment to make the varsity in any sport. Yet, my most lasting disappointment concerning high school athletics was not being able to afford a two-year, red and gold letterman's sweater with a big chenille "L" on it.

High school sports are noted for forging important character-building values on and off the field. In my case, although they helped prepare me for life's games by toughening me mentally and physically, they may not have served me as well psychologically. A teammate nicknamed me "Rochester," after comedian Jack Benny's black valet on his radio show. Although I laughed, I was not amused and scrubbed my face and hands until they bled. Nevertheless, the name stuck and my emotional guard upped a few notches. Years later, while attending a class reunion, someone behind me shouted, "Hey Rochester." Instantly, the long forgotten slight surfaced and I froze. Fortunately, the fellow realized that times had changed and did not approach me.

Annually, Bay Area high school football teams were invited to act as ushers at Stanford and the University of California football games. My teammates, Arthur Honegger and Robert Dal Porto, both of who went on to star at California, had charitable mothers who transported us to the universities. We thrilled at the feats of such gridiron greats as Frankie Albert, Jackie Robinson, and Tom Harmon. My most meaningful impressions, however, were acquired between the parking lots and the stadiums. Pretty coeds and well-dressed students hanging out of leaded-glass dormitory windows were my first clue that not everyone lived in a hardscrabble world. My dreams of a better life began there.

Based on her experience as a student in Mexico, Mother did not know that some high school classes were required and others elective. Accordingly, she only questioned our grades not the subjects. This gave us license to take the easiest courses available. I was a "B" student.

At the beginning of my junior year, our vice-principal, B. J. Callaghan, called me into his office and said, "Henry, you're a good athlete but if you intend to go out for sports in college, you need to start taking college preparatory courses."

I gave him a "Huh?" look.

"Perhaps you don't understand," he continued. "To get into college you need to prepare yourself for higher-level study. I've reviewed your records and have written down the courses you should be taking this year instead of the ones you've signed-up for."

Two years earlier, Mr. Callaghan had helped remove the wire from my shoes. Furthermore, he knew that I had picked asparagus that morning before catching the bus to school; even I could smell me. I glanced at the card and said, "Mr. Callaghan I can't go to college. Who needs this stuff? What's the use?"

"Henry, you don't know what your future holds. You need to prepare for it by getting a good education. In any case, you have the ability to be a good student but seem satisfied to waste your time by taking the easiest courses around."

"Oh, Mr. Callaghan, you and your pep talks." I stuffed the card in my pocket and impatiently waited to be dismissed.

He lowered his head, shook it slowly, and waved me away.

Mr. Callaghan tried to influence my curriculum, but classmate Patsy Miller unknowingly controlled it. My heart clanged whenever she said "Hi" and smiled in my direction. When possible, I designed my class schedule around hers, played to her when competing, and spent many evenings admiring her athletic body, blond hair, and mysterious smile as she roller-skated round Brentwood's American Legion Hall. It still bothers me to recall that the closest I ever came to confessing my undying love was when I asked, "Patsy, would you sign my annual?"

In June 1941, I borrowed Father's white shirt and tie, classmate Howard Silva loaned me a jacket, and his folks gave me a ride to our graduation. As my class of 59 students stood to receive their diplomas, I knew that my parents were not among the proud families waving and craning to snap photographs. Still it was not enough to keep me from scanning the auditorium for signs of them. I never learned if their absence was because I wore Father's only dress shirt or because the gas in the car was needed for work the next day. After the ceremony, everyone gathered in the school lobby for punch and cookies. Preferring not to face the inevitable questions as to why my parents were absent, I took a last sentimental stroll through the halls. Early the next morning, Father, Gus, and I began a job thinning apricot trees. World War II was six months away.

Chapter 2

I Wanted Wings
(1942–1944)

―

We Don't Take Filipinos, Spics, or Niggers

First, schoolmate Roy Tarply died aboard USS *Arizona.* Then, Marines Charlie Cabral and Alvin "Knoxie" Domingo died in action in the South Pacific. Their deaths brought home the appalling difference between a window pennant that displayed a blue star and one with a gold star. Knoxie and Gus were close friends and before long, Gus surprised the family with the announcement that he had enlisted in the Marine Corps. We had always done everything together and it was inconceivable to me that he had not invited me to share this greatest of all adventures. I begged Mother to sign an age-waiver, but she said "No!" with a finality I knew was useless to argue against.

I missed my big brother terribly. Alone in bed at night, I would fall asleep worrying about him; where was he, what was he doing, was he safe, would he come home? Highly censored V-mail letters postmarked "Somewhere in the Pacific" only served to fuel our concern for him. Night after night, with her face grim and the room filled with stern silence, Mother would turn on the radio and have me translate the news reports. When the ordeal was over, no matter what she was feeling—grief, anxiety, fear—she would keep her troubles to herself and wordlessly retreat to her room. Her mournful sobs would cause us to cry in sympathy for her.

The Navy installed a V-12 Preflight Training School at St. Mary's College in nearby Moraga. Naively, I thought that by joining the program I would be permanently stationed there, thus enabling me to help my brother and remain close to Mother. On the eve of my nineteenth birthday, I bathed in the Number 10 washtub, scrubbed my best Levi's on our rippled washboard, and blackened my jackboots with 3-In-One oil. Early the next day, I pushed my second-hand Harley-74 down the street so as not to wake Mother, kick-started it, and headed for the Oakland Armed Forces Recruiting Center.

As I roared along Highway 4, the engine noise between my legs, and the red flames painted on the black gas tank, intensified my macho image; I was ready. Soldiers of all services were reporting for work when I arrived and one directed me to the V-12 program office. The room was empty but for a lone lieutenant slouched behind a desk reading a newspaper and having a cup of coffee and a cigarette. Intimidated by the military trappings, I wanted to leave but a strong sense of patriotism urged me forward. I approached his desk and stood ramrod straight like I had seen them do in the movies. He lowered the paper to eye level, gazed at me for a long moment, then resumed reading. I thought, I must not be standing straight enough, and cranked my head and shoulder blades back a notch.

Finally, he looked again, heaved a sigh, threw the paper aside, took a drag, and blew a blue cloud at me. "Young man," he said, "we don't take Filipinos, spics, or niggers in this program. If you want to join the United States Navy, I suggest you go down the hall. I think they're taking you guys as mess boys right now." The words stung like a whap across the face with a wet towel. No one had ever insulted me so openly before, but what hurt more was that a military officer seated before the flag had done it.

Tears of humiliation and disbelief filled my eyes. Trembling with rage I shouted, "Fuck you, you son of a bitch!" and ran. Chairs scraped in adjoining offices as I rushed by people in the hallway and continued out the front door. On the way home I vowed, "People may think that because I'm Mexican, I'll eat dirt. Well they're wrong and I'll prove it no matter what it takes. There's no way Gus lets anyone talk to him that way and I'll be damned if they'll do it to me." Little did I know.

If it moves, salute it.
If it doesn't, paint it.
If you are not sure, pick it up.
    A Drill Instructor's Order

In January 1943, Phil Zamora, an old Sevoia gang member, and I were drafted into the Army and ordered to report for duty at the Presidio of Monterey. At the end of our first day of hard KP, the mess sergeant complimented my work and offered me a full-time job as a KP Pusher. I accepted; the food was better, the hours shorter, and the work easier than I was used to. Most of my first paycheck went to Father. Aware of the feeling a new pair of shoes gave me, I asked him to buy the kids new footwear.

The work schedule allowed me time for almost weekly visits home but I invented excuses to stay away. Gossip travels fast in a small town and thinly veiled stories about Mother's odd behavior were everywhere. At first, I discounted them as sour-grape sequels to our reputation as a family of eccentrics.

1943, Presidio of Monterey, California. (L–R) Newly inducted U.S. Army Privates: Phil Zamora, Hank Cervantes, Carl Peterson

The viewpoint stemmed from the fact that in a devoutly Roman Catholic neighborhood, we were the only Hispanic family that attended the local Methodist church. Moreover, it was joked about that as a member of the choir, Mother sang the hymns in Spanish while the others sang in English. Rather than ask Father if the rumors were true, I volunteered for extra duty; it cleared my conscience.

One foggy morning, Phil and I were on our way to the post exchange (PX) when he said, "Hey, Hank, *mira* (look). They're looking for pilots."

"Where, guy?"

"Over there, see the blue and yellow sign with the airplane flying off of it? It says, 'Take a test and become a pilot, navigator, or bombardier in the United States Army Air Force.' Let's go take it."

I laughed, "Are you crazy Phil? You know we can't pass no test to be a pilot."

"How do you know we can't 'til we try?"

"I don't, but you know we can't."

"Hey, you can't tell. Even if we don't pass, maybe they'll let us work around the planes. You know, putting air in the tires or fixing them or something. It beats dragging a rifle around."

"Yeah sure, but I told you what happened to me when I tried to go to the Navy pilot school?"

"Look guy, what's the worse thing they can say to us?"

"No, I guess"

"You've heard that before. Come on."

"OK, let's go."

The three-hour examination centered on reasoning, written comprehension, spatial awareness, and perceptual speed. Within minutes, men were throwing down their pencils in surrender and leaving. Phil failed, but I got a 96.

Those of us who qualified were sent to Santa Ana Army Air Field located where Orange Coast College is today. There, we were required to state our preferred classification—pilot, navigator, or bombardier. Then everyone was subjected to eight hours of evaluations that included printed, physical, psychological, and apparatus tests. Only one out of five survived the rigid selection process for pilots. Selection for navigator required applicants to achieve a rating just below that for pilots, and the bombardier classification was less than that of navigator. As a part of their decision, officials also considered service needs and an expected failure rate of 40 percent due to academics, accidents, and physical problems. The war must have been having a bad day when I went through because, much to my surprise, they accepted me for pilot training.

Instruction began immediately. Up at 0510, reveille formation at 0520, breakfast at 0600, physical education 0830, ground school classes at 1000, and lunch at 1100. More classes from 1200–1600, drill and retreat formation from 1600–1700, dinner at 1730, in quarters at 2030, lights out at 2200. Studies included Military Discipline and Courtesy, Mathematics, Naval and Ground Forces, Morse Code, Physics,

1943, Santa Ana Army Air Base, California. Running the 440-yard dash in GI shoes during a camp-out

Maps and Charts, Chemical Warfare, First Aid, and Aircraft Identification. Water survival lessons were taught on a beach now owned by the exclusive Balboa Bay Club.

At noon on Saturdays, streams of cadets rushed to a nearby Pacific Electric Railway station for the long ride into Los Angeles. Olvera Street and East L.A. were familiar locations, but I made no effort to visit there. It was June 1943. Prejudice against Mexican-Americans was widespread. The "Sleepy Lagoon case" in which twenty-two Mexican youths were convicted of a single murder was still in the news, and now the "Zoot Suit Riots" were on. Groups of sailors were cruising the streets shouting slurs at Mexicans and assaulting *pachucos* (flashily dressed young Mexicans; zoot suiters) wearing the exaggerated clothing. I was not aware that any one in uniform had been attacked. Nevertheless, I stayed close to my classmates.

Nights in Los Angeles were predictably boring. Servicemen were everywhere, hotels were filled to capacity, and they even rented the lobby furniture. Some of the older men went to the dime-a-dance ballroom but most of us lacked that level of confidence. We ogled the B-girls at the Lexington Hotel bar until 0200 then went to the all-night Follies burlesque house on Main Street. No one paid attention to the middle-aged strippers backed by an atrocious sounding saxophone, trumpet, and drums. Everyone sat far back wishing only to be left alone and fall asleep. But the catnap only lasted until 0400 when the lights came up and the manager cleared the room by blowing a police whistle non-stop into the microphone. We then hit the streets.

No one who has ever spent the night roaming the streets forgets the feeling. Dead tired and desperate for sleep, we stumbled aboard a Red Car going toward Venice and Pacific Ocean Park. The streets were deserted and the sidewalks silent and shadowy until we reached Beverly Hills. Despite the impossible hour, we always kept a sharp eye out for movie stars while passing through the city. Never mind that after three years of war, any that were still around were in bed after a night out at Ciro's or Mocambo. On the beach, the amusement parks were closed for the night and in the eerie stillness there was nothing to do but re-board the streetcar and sleep during the long ride back to Santa Ana.

On Sundays at 1500, the 13,000-man cadet corps assembled into squadrons and converged on a huge central drill field. Once in place, we checked each other's uniform; cap two-finger widths from the eyebrow, shirt tucked in, tie straight, buttons buttoned, belt buckle centered, and shoes dusted on the backs of our pants legs. Then came the command,

"Ten-hutt!" Like row upon row of owl-eyed mannequins, we stood "at attention" for what seemed forever, body rigid, eyes forward, and arms locked at the side. Meanwhile, the adjutant read the Order of The Day, the band played "The Star Spangled Banner," and the honor guard retired the flag. Anyone who fainted due to the heat, humidity, or a hangover was hauled to the hospital for an overnight stay and a one-way ticket back to the Infantry. As the ceremony continued, the band paraded and took its place before the reviewing stand. Finally, the adjutant provided us welcomed relief with the shouted command, "Pass in review!" Unit after unit marched away until at the appropriate moment our commander called out, "Columns of squadrons, right squadron, right turn. March!"

Off we went; pennants flying, chests out, shoulders back, head straight but eyes cranked right, struggling to stay in alignment. The band repeated "The Washington Post March" several times then launched into the Air Corps song, "Off We Go into the Wild Blue Yonder." Instantly, tears filled my eyes, a huge lump choked my throat, and my chest felt as if it would burst with pride, pride for my family, my people, and myself. My emotional reaction to that song has not changed; it remains constant to this day.

One day we were ordered to pack up. No reason, no destination. We boarded a mile-long troop-train pulled by an ancient coal-burning locomotive that needed a fresh supply of water every few miles. We wandered across the western desert for four days with the windows wide-open and soot invading our nostrils, clothing and bedding. The train finally pulled into a tiny train station at Pullman, Washington. We dismounted and looking like startled chipmunks rather than soldiers, marched to Washington State College.

I Won't Serve Him, He's Indian

WHY I WANT TO BE A PILOT
(by Tommy Tyler, 5th Grade, Jefferson School, Beaufort, South Carolina)

When I grow up I want to be a pilot because it's a fun job and easy to do. That's why there are so many pilots flying around these days. Pilots don't need much school they just need to learn to read numbers so they can read their instruments. I guess they should be able to read road maps too, so they can find their way if they get lost. Pilots should be brave so they won't get scared when it's foggy and they can't see. Or if a wing falls off, they should stay calm so they'll know what to do. Pilots have to have good eyes to see through clouds. And they can't be afraid of thunder or lightning because they are so much closer to them than we are. The salary pilots make is another thing I like. They make more money than they know what to do with. This is because most people think that plane flying is dangerous. Except pilots don't, because they know how easy it is. I hope I don't get air-sick, because I get car-sick and if I get air-sick I couldn't be a pilot. And then I would have to go to work."

During three-months at Washington State, we who had never stepped inside of a college were provided sixty hours of English, geography, and modern history; eighty hours of mathematics and physics; and ten hours of preparatory flying experience. When there was any free time, it was devoted to military training.

For me, little Tommy's worst fear came true on my first flight in a Piper Cub "tail-dragger." My instructor, Mr. Butters, had hardly lifted off the dirt runway when I turned pea-green. He shook his head in disgust, grabbed my cap, handed it to me and said, "Here, use this." I heaved into it and having made his point, he gave me a paper sack to dispose of the mess. His after-landing critique included a bit of advice, "You had better get over it or you won't be in this program long." No need to explain what "it" meant. He knew the ropes, however, and whenever I began getting woozy, he would interrupt whatever we were doing and have me fly the plane. The need to focus on survival rather than my stomach immediately dispelled the lesser of the two concerns. His final written evaluation stated: "Satisfactory. This student shows good judgment but is slow in reaction. Very eager to learn, works hard." Mr. Butters kindly omitted any mention of my tendency to barf at the slightest provocation.

1943. Cracking the books at Washington State College (now University)

Piloting a plane involves more than reading numbers and not being afraid of thunderstorms. Flying rests on a structure of the laws of physics and one has to know how they apply if he intends to be around to collect the good salaries pilots make. In the classroom, my past came back to haunt me. "What's the use? Who needs it?" I had once said. I did, big time!

Early one morning, the last notes of our wake-up song, Glenn Miller's "American Patrol," had just faded from the speaker system when it barked, "Cadet Cervantes report to Lieutenant Lewis, on the double." Our training officer said, "Cervantes, you've only been here two weeks and you've already failed two tests in Theory of Flight. Keep this up and you're going back to the infantry, which is where you probably belong." He continued, "There's a professor here in town who's volunteered to help near-failures like you. Here's his card. Go see him tonight; but if he can't help you, you'd best pack your bags."

Professor Rodriguez was a Cuban psychology professor and after three hours together he said, "Enrique, apparently you've acquired the discipline necessary to do stoop labor under a hot sun. But you have yet to learn the equally demanding discipline necessary to sit in a schoolroom and work with your brain. A good memory is important to fly an airplane, and I intend to teach you how to study." The professor enabled me to squeak by at the bottom of my class.

On our final weekend at the school, three classmates and I hopped on a bus bound for nearby Moscow, Idaho. Intent on celebrating our completion of the course, we swaggered into the first saloon and one of the fellows ordered, "Bring us four beers." The barmaid looked us over, fetched three bottles, and set them on the bar before them. Puzzled, we looked at her wondering how she could have misunderstood the order. He asked, "Say, where's the other beer?"

She turned sideways, jerked her thumb over her shoulder at me and said, "I brought you all one. But I won't serve him, he's Indian." My buddies doubled over with laughter and she joined in, slapping the bar to vent her glee. I flushed, but rather than argue the finite difference between a Mexican and an Indian, spun on my heel and stomped out. The others caught up with me and we found a less discriminating place in which to drink. The party lasted past the departure time for the bus to Pullman, and we had to walk home. It was a ten-mile hike but no one mentioned the bar incident; I took secret delight in my friends' discomfort.

A week later, we entered the formal flying training program at Thunderbird Field near Glendale, Arizona. Before being released to enjoy the excitement of flying solo, students were required to master the spin-recovery procedure. When I began this phase of instruction, my flight instructor said, "Follow me on the controls and I will demonstrate and talk you through the maneuver." He cut the power, raised the nose high, waited for the airspeed to bleed off to zero, kicked the rudder all the way in, and we winged-over into a spin. Suddenly, all the pleasures of flying disappeared. The open-cockpit PT-17 began spinning like a platter, and a whirling tapestry of parched desert and green cotton fields came rushing up to meet us. He allowed it to go four turns. As we resumed level flight, I vomited all over the instrument panel and myself. I thought, enough of this, I can hardly wait to get on the ground. Not a chance; I continued to slip and slide around in my mess for an hour. The temperature was well over 100 degrees when we landed, and the ground mechanic apparently detected the foul odor from ten feet away. He motioned me to stay put, fetched a sponge and a bucket, handed them up to me, and said, "He who throws up, cleans up."

My problem persisted. All I had to do was smell the odor of doped fabric and burnt engine oil, and wave upon wave of revulsion would rise in my stomach until I upchucked. Cadets were quitting for various reasons, and only pride stood between them and me. Whenever a cadet was seen going to the office, we knew that he was about to quit or be washed out; and I did not want to be seen quitting.

Thanksgiving Day came and many local families invited cadets into their homes for the dinner. A good hearted family selected me and we agreed to meet at Adams Hotel in Phoenix. I was in the lobby waiting, when I noticed a Mexican family seated nearby. Their eldest son appeared to be a newly minted infantry second lieutenant and was the first Latino military officer I had ever seen. Their pride in him was obvious and I pictured my parents in a like setting. I vowed, "Mud, flood, or blood, you're going to stay in this program, even if it kills you."

Now slightly smaller, our class received basic flying training at Marana, a tiny airfield twenty miles north of Tucson. It is not inconceivable that a group of Mexicans found the most forlorn place in the area, erected some two-by-four and tarpaper shacks, scraped a block of desert flat for a runway, and named the jumble Marana as a joke on Los Americanos. In Spanish *marana* means "sow" and the name fit like a glove.

Three months later, we were loaded into a caravan of GI buses and sent south to another unknown destination. The rickety parade was beyond Tucson when someone saw a UC-78 twin-engine "Bobcat." The ungainly trainer confirmed what many of us suspected. We were bound for Douglas, a twin-engine, advanced flying school on the Arizona-Mexico border.

Early on, Mexican children learn that being Spanish is acceptable; Mexican is not. Accordingly, in a constant effort to meld in, I encouraged my classmates, who wanted to anyway, to believe I was Spanish. The lie worked well enough until the weekend that three of us crossed the border to visit Agua Prieta, Mexico. It was my first visit to my ancestral homeland and I was excited. The air was filled with smells of refried beans and corn tortillas, people were speaking my home language, and men were dressed much the same as I once did. Yet it was disturbing; the Mexican in me identified with them and the American felt embarrassed. I had a strong urge to acclimate but that was out of the question. Instead, I agreed with my friends that one turn up the main street was enough; we could do without its curio shops, tawdry bars, and sex shows. As we neared the border-gate, a pretty, young streetwalker propositioned me. Rather than risk loss of status by revealing my ability to flirt with her in Spanish, I replied, "No thanks." She sensed my intent to deceive and screamed, "*Vete, no quieres que los gabachos sepan que eres pocho*" (Go, you don't want them to know that you're Mexican). To my friends she said, "He Mexican, he no want you to know." Word of the incident spread back at the airfield, and I became a convenient target for the slurs and jokes about Mexicans that free-flowed in class. I endured the humiliation as part of the price for being there.

Before graduating, one of the final tests was a night cross-country flight. A standard plan required that one student fly and the other navigate from Douglas to El Paso, switch seats in midair, proceed to Cochise, make a full-stop landing, take off, and return to Douglas.

Cadet Darrell Cole and I were paired and scheduled to be the last off at 0200. We tossed a coin to determine who would have the fun of landing at Cochise; I lost and climbed into the left seat. We arrived over El Paso, exchanged seats, and I became the navigator. It was not much of a test; powerful beacons were situated every 10 miles along the airways and on a clear night one could see three or four ahead. Cochise was a postage stamp-size emergency strip and as we began our approach to the field, I warned Cole that he was too steep and too fast. He ignored me and we landed far down the strip. The "bamboo bomber" smashed through a fence, nosed-over, and skidded to a stop upside down. Everything went pitch black and the sickening odor of gasoline invaded the cabin. We clambered out and ran into the desert just as the plane erupted into sky-high flames.

As we sat in the hot sand and watched the blaze, no one came to our rescue—we were out in the middle of nowhere. The flames subsided and the two blackened engines emerged from the ashes like twin headstones to our flying careers. With nothing to do but worry about scorpions and listen to the mournful howl of a distant coyote, we waited and waited. Hardly a word passed between us but none was needed, for we each knew what the other was thinking; that the crash would grease our path back to the infantry. This was a given; however, our more immediate concern was a rumor that cadets who damaged aircraft due to pilot error were required to reimburse the government for the cost of repairs. And we were wondering what a UC-78 was worth and who would pay how much for the pile of ashes before us. Our instructor landed about noon and without shutting-down, motioned us aboard. While viewing the ashes he assumed that I made the landing and said, "Well compadre, you really screwed up this time. When we get back, you might as well pack it up and head back to old Mejico." I was too dejected to be insulted or protest my innocence.

The following night the first entry on the flight schedule read: "LT. MOTHERSBAUGH/CERVANTES, AT-6, 797, X-C, ELP, CHECK RIDE."

Mothersbaugh was a cadet's worse nightmare. He stood about 6'4" had brush-cut blonde hair, a pencil mustache, and looked down at mere mortals with piercing blue eyes and detached arrogance. Most of us headed in the opposite direction whenever we saw him coming, but I couldn't evade him this night. He strode through the ready room with a seat-pack parachute over his shoulder and with a head-bob motioned me to follow. I chased him to a single-engine trainer where he waved me toward the back seat as if shooing a fly. His contempt for the world seemed to include the plane for he kicked the tires, whacked the propeller a couple of times as if daring it to fall off, and climbed in.

It was my first time in an AT-6, so I assumed that the sole purpose of the flight was to "fill a square" in order to wash me out. Nevertheless, determined to do my best, I studied the cockpit. Tense as a cornered cat, I waited to be tested. Mothersbaugh took off, buzzed a couple of farmhouses, practiced acrobatics, whistled a few old tunes, talked to himself, returned, and landed. He completed the flight form, climbed out, and headed back toward the office. His scorn could not have been more obvious; he hadn't said a word to me during the entire flight. Dejected, I followed along, watching his parachute bounce off his butt when he suddenly stopped and I stumbled into him. He steadied me, grinned and said, "Good ride, Harry, you passed." (Twenty years later, I met Colonel Mothersbaugh at a conference at Hill Air Force Base, Utah. His demeanor had not changed, nor did he make any effort to recall the flight. I thanked him anyway.)

A week later, Cole and I were summoned to the Base Finance Office. A corporal placed a "Statement of Charges" on a counter before us, checked two blank lines at the bottom of the page and said, "Read this and sign here." The form certified that the UC-78 had been worth $17,000 and that we judged it to be "beyond economical repair." In a quavering voice Cole asked, "Do we each pay half?" The corporal burst out laughing, but a sergeant who overheard the question came over and said, "We need you to sign the statement in order to Class 26 (write off) the airplane. Don't worry about it, you two are lucky to be alive." We signed and waltzed out arm-in-arm. Cole left the next day.

∞

Graduation Day

Mercifully, graduation day came and we marched onto the stage of an all-purpose gym for the event. Snickers and guffaws erupted from the audience when I appeared. After months in the desert sun, my skin had turned mahogany and I stood out like a chocolate brownie in a box of oatmeal cookies. The ceremony opened with a deafening recording of "The Star Spangled Banner" followed by the standard patriotic ritual. Then a fat colonel who waddled like he had a load in his shorts took center stage. He administered the oath of office and as the adjutant called out our names, presented us with silver wings: "Flight Officer Jack Warren Brown, Flight Officer Raymond Emmett Burke, Flight Officer Henry Kre-Kervanes"—he rolled his eyes and continued.

College-educated cadets were commissioned second lieutenants and the rest of us were appointed to the lower rank of flight officer. No matter, it was 27 June 1944; I was 20 years old and on top of the world.

* * * *

My next station was to be the B-17 Co-pilot Transition School at Las Vegas Army Air Field, Nevada. We were all given ten days to report for duty, so my roommate, Lieutenant Jack (John R.) Chandler, and I promptly boarded a Greyhound bus bound for Los Angeles. Thrown together by alphabetical coincidence, we were friends but unlikely travel companions. Although we both hailed from the Bay Area, scuttlebutt had it that Jack belonged to *The Los Angeles Times* Chandler family. He refused to discuss the rumor, nevertheless, everyone believed it because we knew that he attended the University of California at Berkeley's School of Journalism. Our common bond was Jack's love of rodeo horses and my lie that "Silver" was a magnificent stallion on the ranch we owned in Fresno. As we chatted along the way, Jack confided that he and his mother were at odds because without informing her, he had transferred from the Berkley campus to the one at Davis, in order to study Animal Husbandry. She learned of his whereabouts when his draft notice arrived at their home.

We arrived at the Los Angeles Union Train Station just in time to buy two of the last remaining tickets on The Lark, an overnight train to San Francisco. Aboard the coach car, I had an aisle seat and Jack and a sailor were assigned seats facing me. A prim, thirtyish-looking woman claimed the seat to my left. Everything about her spoke of big bucks—luxuriant honey-blond hair, flawless makeup, crystal-blue eyes, a stylish pearl-gray silk dress, and a brilliant wedding ring set. She sat down, haughtily sniffed

1944, Douglas Air Base, Arizona. (L–R) Hank with Aviation Cadets Raymond G. Burke and John R. (Jack) Chandler

the ozone layer and turned to gaze out the window. I dreaded the prospect of having to sit by her and shifted uneasily, looking for a comfortable position in which to sleep without disturbing her. She noted my movement, tucked her skirt under her legs, and returned her attention to a row of boxcars next to us.

After a while, Jack's new uniform caught her eye and she asked, "How long have you been commissioned?" Jack blushed and said, "Seven and a half hours. We graduated from flying school this morning, and we're on our way home." She gave him an empty smile and said, "Congratulations, my husband's a Navy commander." That took care of that. The sailor straightened up a bit and everyone went back to staring into space.

Suddenly, the train jerked violently and began to lurch, sway, and wobble forward. Initially she and I asked forgiveness whenever we jostled one another. But as we continued to shake, rattle, and roll in discordant harmony, our apologies became meaningless so we forgot about the niceties and just went along with the ride. The train accelerated and, as the car's oscillations became more rhythmic, her buoyant breasts, although well covered, began swaying seductively. I hadn't been near a woman for a year and casually dropped my arm across my lap to hide my reaction. Apparently, the motion reflected in the windowpane; she frowned, contemptuously tossed her head and, with an emphatic bounce, turned her back to me.

Gradually, a languid Pacific and the warm afternoon sun combined to soften her attitude. Once, when our hands brushed, I gave her a cartoon frown and she surprised me with a faint smile. The constant clickity-clack lulled Jack and the sailor to sleep and, as dusk turned to twilight, a feeling of privacy deepened between us. Time passed and somehow, without knowing how it came about, every time the car swayed our shoulders touched. Her warmth excited me; my body grew rigid, my heart began to hammer, and I found myself gently massaging my left thigh. Suddenly the wheel-noise grew louder and we plunged into a tunnel with a roar and an intense odor of coal smoke. Immediately, she stood up, reached into an overhead rack for a train blanket, paused momentarily to accentuate the silky contour of her breasts, boldly looked into my eyes, and sat down. She covered herself with half of the comforter, extended the other half toward me, and I overlapped my left side with it. We clasped hands beneath it and as we emerged from the tunnel, continued to silently stare straight ahead. No words were needed, her cool, more experienced hand conveyed universal messages.

Aroused by her boldness, I tried to bridge her thigh with our grip but that set-off a concealed tug-of-war that she ended with a light slap of the hand. Night fell and the overhead lights went off. She punted her shoes, reclined on the seat, faced me, and nestled into my arms. Jack and the sailor sounded as if they were asleep but I doubted their light snoring.

Morning sunlight awoke me with a start. Imogene was in my arms fast asleep with her legs sprawled akimbo. Two elderly ladies stood in the aisle sniffing toward us with utter disgust written on their faces. I stared them down and with a parting humph of disapproval, they pitter-pattered away clutching their purses to their chests. The rattle of the newspaper cart awakened Imogene. She sat up. Her hair looked like a tangled haystack, she had mascara-ringed eyes, was crimson from nose to chin, and missing buttons exposed ample cleavage. Blushing fiercely, she patted her hair down, gathered herself as best she could, and with her breasts heaving with every step, bolted for the restroom. To spare her the embarrassment of having everyone stare at her, when she returned, I held the blanket aside and opened my arms wide. She resumed her previous position and closed her eyes. An hour later, I gently shook her awake. Imogene smiled, kissed my chin, pulled my head down and murmured, "When we get there, why don't we go to my place and get comfy and relax?" I whispered transparent excuses as my interest was changing from romance to the excitement of what was awaiting me at home.

We were due to arrive in San Francisco soon and within a few hours a scene I had imagined many times would take place. I intended to pin a pair of miniature silver wings on Mother's dress and say all the things I had never said before. How much I loved her, how her values had inspired me to reach my goal, and how deeply I appreciated all the sacrifices she had made on my behalf. This would be her glory day, not mine.

Morning sea mist was drifting over the foothills as the train creaked slowly into the station and groaned to a stop. Immediately, the sailor stood, gave me a huge smile of approval and left. Jack went to retrieve our bags. Aware of the furtive glances being cast in our direction, Imogene and I were clumsily shaking hands and muttering words of farewell when Jack returned. Without a word to her, he handed me my bag and pushed me to the exit. Almost next to the train stood a long black Pierce-Arrow limousine. And beside it, a tall well-dressed woman and a uniformed chauffeur were anxiously scanning the multiple streams of alighting passengers. Jack dropped his bag at my feet and sprinted to the woman. She opened her arms wide, gathered him in for a long moment, then tearfully stood back as he pirouetted to show-off his new uniform. Jack introduced me to his mom and Charles, her chauffeur, and she invited me to join them. As the Pierce Arrow slowly inched its way out of the station, they got into a lively three-way conversation, while I, cowering under my first contact with wealth, shriveled into the leather-lined seat and turned to gaze out the window. There stood Imogene, hands on hips, slack-jawed with disbelief, staring back at me.

As we neared Market Street I said, "Would you please drop me off here, the Greyhound bus depot is just up the street." Mrs. Chandler asked, "Where do you live dear?"

"In Oakley ma'am. It's across the bay in Contra Costa County."

"Oh," she said, "I've never heard of it. It's all farm country out there. Does your family own a ranch?" She continued before I could reply. "Oh, don't worry. Charles will take you home. Won't you, Charles?" "Yes ma'am," Charles answered.

I remained silent, more disturbed by their unintended extension of my mental discomfort than the prospect of a long bus ride home. We cruised up Nob Hill where we entered the porte-cochere of an expensive ante-bellum style home.

Charles insisted that I sit in the back seat and we returned to downtown. As we neared Market Street, from my throne-seat I said, "Charles, Oakley is about seventy miles away. Why don't you just drop me off at the station?" He shook his head. "Well, okay then, cross the Bay Bridge, get on Highway 24, and it'll take us there."

We crossed Oakland and began our ascent up Fish Ranch Road to cross the hills that separate the Bay Area from the Diablo Valley. Tired and spent from the train ride, I fell into fitful sleep. Sometime later, Charles blew the horn and pointed to a road sign that read, "Oakley: Pop. 824." In quick succession we passed Shorty's Signal Station, Olney's Merchandise Store, the Oakley Hotel, Ben's Place, and the boarded-up Oakley Theater. Dal Porto's Tractor and Chevrolet Garage anchored the three-block-long "downtown." As we passed a display of farm implements I said, "Charles, please pull over here."

He stopped, looked into the rearview mirror and asked, "Are we near the ranch yet?" Rather than reply, I jumped out, shouted my thanks, and ran across the highway. Our house was only two blocks away, but I did not want Charles to see it.

A Mexican stepping out of a fancy car is big news in a small town. I could sense people I'd known for years peering at me out of L & D Market, Kempthorne's Rexall Drugs, and Ike's Acme Bar. I avoided all eye contact. During three years of war, no other local had become an officer much less a pilot and I wanted Mother to be the first to share my accomplishment.

No one was home, so I didn't go in. After being away for a year, I felt more like a visitor than a returning family member. An old lawn chair that time had fixed in place under a fruit tree was still there, so I flopped into it and again fell into a deep recuperative sleep. I awoke suddenly, realizing that in the rush to get away from Charles, I had overlooked booking a room at the hotel. The house could not possibly hold me; it had to be straining at the seams with my mother, father, grandmother, and five teenage siblings.

Everyone but Mother was home when I returned from the hotel. No one mentioned her, so I took it for granted that she was at church. But when the sun set and she still hadn't come home, I asked no one and everyone, "Where's Mama?"

Father said, "I'm sorry that we didn't write, but we know what you've been doing and didn't want to worry you. Two months ago your mother left the house in the middle of the night, and we found her walking down the center of the highway in her nightgown. A semi narrowly missed her, and Joe Jesse helped me get her committed to the state mental hospital at Agnews." Stunned, I cloaked my distress with silence.

The next day, Father and I visited the psychiatric wing of the Agnews State Mental Hospital. When the ward nurse saw my uniform, she fluttered, "Oh my, we didn't know that Mrs. Gutierrez has a son who's a pilot. This is wonderful. She had shock therapy this morning and may still be disoriented, but I'm going to get her anyway. Seeing you will be good for her." A locked door opened and Mother shuffled out on the nurse's arm. I had to look twice to assure that she was my mother. Gone were her intelligent eyes and unbounded energy. She was thin and frail, the flesh on her arms had shriveled, and her once black hair was snow white and cut short. Starved for her maternal love, I embraced her and whispered, "*Hi Mama, soy tu hijo, Chacho.*" (I'm your son, Chacho.)

For a year, I had dreamed of the moment she would see me in my new uniform and admire my accomplishment in the same way as Mrs. Chandler had admired Jack's. But her stoic expression never changed;, her eyes remained fixed on what only she could see. I began to cry, and we went out to the car for privacy. As I held her hand in helpless silence, Father pointed beyond the perimeter fence. Through anguished tears, I recognized the orchard where we had once picked prunes to survive and realized that we were in the complex of Spanish style buildings we had once wondered about. I pressed my eyes shut to stop the pain. How in God's name could it possibly be that we were happier then than now? Back in the ward, I buried my head in her shoulder, still desperately searching for the mother I once knew. But it was not to be. Time came to leave and I gently whispered, "I love you mama. Gus is all right, and I promise you that we'll be back soon." With stony silence, as if she had endured me long enough, my dear mother turned away, the nurse took her arm, and they slowly disappeared behind the locked door. I was devastated.

I swallowed my tears as we went to see her doctor. He said, "You say that Maria is your mother? I recall a report that her father died in our Stockton facility and here you are an Army pilot. Hmm, this is very unusual. I wonder if this concerns them? In any case, Maria suffered a severe mental breakdown. She needs to be free of the daily stresses she faces living at home and is much better off here. We provide her a strong support system, healthy meals, daily exercise, and normal social contacts. I think it's fair to say that she will need to be with us for an extended period of time." The doctor's prognosis proved correct, Mother remained in mental institutions during most of my military career.

I felt abandoned and blamed it on my biological father. He hadn't ever bothered to come see us, not even out of curiosity. I thought, I'd like to get that son of a bitch in a strangle hold, rub my success all over his face and say to him, "You deserted us, but I did this with the help of my mother and a man who was more of a father than you could ever be, you bastard." Oh, how I wish I had shared the thought with my stepfather. Surely it would have bonded us more closely. The chasm was too great, however, and we rode home in somber silence.

Father dropped me off at the hotel, and I went into a bar called Ben's Place. The bartender, Wally Whitman, had known me since I was a kid. Over a beer he said, "Stick around, your *paisanos* (countrymen) will be in soon. They're out in the Delta picking tomatoes. We talk about you all the time. Boy, they're going to cream their jeans when they see you in that snazzy uniform." I didn't share his confidence. Would they be proud of what one of their own had done? Or would they consider me disloyal for trying to rise above our status?

Fidel, Jose, Cockeye, Tiofilo, Flaco, Andrew, Macario, and a couple of others came in. They looked like startled raccoons wearing heavy mascara. Black peat grime clogged their eyelashes and ear-hairs, shirts were streaked with salt, pants legs were tied at the ankles, veils of silt sifted to the floor when they moved, and they smelled like dead cats. I had to think hard to remember that I too had once come home in like fashion.

We had been friends. I had slept in their homes and, although they could ill afford it, their mothers had insisted on serving me breakfast at four in the morning prior to our going out to pick asparagus. But time had stood still for them while I had been molded into a far different person than they once knew. Moreover, I had not spoken Spanish for a year and the novelty of over-using the word "sir" and flying jargon had yet to wear off. Initially, they only seemed mildly annoyed with the new me. As the beer flowed, however, their patience thinned and sarcasm crept into their voices.

Finally, Ceferino, his eyes narrow with resentment, said, "*Ya ni hablas Español* (You don't even speak Spanish anymore). You got the big head just because *los gabachos* (foreigners of North American extraction) let you wear that fancy uniform. Whose ass did you kiss to get it?" The others closed in, "Yeah guy, you're not so hot. What makes you think that you're better than we are?" After all I'd been through, their words hurt, and I thought, I don't belong anywhere. Mexicans put me down because I'm an officer and officers put me down because I'm Mexican. It's bad enough being insulted by strangers but I sure as hell don't have to put up with it from so-called friends. I threw some money on the bar and stalked out. Behind me someone said, "*Que se vaya.*" "*Simon, que se vaya*" (Yeah, let him leave). Wally could only shake his head as scornful laughter trailed me out the door.

It had been a long trying day. I trudged up the hotel stairs to my room, opened the door, and stopped short. The room was a shocking pink hue from the red neon Oakley Hotel sign buzzing outside the window. The sight reminded me of a night Gus and I were wandering around Stockton. We were strolling past a seedy hotel known to be a whorehouse when he dared me to step inside. Ever since we were children, accepting his challenges had provided me a means to boost my self-esteem and I usually accepted them. A little bell attached to a scrap of yarn tinkled as I opened the door. Immediately, a young girl clad in pink bra and panties appeared under a red light at the top of the stairs. She started to wave me up, but stopped with her arm in midair as if taking an oath. We gawked at one another. Sarah had attended church Sunday school with us back in Fresno;

our grandmothers were best friends. She screeched, "Get out of here! Get him out of here!" I bolted past Gus like a frightened rabbit, and he caught up with me a block away. Worried that word of our misconduct might somehow get back to Mother, we immediately returned to Oakley.

I went to the window and opened a pair of calico curtains. A swarm of moths and june bugs were waging war against the sign. As I watched them fling themselves at the light, "What ifs?" flooded my mind. What if that doctor tells the Army that my mother is in a mental hospital? Will they ground me? What if word gets around, will other pilots refuse to fly with me? What if, at a flight physical examination, a doctor asks, "Have you or anyone in you immediate family ever had a stroke or suffered a mental illness?" Should I answer truthfully? What if I decide to get married, should I confess that Mother is in an insane asylum and my grandfather died in one? Who would marry me then? No, I decided, if I tip-toe away from the family shadow, keep my mouth shut, and that doctor doesn't talk, maybe it will all work out. A Greyhound bus was due by soon. I packed and hurried home to bid the family farewell. There were none of the tearful good-byes normally shared when a son leaves home, possibly forever, only resigned silence. They knew that my vacation had eight days to go but, rather than stay and at least provide moral support, I was running away.

Aboard the bus, I tried to sort out my sense of loss, disgrace, and guilt. But self-analysis is impossible when one is awash with self-loathing. Slowly, deliberately, I punctured my palm with the clasp of the miniature wings. I hadn't pinned them on Mother's gown because I was ashamed of her.

At Las Vegas Army Air Field, the registrar at the B-17 Co-pilot Training School said, "You're early, we aren't prepared to handle you. Come back in seven days, we'll see you then."

With a week to burn, I found a small motel room and began hanging out on the Las Vegas Strip, which then consisted of two resorts, Hotel Last Frontier and El Rancho. At the Frontier, a rumba band featured a sexy young Mexican vocalist named Norma Hernandez. Norma was a Los Angeles girl and had little in common off-stage with the other members of Eddie Gomez' Puerto Rican band. Though beautiful, at least some of Norma's notable popularity could be attributed to the glittering, skin-tight, floor length gowns that she wore. She captured my attention and my coloring and rank attracted her, so we began dating.

One night after she got off work, we encountered my classmate Ted Johnson and his date Dee—they had just met. As the evening progressed, we learned that despite Dee's bouffant hair-do, false eyelashes, and sexy body, Dee was only sixteen. She followed that bit of news with a comment that when she got home her father would probably whip her for staying out late. Ted suggested that they get married to spare her the beating. Dee accepted.

At the Clark County Court House a cleaning lady said, "My lands children, it's four in the morning. But if you can't wait, go downstairs and see the jailer, he'll marry you." Holding hands, we gaily skipped down a flight of dirty marble stairs to a tiny office that reeked of old cigar butts, urine, and stale sweat. A white Ne-Hi Soda wall thermometer was stuck at 114 degrees, which accounted for the burly jailer being in a dirty undershirt and the beads of sweat clinging to his armpit hairs. He welcomed us, gargled into a spittoon to clear his throat and began the ceremony. The bride popped her gum in rhythm with the reading of the vows and a holding tank full of jeering drunks provided background.

As quickly as it began, the farcical rite ended. Ted paid the jailer five dollars. I do not recall that he questioned Dee's age or that they signed any documents. The newlyweds had an hour together before Ted and I had to get back to the base and prepare for our first day of flight training.

So Long, It's Been Good to Know You

Handsome and wonderfully reliable, the Boeing B-17 Flying Fortress had four engines, a cruising speed of 190 mph, weighed 50,000 pounds, and could carry six tons of bombs 1,200 miles. With thirteen .50-caliber machine guns for armament, the aerial battleship was one of the most effective bombers ever built.

During the month we were stationed in Las Vegas, returned war veterans taught us cockpit flight duties. While in the back of the plane, fledgling aerial gunners learned their trade by firing .50-caliber machine guns at sleeve targets towed by B-26 twin-engine Martin Marauders. The Women Air Service Pilots (WASPs) who flew the tow planes had "one of the boys" status at the bar. Not only because the gunners occasionally missed the "Rag-mop" and hit the plane, but because the B-26 was know as a "killer" when on a single engine. My appreciation for the dangers they faced became more personal when I learned that a school chum, Marie Jacobson, had joined their ranks.

Early one morning I went up with an instructor who appeared to be half-gassed from a night out on the town. He took the B-17 to altitude, pointed to two distant peaks and said, "I'm going to take a nap. Fly back and forth between those two mountains and wake me up in four hours." With that, he crawled down into the catwalk and went to sleep. Mountains differ in appearance from different angles and I promptly got lost. Three hours later, the instructor returned to the flight deck and took over. He made a couple of 360-degree turns, gave me a withering glare and said, "You've got it, hold a heading, any heading." After some serious triangulation with the radio compass, he determined that we were over Idaho well on our way to Canada. A chorus of privates and corporals loudly criticizing my flying skills added miles to our long flight home.

From Los Vegas, we were sent to an Army air field in Lincoln, Nebraska, where we were taught the different skills required to fight a war in a B-17 and were randomly assigned to nine-man crews. The officers on our crew were Pilot, First Lieutenant Joe Carl Martin, a former oil well roustabout from Houston; Copilot, me; and Navigator, First Lieutenant Antonio (Tony) Picone, a husky ex-Detroit cop. The enlisted men, all sergeants, were Flight Engineer-Top Turret Gunner William (Dude) Dudecz, Radio Operator-Gunner Norman Larsen, Togglier-Gunner Ralph Spada, Waist Gunner Matthew (Matt) Schipper, Ball Turret Gunner Celeste (Les) Rossi, and Tail Gunner Paul Gerling.

After a few days, we were hustled off to Rapid City, South Dakota for three months of combat crew training. Primarily, we learned formation flying, bombing procedures, and crew coordination. One moonless night, we were one of several crews flying in a racetrack pattern over a practice bombing range. Alone in the cockpit, I became disoriented and assumed that the wing light of a B-17 flying away from a star was a plane flying directly toward us. The apparition was so real that I immediately rolled the bomber into a diving turn to avoid what appeared to be a certain midair collision. It's been said that, "Flying is hours and hours of boredom interspersed with moments of sheer terror." That was my first "moment," there would be more.

In late December 1944, we returned to Lincoln AAF to complete final processing for overseas duty. The last item on the agenda required that we go by the legal office to complete a last will and testament. The vast majority of us did not own anything of value, so we had little if any need for a will. Nevertheless, it was a shock for a twenty-year-old to face up to his mortality and most of us left the office feeling decidedly more adult and fragile than when we arrived.

On Christmas Day, I went over to Ted's and Dee's to share a hot toddy. I went to the old apartment house and rapped on their door. Dee cracked it open, peeked out and quickly shut it. Through the door she said, "Hi Hank, Ted's out." "That's OK, Dee," I said, "I just stopped by to wish you two a Merry Christmas. I'll come back another time." Dee opened the door, grasped my hand and yanked me in. The room smelled of burnt bacon, the bed was undone, two half-opened suitcases were on the floor, and wash was soaking in the sink. Dee hesitated then turned to face me; she looked like some kind of ghoulish clown. The left side of her face appeared to have been hit with a baseball bat and the right was made-up as if she were about to go out. She lisped, "Ted beat me up. He tried to make me do something dirty, but I wouldn't do it. I wish I'd gone home that night even if my dad had hit me." Without asking for details I said, "Dee, I'll give you the money if you want to go. How much do you need?" She thought for a moment then said, "No, you guys will be going overseas soon, and I want the $10,000 if the bastard gets killed." He did.

"Jingle Bells" had hardly stopped playing in Lincoln's lone department store when we were certified "Combat Ready" and put aboard a train. We weren't told where we were going and were ordered to keep the window shades drawn. Our attempts to identify towns we passed through were useless because all location signs had been removed as a precaution against spies. About all we learned was that with every stop, the length of the train grew until it appeared to be about a mile long. Several nights later, the train ground to a stop beside a long, dimly lit, wooden warehouse. We were rushed inside, lined up in rows and while Red Cross ladies served us coffee and doughnuts, GI's handed everyone a card with a number on it. Then a sergeant ordered, "Pick up your bags and follow me."

As we surged forward, multiple doors on the opposite side of the warehouse opened and we shuffled out to a huge platform. Before us, barely discernible in the darkness, was an immense, grimy black wall. It seems incredibly naïve to me now, but it took us a while to discern that we were facing the hull of a huge ship. Down the line, multiple streams of soldiers struggled up the gangways with their gear and we joined them. Aboard ship, sailors directed us to the cabin number printed on our cards. Seven double-decked bunks were crammed into our small stateroom and I quickly claimed an upper by a porthole. Minutes later, a sailor entered the room and in a Cockney accent said, "Let me have your attention please. You gentlemen have just departed the Boston Port of Embarkation and are now aboard *Ile de France*. This is a French ship manned by the British Royal Navy. Until we get underway, please do not leave this room for any reason unless ordered to do so. Thank you, ta-ta."

Only a lower bunk by the bathroom door remained open and everyone silently appreciated not having it. With false cheerfulness someone said, "Hey, it's New Year's Eve. Let's celebrate!" No one reacted. We just lay in our beds and stared at the ceiling or the cot above, each lost in his thoughts of a distant world called home. The magic hour passed and we opened the portholes to watch the endless columns of men that continued to come aboard. Nearing dawn, one gangway was cleared and MPs began prodding about two hundred chain-linked GI's up the aisle.

An hour later, a small, baby-faced, blond infantry first lieutenant came into our room. He looked like a little kid playing soldier. His olive drab shirt bagged, the belt-loops on his pants were bunched around his waist and his pants-legs were tucked into the tops of his combat boots as if to help hold them up. He dropped a Musette Bag (shoulder bag) on the empty bunk and turned to look around. We gaped! For pinned above his left shirt pocket was a Combat Infantryman Badge and beneath it, a pale blue ribbon with tiny white stars: the Medal of Honor. He smiled at our astonished faces and left.

Lieutenant David Waybur grew up in Fremont, a small town not far from Oakley, and we became friends. In July 1943, Dave was a squad leader with the Third Infantry Division in Sicily. One night, he and his men were in three jeeps traveling up a narrow mountain road when they encountered four enemy tanks coming the other way. Dave jumped out with his .45-caliber Tommy Gun in hand and while standing in bright moonlight, poured a stream of bullets into the open ports of the lead tank. He killed the driver and the out-of-control tank tumbled into a stream below. He sent a man for help then led his people in a two-hour battle with the remaining tanks. Reinforcements arrived and the tank crews took to the hills. Seriously wounded, Dave was recuperating in a hospital in North Africa when General Mark Clark presented him the medal. Dave was sent home to completely recover and while there married a beautiful girl whose dad who also happened to be rich (their wedding present was a new Cadillac convertible and a honeymoon in Palm Springs). Back on duty, the handsome hero was assigned to a contingent of movie stars selling war bonds. He soon tired of that and requested a job training recruits at Fort Leavenworth, Kansas. That didn't work either. Dave knew that once soldiers leave boot camp, they are seldom required to march in cadence. So rather than teach the recruits parade ground etiquette and spit and polish housecleaning, Dave taught them battlefield survival skills. After two reprimands for the same offense, Dave requested a transfer back to his old combat outfit. Upon his arrival at the port of embarkation, the commander placed him in charge of a rag-tag collection of GI's who kept going AWOL to avoid the war. His orders to Dave were simply, "Get them there."

Our second day out, some of the prisoners missed the daily lifeboat drill and the troop commander chided Dave for it. Upset, Dave went to check out the problem and I tagged along with him. Along the way I asked, "Dave, what's wrong with these guys? Why don't they want to do their part?" "Hank," he said, "they only have one problem. The bastards are afraid of dying." Dave's demeanor had changed from a baby-faced kid to a tough, no-nonsense leader. As we descended into the bowels of the ship, the rhythmic engine pulse increased in intensity until it became a rumbling reverberation that penetrated into the soles of my feet. It seemed impossible to go any deeper, yet we did. Finally Dave opened an unmarked pressure door, and we were hit with a blast of hot humid air that almost knocked me back. The colossal engine room was a Dante's Inferno of throbbing, roaring masses of machinery and the surrounding walls were stacked eight high with stretchers. Seasick soldiers occupied many of the stretchers and long glassine strings of slime and spittle were dripping down from one bunk to another. Dave had no sympathy for the malingerers. He blew a police whistle and shouted for the men to, "Fall in!" Only a few men responded, most just turned their backs to him.

Dave said to me, "Let's go." More than 14,000 men were aboard the ship so he easily recruited about 50 six-footers. He issued the men nightsticks and had them roust the prisoners out to the wintry, windswept deck. The men were held there while their living area was hosed down with seawater. Dave's problem did not reoccur.

Back in our cabin, I asked Dave, "Where do you keep the rest of your luggage?"

He pointed to the Musette Bag and said, "This is it. I don't have anymore."

"Go on, you can't live with what that little thing holds."

Dave chuckled, "Here, I'll show you."

He spilled the contents on the bunk: four sets of underclothes, family pictures, two pairs of silk stockings given to him by actress Carole Landis, toilet articles, and an industrial size bottle of green Mennen's after shave lotion.

I pointed to the bottle and said, "I understand the other stuff, but what the hell is that for?"

He replied, "We're not like you guys, we don't have flunkies to help us. In the infantry, we carry everything on our backs and I only take essentials."

"OK, I'll bite. So why is a quart of after shave so important?"

"Well, when we liberate a town, I find a nice looking girl to spend the night with. And if there's no soap and water handy, I douse myself with the bug juice, she does the same and we get on with it. That stuff's better than Lysol, it'll kill any stink."

I hope Dave got to use all the Mennen's. He died three months later while fighting in Germany.

On our seventh day out, I awoke to find us slowly gliding up the Firth of Clyde to Glasgow, Scotland. Upon landing, the ground troops continued on to the continent to join infantry units fighting there and the airmen were processed into bomber and fighter units of the Eighth Air Force at the Valley Repl-Depl (Personnel Replacement Depot).

That night in the officers club, upon hearing that our crew had been assigned to the 100th Bomb Group, a home-bound veteran of the air war told Joe, Tony, and me that the 100th was a hard luck outfit. He called it the "Bloody 100th" and said that the Luftwaffe had a vendetta against the group, repeatedly singling it out for attack. Apparently, the vendetta resulted from a pilot of a crippled B-17 who lowered his gear as a sign of surrender only to then have his gunners blast the German fighters as they came in close to escort the B-17 down. Others confirmed the story; but it was common practice for veterans to "flak-up" replacement crews, and we were so green the tale didn't particularly impress us. A day later, our crew boarded an overnight train that delivered the morning milk and fresh flight crews to airfields along Bomber Alley.

Chapter 3

Aerial Combat
(1945)

―

The "Bloody 100th" Bomb Group

"Diss, next stop, Diss. Yanks, this is your stop." We exited the train in total darkness and climbed aboard a 6×6 GI truck idling nearby. The driver turned on two dim blue running lights and sped off, twenty minutes later we skidded to a stop. The GI came around, let down the tailgate and said, "Lieutenant Martin, this is the 349th Squadron officers housing area. You and your officers get out here. Follow that path, it'll take you to Hut 15 where you'll find three empty bunks. Oh, yeah, I'd be quiet going in. We're flying a mission in the morning and that's where Lieutenant (Thomas E.) O'Neill lives. Boy, has he got a short fuse."

Joe, Tony, and I slipped and slid to a one-story, concrete-slab building. The wood door creaked as Tony cracked it open. He stopped, we listened, no complaints, so we tiptoed in. On the wall, a glowing red "ALERT" light confirmed the driver's warning. We switched on our gooseneck GI flashlights. Two rows of beds lined the length of the room and all appeared occupied except for three side-by-side. Each was stacked with two GI blankets and three straw-filled biscuits. As we prepared the beds our flashlights illuminated candle-smoke graffiti scrawled on the chalk-white ceiling: Frankfurt, Berlin, Merseburg, Bremen, Leipzig. I turned off my light and got into bed fully clothed. Lonely and homesick, I wanted something familiar touching me. As I stared at the ceiling, the graffiti seemed to have been applied with florescent paint for I swear it was visible. I wondered who slept here last. Was he a prisoner, dead, missing? Will I end up with him or return home? I was mulling the questions over in my mind when the barracks door opened and a GI came in. One after another, he went to several bunks, nudged the occupant and whispered, "Sir, briefing at 0400." The fellow across the aisle rose, turned on his flashlight, dressed and without a word to anyone, went out to meet his day. The distant roar of R-1820 engines being pre-flighted lulled me to sleep.

Later that morning we learned that in addition to the 349th, the 350th, 351st, and 418th squadrons comprised the "Bloody 100th" Bombardment Group. Our airfield was a former Royal Air Force (RAF) installation named Thorpe-Abbotts and we were in East Anglia about ninety miles from London.

That afternoon we flew the first of four orientation flights over the British Isles. On the fourth, we were up practicing formation flying with five other crews when an unidentified voice on the radio said, "Close it up, close it up." Joe said, "We're in position. I wonder who he's talking to?"

Just then, an old, stripped-down, hack B-17 overtook the formation and sailed off ahead of us. The voice on the radio said, "This is Colonel Jeffrey. If I can run a B-17 through there, God help you when they get hold of you." No need to explain who "they" were.

1945, 100th Bomb Group, England. On missions, pilots typically wore: long johns, electric-heated "Bunny Suit," uniform, flight suit, flight jacket, fleece-lined boots, escape kit and a .45 caliber pistol. In the cockpit, they donned a radio headset and throat mike, oxygen mask, gloves, water life preserver, and parachute harness. In combat, they added a steel helmet and a steel-plated flak suit that resembled a catcher's chest protector

It was rare for a B-17 pilot to be older than thirty. Most of us were barely into our twenties and Colonel Tom Jeffrey was no exception. Short and well built, he was about twenty-eight, handsome, with Chestnut hair, a close mustache, a bit of a twang in his voice, and a slight swagger to compensate for his stature. We had already heard that he was tough but that was OK, he held the key to our survival and we went to work.

That night, after dinner, I invited Carl and Tony to go checkout the town of Diss. They were newly married, however, and had no interest in chasing women. I flagged a truck headed toward the main gate and the driver motioned me into the cab. As we sped toward Diss, I idly asked him, "Is this a regular run into town?" "No," the driver replied, "I'm going to the train station to pick up a new crew." I said, "Oh, it's awfully quiet in back, I'd think that at this time of day you'd have a truck load of guys going into town for a good time." He eyed me and said, "You must be new. No, there's nobody back there. We don't go into Diss unless we have to, but you might like it."

Something in his tone of voice made me uncomfortable so I dropped the subject. We parted at the station and I strolled up a hill toward Diss. Along the way, a tweedy looking woman who appeared to be on her daily constitutional overtook me and slowed to my pace. She chirped, "Are you lost, Yank?" "Well, yes and no, ma'am," I replied. "I hear there's a dance at a place called the Corn Exchange. Am I headed in the right direction?" "Yes," she said, "it's a large yellow building past the summit, you can't miss it. But the doors do not open until eight. Have a nice time and come back again." She resumed her pace.

I roamed the town until nightfall but no one seemed interested in a lonely Yank and I returned home. The next morning I asked a couple of veterans, "Where do you guys go to have fun in Diss?" They look at me a little strange and one said, "I don't know, we don't go there much."

That seemed odd, so I posed the question to the barracks' leader Captain Will Murray. Will said, "Henry, a Negro Army engineering outfit is stationed near Diss and it's 'their' town. We don't go there unless we have to." Will also clarified my question on "Escape Cards." We had been told to report to the photo shop to be photographed in a civilian coat and tie. The photos were used to create fake identification cards for possible use if we went down. Will said, "Forget it, the photo shop has been using the same coat and tie for so long and so many crews have gone down that the Germans don't even bother to interrogate our guys. The jacket and tie give

1945, 100th Bomb Group, England.
Capt. Will Murray, Salinas, California

them away as being from the 100th and off they go to prison camp. Don't even bother."

I also forgot about Diss. In time, I found that most Englishmen assumed me to be Italian and professed to harbor no prejudices against African-Americans. They seemed, however, to do so against East Indians, and if all that was not perplexing enough, they thought that being Mexican was exotic. It was all too much for me; I stayed home unless the flight schedule permitted a trip to London.

* * * *

Winters in England can be brutal. Powerful storms sweep in off the North Sea, temperatures plummet and everything and everyone seems to be made out of square parts. It's a time best suited for lying before a crackling fireplace in leisure clothes, with soft music in the background and a loving girl in your arms. Dream on.

It was 0600, 19 February 1945. The skies were dark, cold sheets of water lashed across the ramp and everything looked strange. Eight to ten B-17's were staggered on opposite sides of Runway 28 when a green-green flare arched high from the control tower. Immediately, four giant water rooster-tails spouted behind FireBall Dog 1. The heavily laden B-17 lumbered down the strip, broke ground, and rumbled out of sight. Precisely 25 seconds later, a second bomber went, then another, and another. Each departure set off a cacophony of screeching, squealing brakes, and engines roaring alternating power blasts as the line of waiting planes moved forward. We reached the number one slot and Joe taxied ahead a bit. We locked the tail wheel, set the brakes, and gently coaxed the throttles full open. As the engines reached full song, blue fire poured from the superchargers and the plane began bouncing in its desire to fly. On the hack, Joe released the brakes and we had no sooner lifted off than we entered the clouds. Wheels up, flaps up, set climb power. We began a shallow left turn.

We corkscrewed up and around a nearby radio beacon called Splasher 6 and emerged from billowing clouds at 12,000 feet. Soon the wing lights of all the 100th's thirty-six B-17s could be seen forming into four squadrons of nine aircraft each. As we continued to climb, the squadrons formed into one group layered and staggered horizontally and vertically. For the remainder of the flight, we maneuvered in unison with no space between us for zigzagging. By doing so, the amassed firepower of more than 430 closely spaced, heavy machine guns would contribute to the defense of the group. When the last B-17 was in place, the 100th joined the 90th and 390th Bomb Groups to become the 13th Combat Wing. The formation commander then led his 108 B-17s to a designated spot within the 16 groups that comprised the 3rd Air Division. Up and down Bomber Alley the 1st and 2nd air divisions formed in like manner and nearly an hour after takeoff, the bomber stream made a sweeping turn east and we headed toward so-called "U.S. Highway 1," our usual flight path into Germany.

1945, 100th Bomb Group, England. Lt. Joe Carl Martin, Houston, Texas

Twenty minutes out over the North Sea, the VHF radio crackled, "Gunners, cleared to test fire." Our plane reeked of burning cordite and shuddered like an old pickup speeding over freeway lane markers as the gunners jack-hammered fluid streams of tracers into the darkness. Suddenly, a distant explosion lit up the sky and flaming debris lazily drifted down as if in slow motion. Tension-edged questions crowded the intercom, "Was it a B-17?" "Did a gunner shoot it down?" "Are there enemy fighters in the area?" None of us had any answers and VHF radio silence was strictly enforced so we dropped the subject and concentrated on our jobs.

As we neared the enemy lines, Dude helped Joe and me into our flak suits. The armored vest resembled an over-sized catcher's chest protector and along with them, we wore a steel helmet that resembled a German infantry hard-hat with earflaps. We had not trained with the equipment back in the States and, although we had been briefed on it since our arrival, I was reminded of the first time I donned a football uniform and helmet back at Liberty High: macho, tough, ready to challenge anyone. Dude donned his equipment and returned to the top gun turret. Meanwhile, up in the egg-shaped Plexiglass nose, Ralph and Tony were arguing about the best way to get maximum protection from their battle gear. "Damn it Tony," Ralph was saying, "I'm telling you, they shoot at us from the ground. If we spread both suits on the floor they'll protect us better." Bridegroom Tony replied, "You do what you want with yours. I know where mine's going." He sat on it and wrapped it around his crotch.

Within a minute, rivulets of moisture began to trickle down my forehead and the back of my neck. It wasn't sweat; I was scared but not that much. Joe had the same problem. I mopped my face with my sleeve and that made my eyes burn. I unsnapped the oxygen mask, the odor was unmistakable—it was urine. Joe moaned, "Here you take it." Aaaaarrgh! Retch! Bleah! Ptooie, Ptooie.

No need to ask what happened. Either Tony or Ralph had peed into the forward relief tube. It was plugged but he could not stop so the urine spilled on our battle gear and froze. Joe was very religious and his ultimate expression of frustration was "Dad gum it." I was not similarly encumbered and barraged the two morons with every profane word I could think of. The only reaction to my outburst was a lot of ill-disguised snickering over the intercom. Who said that war isn't hell?

We arrived over the "initial point" from where the group wheeled into a twenty-or-so-mile run to the target. From his perch, Ralph maintained a sharp eye on the lead ship. There, the bombardier acquired the target and opened his bomb bay doors. An ocean-like roar announced that Ralph had opened ours as well. The bombardier continued to make final adjustments to his Norden bombsight until their bombs released. The moment their bombs appeared, we lurched upward as Ralph dropped ours and called, "Bombs away." Within seconds, Ralph was back on the intercom, "Hey, I can see the flashes of our bombs hitting the target." His companion Tony said, "Get your head back in here you dummy. Those aren't bomb-hits, they're shooting at us."

Puffs of black smoke shaped like little Casper the Friendly Ghosts dappled the sky around us. The tiny clouds seemed insignificantly small and incapable of creating all the horror stories we had heard. *Whumph! Whumph!* Suddenly, very nearby we saw two red flashes of fire, felt the con-

1945. B-17s of the "Bloody" 100th Bomb Group en route to a target

cussions, and flak rattled off the paper-thin fuselage. Until that moment, the idea of going to war had a new and exciting feeling to it. Now I felt naked; my knees met to protect my groin, my shoulders hunched, my elbows tucked in and my neck shrank in an effort to hide my body under the flak suit. I also thought of removing my feet from the rudder pedals but I already felt like a pretzel and it is impossible to fly formation that way. I sat up and said to myself, "To hell with it, if it's going to happen it's going to happen, do your job." Hundreds of explosions blended into a dense cloud of greasy black smoke that we passed through and returned home. During debriefing, old hands judged the flak over the target as "severe."

* * * *

Two days later, the deluge had not let up when a 6×6 crew truck dropped us off at *The Squawkin' Hawk*. She was the oldest bomber in the 100th. Rather than the natural metal finish of newer B-17s, it was painted a creamed-coffee color, bright aluminum patches marked past wounds, the engines dripped oil, and stenciled beneath the pilot's window were seven black swastikas. We unloaded our flight gear and hurried into the ground crew tent. Everyone crowded around buttback to a fifty-gallon drum that had been converted into a waste-oil stove. Joe and I reviewed the aircraft maintenance records with the crew chief. Meanwhile, the gunners disassembled their machine guns, carefully wiped the mechanisms free of preserving oil, re-assembled the weapons, and installed them at their positions aboard the plane. Because temperatures in their areas of the plane were much colder than ours, each gunner donned a bulging, binding, sheepskin-lined leather flying suit, a Mae West life preserver, parachute harness, throat mike, and a warm leather helmet with an installed radio headset. Overwhelmed by the sheer bulk of their equipment, they moved about like awkward turtles — and they had yet to don their battle gear.

Soon it was time to go. Dude, Joe, and I slung our flak suits and steel battle helmets up and aft of the nose hatch door, chinned our selves up and in, crawled over the equipment and up to the cockpit. The seats felt like a well-worn shoe and smelled like one.

We started the engines and waited for the yellow flare to arch up from the control tower-a signal for the planes to taxi out for takeoff. Ever so slowly, we inched forward prepared to merge into our designated position in the parade of B-17s going by. Our spot came up and we trundled toward it. Suddenly, *The Squawkin' Hawk* lurched and stopped with the wings canted over as if in a steep right turn. We shut down the engines and got out. The left wheel was on the concrete pad but the right one was mired in mud up to the axle.

We were under the wing watching other planes find alternate routes to the runway when the group engineering officer, Major Eugene Rovegno, arrived in his jeep. The dark-skinned, bald-headed son of Italy had a Roman nose, an irreverent mouth, and a well-known reputation for telling pilots "how the cow ate the cabbage." If that were not intimidating enough, his nickname was Butch and his Ike jacket sported gold Marine pilot wings, a World War I Victory Ribbon, and a row of overseas bars that extended to his elbow. He was the kind of senior officer every junior birdman instinctively knew to avoid.

With hands on hips and legs widespread, he stood in the downpour and evaluated the situation. "Well you two really screwed up this time," he said to Joe and me. "Don't just stand there, get some shovels and dig it out." Joe turned to the crew and said, "Come on men, let's get some shovels and dig it out." Rovegno interrupted him, "Why are you asking them to do it? You did it, you do it." The crew backed into the shadows as Joe and I found a pair of shovels and frantically began digging grease-slick mud away from the wheel. The major watched us for a minute, had a quick discussion with the crew chief, then drove away.

We were soaked to the skin with sweat and rain when the sergeant emerged from his tent and said, "Stop digging, we'll have to de-fuel and unload the bombs before we can tow her out." Rovegno had purposely embarrassed us for his benefit since he would have to do the real work. We stomped the mud from our boots, collected our gear and like a couple of drenched turkeys trying to act nonchalant, went splashing through lake-like puddles back to the ready room. The crew trailed well behind, carefully avoiding every puddle and grinning at every passerby.

* * * *

It was dark and windy as we climbed into what had become "our" B-17G. She answered to three-eight-five-one-four and her official call sign was Kidmeat J-Jig. She was better known, however, as *E-Z Goin'*. An unknown "nose-art" artist had emblazoned the name on her nose, and beneath it added a turtle with funny eyes and a gleeful smile blithely hauling a bomb balanced atop its shell.

The Munich rail yards were the target for the day but by the time we arrived, the Germans had obscured the area with a smoke screen. Rather than risk hitting the nearby Dachau prison camp, we randomly elected to bomb the city center. On our return flight, we were treated to the sparkling majesty of the snow-capped Swiss Alps on a sunny day. As I gazed at their towering splendor, all I could think of was the destruction we had left back in Munich.

* * * *

On our fifth mission, a massive force of over 1,100 bombers attacked several targets in the Berlin area. The 100th hit the Alexanderplatz railroad station. In addition to it being our first visit to the famous target, the mission also had personal significance as it qualified me to apply for a battlefield commission. The rank of flight officer was equivalent to warrant officer, which technically was an enlisted grade. Our rank insignia was blue-and-gold bars and a cap emblem that resembled a rooster in the act of relieving himself. To be considered for the promotion to second lieutenant, flight officers were required to travel to Elvenden Hall, seventy miles away, on an off duty day no less, and meet a Direct Commission Appointment Board. Not only was this inconvenient but the process had a Catch-22 aspect to it. Flight officers and second lieutenants received the same basic salary. Commissioned officers, however, received a 10 percent increase for overseas service, whereas flight officers, like all enlisted men, received 20 percent. Accordingly, the promotion amounted to a 10 percent cut in pay.

Given the advertised longevity of 100th air crews, I did not consider it cost-effective to miss a couple of nights in London for that kind of advancement so I forgot about it. In retrospect, the decision undoubtedly cost me a promotion by the time I retired. Nevertheless, I would do it again, for I matured much faster on the streets of London than in the skies over Germany.

Members of the crew seldom socialized together. Tony and Joe kept to themselves as did the enlisted men. Consequently, whenever we received a three-day pass, I visited London alone. During daytime, bombed-out buildings and a kaleidoscope of military uniforms gave London a decided wartime appearance. At night, however, the city appeared to take on an eerie, carnival-like atmosphere. When the pubs closed, people spilled into the streets and women were easier to find than taxicabs. Everywhere one turned, girls offered their hospitality; some for a price, some for free, and some would even do it in doorways. But I didn't judge them harshly; bombs hadn't been falling on my hometown for four years.

It was a perfect Sunday afternoon, the sky was Wedgwood blue, the humidity was down and I was exploring London's dizzying patchwork of streets that make no sense at all. In the Soho district, the old-world architecture of a little tea shop drew my attention. I peered through a window and immediately on the other side was a handsome, aristocratic-looking woman who appeared lost in thought. I edged over for a better view. She sensed the attention and riveted me with a penetrating stare.

Caught in the act, I offered an embarrassed smile and shrugged my shoulders as if to say, "Hey there's no harm in looking." Surprisingly, she nodded an invitation for me to come in. I did so and introduced myself to Helena Randwick. Helena had blonde swept-back hair, pale blue eyes, a closed-mouthed smile, and bad teeth. Clearly from a world of privilege, she held her head high and in an accented voice told me that she was Norwegian by birth and married to a Royal Air Force (RAF) pilot. She ordered me "tea and scones" and a young girl served me a cup and four tiny slices of jellied toast. They were hardly a mouthful and, eager to flash the money in my wallet, I wolfed them down and asked for more. The waitress leaned close to me and whispered, "Sir, there is a war on and we really must conserve in order to take care of all our customers." Red-faced, I stammered an apology and Helena smoothed over my blunder like a mother offering an excuse for an ill-mannered child. Helena lived in nearby Mayfair, and after a pleasant conversation I walked her home.

Well before we arrived, I knew there was no chance that she would invite me in. She shook my hand goodbye and disappeared into an entrance that looked more like a private club than an apartment building. We had not set a date, nevertheless I returned to tea shop the next day. Helena was there and seemed genuinely happy to see me. After the requisite cup of tea she asked, "Would you like to go to the cinema?"

"Sure," I said. "What would you like to see?"

"*A Guy Named Joe*," she answered. "It's at the Lyceum Theater."

"Great, I'd love to see it." No need to mention that this would be my third viewing of the film.

At the box-office, she insisted that we sit in the balcony. The cheap seats seemed out of character for her but once the feature started the reason became apparent. "What was that? What did she say?" "What does that mean?" The whispered questions lasted the entire film. We had a good time and upon our arrival at her building, she invited me into their apartment.

The flat had dark wood walls lined with impressive plaques and paintings, floor-to-ceiling bookshelves arrayed with gold-embossed leather bound books, porcelain hanging lamps provided subdued lighting, and everywhere were photographs of a fair-haired RAF pilot. Over tea, she spoke about her husband for the first time. He was a squadron leader stationed nearby, they had been married seven years, were devoted to each other, and before the war, he had held a position in the office of the Lord Mayor. She sounded convincing but her eyes told me that she wanted more than he had left after a hard day in the air. We began an affair.

Our dates were keyed to their mailbox. Slot open meant safe. Slot closed, he's home. One day I went by to check on her availability and the slot was open. I rushed by florid-faced old men snoring in the lobby, ignored the lift to take the stairs two at a time but stopped short at the landing. Tacked on the door was a small black wreath. I considered ringing the doorbell to offer condolences but thought better of it and quietly retreated.

Two months later, I was leaving the Lyceum Theater when I met Helena coming in on the arm of a handsome RAF pilot. She dropped his hand, took a step in my direction, blinked and said, "Henry, I--I had no idea you were in town." Feeling helpless, I looked over her shoulder and unsuccessfully tried to compare her companion to the fellow in the photos. She only hesitated for a moment before her sophistication took over. With finality in her voice she said, "So good to see you again leftenant, goodbye." She rejoined him and, as they went on, I turned, admired her once more, and smiled at the memories.

∞

Jet! Jet! Jet! What's That? I Dunno

The 100th was at 29,000 feet leading the 3rd Air Division to a factory near Brunswick, Germany, and six of us were ahead of the group dropping chaff, metalized strips that helped mask our planes from the radar the Germans used to aim their cannons.

I was flying in close formation with our leader, Captain Jack W. Trasher. As we droned along, I admired Jack's B-17G, examining its gleaming fuselage, fresh insignia and squadron code markings, the first smudges of soot behind the engines, and the new staggered waist windows. The tail gunner appeared to wave at me but I didn't return it, why bother. Flying a B-17 no longer required total absorption. To tell the truth, the job had become a bit routine. *E-Z Goin'* trimmed well, the controls were smooth and the engines reliable. Whereas older planes gave off a telltale odor of hydraulic fluid, sweat, and dirt, *E-Z Goin'* still had a new-car smell. I felt like cocking my hat back, putting a stick of chewing gum in my mouth and sticking my elbow out of the window.

My mind wandered. I recalled a professor's daughter I'd met in London the last time there. We'd had sex on her living room floor while her grandparents were upstairs. Still, I wondered if I was really her first man as she claimed or if she said that to all her men. Yet she had given me a studio photograph and begged to come live near the airfield. I decided to see her again.

Suddenly, someone broke radio silence—and my erotic daydream—by shouting, "Jet! Jet! Jet!" I asked Joe, "What's that?" He replied, "I dunno." Off to our left, two sleek, shark-like fighters with swastikas on their tails zoomed into view. They didn't have propellers churning the air and were moving faster than anything we had ever seen before. No one had ever shown us a photo or silhouette of such a machine, or warned us that the Germans had a new, twin-engine, swept-wing fighter called the Me-262, with an unknown propulsion system, that trailed black smoke and was a hundred miles an hour faster than anything we had.

Pow-pow-pow-pow-pow! Smoking cannon shells stitched bright jagged holes across Jack's left wing and the attackers dived down and away. Flames erupted and Jack sideslipped the plane in an effort to douse the blaze. That didn't help, so he returned to straight-and-level flight and the fire intensified. As expected, crewmen came tumbling out of the escape hatches; one, two, three, four, five, six—six—six, *boom!* The plane exploded with Jack still visible at the controls. He and two men died.

When a stricken B-17 plunged to earth, it usually dived or spiraled down with a certain elegance that glossed over the fact that inside, terrorized men were reeling around like dice in a tin cup. When one exploded, however, huge assemblies, parts and pieces, and flaming fuel and oil flew off in all directions and the crew was blasted into space like so many scarecrows! As we staggered through the shock wave, I caught my breath, my stomach-muscles knotted, my body went rigid, and I got goose bumps. A moment later, nothing! All traces of the explosion were behind us and I was flying formation with a hole in the sky.

Dismayed, Joe and I glanced at one another then looked away. One never felt more alive than when he had cheated death and it was embarrassing to find yourself elated when friends were dying. You felt a need to apologize to someone—anyone—for them being killed and you being spared. Joe took the controls and my adrenaline level slowly returned to normal.

The horror of a fire at altitude never fades. The air is so clear up there that fire appears brighter and deadlier than on the ground. It is the death fliers fear most and the memory remains coiled and ready to strike when least expected. Don't ever let some macho pilot tell you he doesn't know the meaning of the word fear. All who fly have had full-body bear hugs with it. As they say, however, "The difference between pilots is their ability to handle fear. And if you can't, you shouldn't be one."

With Jack gone, our deputy-leader assumed command and immediately pushed over into a steep dive. It felt like I was back in the front seat of the Great Dipper roller coaster on the beach at Santa Cruz, California. *E-Z Goin'* shuddered in protest as the airspeed indicator needles passed their red-lines as if they didn't matter and the altimeters twirled backwards at an alarming rate. Exceeding the speed limit was more than the pilot of one plane could stomach and he backed off. We pulled out of the dive at 15,000 feet and had an uneventful flight home. Upon landing, all the planes in our element were inspected for structural stress damage but not was found.

Later that evening, we were washing up for dinner when the laggard pilot came by and accused the leader of having abandoned him. The captain replied, "Pal, if it's ever a choice between you or me going down, I hope it's you." No one else said a word.

Jack was the All-American type: tall, blond, and handsome. He bunked across the aisle from me and only the night before I had watched him kiss a photograph of a dreamy looking girl and say, "Only two more baby, two more, and I'll be home." For me that moment symbolized the ultimate tragedy of war; so many dreams lost, so many futures wasted.

* * * *

On March 15th, we bombed the rail yards in Oranienburg, a suburb of Berlin. Following the raid, *The Stars and Stripes* reported in part, "Thousands of bombs hit the target." That may be true but apparently the reporter missed seeing the 100th's strike photos. All we did was save some German farmer from having to plow his potato patch.

The Russian armies had backed-up thousands of civilians into Berlin and on March 18, 1,300 bombers and 700 fighters lifted-off for what would be the 100th's last sweep against that city. Perhaps the Germans sensed that our bombing systems were set to deliver the bombs at maximum intervals across the city, for there was no need to answer any "Are we there yet?" questions.

It has been said that the Germans deployed 10,000 cannons against the Anglo-American bombers and on that day it seemed like all of them were there. We were at 33,000 feet and from miles away, a huge, ominous, oily, black cloud defined the target area. I glanced back as we turned on the bomb run. As far as I could see, the sun was glinting off a parade of planes that extended back to the horizon. Hours would pass before the last B-17 bombed the city. We adjusted our flak-suits, scrunched down our battle-helmets, and the formation closed-up.

Suddenly, from out of the sun, four Me-262s pounced on our badly strung-out low squadron. Someone reported that *Sky Chariot* had lost its left horizontal stabilizer. When last seen, Lieutenant Rollie King was going down under control but under attack. We later learn that six crewmen bailed out before the B-17 went into a violent spin and exploded.

Our new ball-turret gunner, Sergeant Alfred E. "Mouse" Collins, who had replaced Lee Rossi (grounded due to injury), called on the intercom, "My guns are jammed. I'm coming out." The odds against pilots getting out of their seats in an emergency, hooking on their parachutes, and successfully making their way through a narrow aisle to the front hatch or bomb bay to bail out were extremely high. But given the centrifugal forces of a spinning plane and the cumbersome clothing the gunners wore, for one of them to exit the ball quickly had to take an act of God. Nevertheless, Joe said, "Mouse, stay where you are and keep tracking. If incoming fighters see your guns stowed, they'll attack us from that direction. And you other gunners, keep your guns moving. Let them know we're watching them." Mouse stayed put.

Lieutenant Merrill Jensen's plane was sighted with his number four engine shut down and missing about five feet of one wing tip. Jensen headed for Poland where, we later learned, he landed safely.

Sweet Nancy II had two engines shot-up. Lieutenant Edward "Duke" Gwin dived away from the formation. All seemed to go well for a minute then the plane nosed up at a steep angle, the tail broke off and the two assemblies spun down. Only one chute was seen. Duke Gwin and his crew had been with us since Lincoln.

Pathfinder took several cannon hits in the left wing. The fuel tanks ignited but the pilot, Lieutenant Paul DeWeerdt, maintained control while his men bailed out. The plane exploded and amazingly Paul was the only survivor. Parts, parachutes, and bodies floated by as we entered heavy flak. Elsewhere, a B-17 was seen on fire and the copilot crawled out through his side window. He appeared to miss the propeller, slid back down the wing, and slammed into the horizontal stabilizer. He hung there like a staple then fell away as the plane blew-up.

A later issue of *The Stars and Stripes* reported that over 80,000 civilians died in the raid. The 100th lost thirty-eight men.

Three days later, the 100th went after a tank plant in Plauen, Germany, and we were assigned to fly the tail-end-Charlie position in the low-low squadron, the infamous "Purple Heart corner." Along the way, a lone B-17 appeared to our left. It presented a more inviting target than we did and for that, we were silently grateful. Predictably, two Me-262's attacked them from six o'clock high. The bomber absorbed the hits and the jets over-ran it then turned left. The 100th's gunners fired a barrage and a trail of silvery cowling, parts and pieces, tumbled lazily downward as the two disappeared into clouds. In the squadron above us, a Me-262 came in from five o'clock high firing at Lieutenant Bernard Painter's B-17. At the same time, a P-51 was closing on the jet's tail. The B-17 exploded and the 262 climbed so fast that the P-51 appeared to be flying through molasses. Hard to believe, but again, Painter was the only survivor and became a prisoner of war. That Me-262 pilot's demonstration of his 560-mile-per-hour jet over a 440-mile-per-hour P-51 was not lost on us. We were still in awe of his performance when a Me-163 rocket-powered fighter, shaped like a beer-barrel, shot up through the formation and disappeared into a cloud layer above. That really brought out the, "Wows!" and the, "What was thats?" No one had answers, so we continued plowing toward Plauen where we smashed a tank factory then returned home. The 100th's gunners claimed one fighter shot down.

On March 24, 1945, more than 1,600 C-47s and 1,300 gliders were poised to land troops on the far side of the Rhine River. We were awakened much earlier than ever before. Our job was to bomb German-held airfields in Holland to keep their fighters grounded. At 0400, we were briefed for the first of two missions scheduled for the day but our baby-faced tailgunner, Paul Gerling, caused us to nearly miss the first takeoff time. Paul had witnessed much of the action over Berlin from his isolated outpost in the tail and before this mission confided to me that he wanted to quit flying. As the informal personnel officer for the crew, I persuaded Paul to visit the Padre and accompanied him there in order to keep it a secret from the others. The priest assumed that we both needed jacking-up and worked me over as well. On our way back to the plane, I mentioned that the benediction probably benefited me more than it did him, so Paul reversed our roles and told the crew that he had taken me. We post-holed the runway at Steenwijk, Holland, and were home by noon.

At 1400 we took-off again to bomb an airfield at Ziegenhian. The group was spiraling up into formation when a sky full of RAF Lancaster bombers emerged from the haze headed directly for us. The RAF did not fly in geometric patterns as we did. They assembled in no particular order, and everyone departed in the same direction at the same time. We tried to close ranks and force the ungainly "Lancs" to circumvent our half-formed group. Instead, they remained on course and a minute later, thirty-six bomb-and-fuel-laden B-17s at climb speed were going every which way with everyone struggling to avoid each other, dodge the "Lancs," fight the prop wash, and not stall out. It was another moment of terror.

A week later, the 100th's target was an oil refinery near Zeitz. Luftwaffe fighters were attacking groups ahead of us and I was tucked-in-close below and behind Lieutenant Arthur Larson's plane in the element ahead. Light flak sprouted among us as we began the bomb run. Suddenly, Larson's number three engine separated from the plane like a plucked grape and fell away with the propeller spinning wildly. Instantly, severed electrical wiring harnesses began discharging angry blue sparks and flailing rubber snakes were spewing oil and high-octane gasoline. Tony shouted, "Everything's there, get away from him, he's going to blow-up." Another crewman with a view of the plane yelled, "Get away!" "Get away from him!" I was faced with a dilemma: should I bank and possibly alter the trajectory of our bombs or stay and risk being damaged? Larson resolved the question; he banked away then resumed level flight. A moment later his rear escape door flew off and a crewmember bailed out. The man immediately opened his parachute and as he floated away, we all agreed that he would never survive his trip to earth. If flak or anoxia (oxygen depletion at high altitudes) didn't kill him one of the following planes surely would. If he survived that, chances were that civilians on the ground would hang him as they had others. Meanwhile the flak stopped and Larson appeared to have the plane under control. Our leader called him, "Stay with us, it's not far to the airfields behind Patton's army. We'll spot a good one for you to land." "No," Larson replied, "I think we'll keep going east and see how the Russians are doing."

The B-17 disappeared into the haze and we returned home. Upon entering the barracks, we found the squadron adjutant packing Larson's belongings. He had already stowed Navigator Lieutenant Watterson's and Bombardier Lieutenant Dineen's stuff and Joe said to him, "Hey, stop that. Those guys landed in Russia, they'll be back soon. The guy you need to pack up is the tail gunner. He bailed out over the target and there's no way he made it." The adjutant ignored him and continued to carefully examine and place each item into a new duffel bag. Tony said, "All right then. If you won't stop, let us collect our chits." Chits were vouchers for items of like value that we exchanged with officers on other crews. For example, we'd exchange a radio for a pair of sheets, a jacket for a bike, or fleece-lined boots for a trench coat. When the fellow went down, we presented the chit to the adjutant and he allowed us to take possession of the item before packing the remainder for shipment home. Occasionally some wise-ass would give chits for the same item to three or four guys and when he went down, a big argument would erupt over who rightfully owned it; talk about a lack of integrity.

Two weeks later Technical Sergeant John. E. Kaiser, the tail gunner who bailed out, surprised us when he entered our barracks. As we listened in awe, he related this story: "The trip down was no sweat. But I no sooner hit the ground than a bunch of farmers waving axes, pitchforks, and shotguns came after me. I had to run a mile in my boots before I came to a gun emplacement. A bunch of old guys and kids were shooting at you guys so I jumped into the revetment. They chased the farmers away then searched me for cigarettes. They let me keep one, so we all lit-up and I laid back and watched them shoot at you guys. They were pretty good, my only worry was that some dumb togglier might miss the target and hit me. They put me in the town jail and a couple of days later an English-speaking German showed up. He asked if I was OK then told me that our plane crashed and everybody died. He showed me Lieutenant Larson's dog tags, wedding ring, and stuff like that from all the guys. The Russians let me out."

The Eighth's next targets were the submarine pens at Kiel. As we approached the Baltic Sea location, the group entered heavy cloud cover and everything became downright eerie. We were flying half-instruments and half-formation with blurred outlines of nearby planes looming and disappearing like threatening shadows. Nevertheless, the clouds were a blessing in disguise. For during one brief period of clarity, we saw some enormous explosions that appeared to be about the size of a house. Later, some said that a battleship fired at us. While others claimed that it was a "Big Bertha" cannon mounted on a railroad flat car. After what seemed an eternity, the lead bombardier called out "bombs away" and Ralph toggled our bombs into the murk. The group continued on the same heading until we suddenly emerged into sparkling blue sky.

We were far out over the North Sea and as we turned for home, Lieutenant Bill Baldwin's bombs had not released over the target so he left the formation and dropped them. Time passed, then Baldwin announced, "I'm low on fuel. We'll try to make it home alone." For no apparent reason, he lowered the landing gear, began a letdown and turned toward Belgium. His last transmission was, "I'm down to 80 gallons and about fifteen minutes from land."

Later we learned that he flew over the Frisian Islands at about 5,000 feet. The German flak gunners stationed there were famed marksmen and they set the B-17 on fire. Three men bailed out, but Baldwin and five others died in the explosion. Of the three that escaped, two survived water landings and were taken prisoner. The other, a gunner named Goodwin, landed on the ground but may have been killed by the Germans. He had vowed never to be taken alive—he would rather fight it out.

Why do they have to use the word easy?
If one man suffers fear, a wound, or death
It wasn't easy.
(An unknown soldier)

The next day's issue of *The Stars and Stripes* stated in part, "... 750 Fortresses escorted by 650 Mustangs rumbled through solid clouds to hammer three U-boat yards at the German Naval Base at Kiel. Bombing was by instruments. Action was light. One bomber and three fighters failed to return."

From his sack, Tony read the article aloud then said, "Action may have been light for that son of a bitch sitting in his newspaper office. But I'll guarantee you that for the thirteen guys that went down, it was a hell of a day of war."

Contrary to the published report, reconnaissance photos showed that we had not "hammered" anything and the planes were prepared for a return trip the following day. However, overnight a spy plane photographed some Red Cross barges loaded with prisoner of war supplies docked near the pens. Consequently, we were assigned targets across the river from the pens. Good thinking, we missed again.

On April 6th, the planes were loaded with thirty-four 150-pounders and two incendiaries, and we bombed the Leipzig rail yards. The 1,200-mile flight was uneventful and as the group neared the white cliffs of Dover, we on *E-Z Goin'* were laughing and scratching about the "milk run." The formation entered low clouds and we broke out at 500 feet in rain and fog. Everyone scattered. Given the number of airfields that were crowded into Bomber Alley, it does not take much imagination to visualize the low-level chaos this created. B-17s and B-24s, all on low-fuel, were everywhere looking for a place to land. It was like playing a deadly game of dodge ball in an arena bound by clouds on one side, and death-dealing church steeples and radio towers on the other. We played chicken with other pilots to enter the traffic pattern and as we touched-down a B-24 crashed into nearby woods while trying to land on our inactive runway. A furious fire illuminated the clouds and all aboard died.

Fortunately for us, the German jets materialized far too late to alter the outcome of the war. As it was, every time we saw one, someone in the group went down. Their victories were too few, however, to achieve any decisive results. The glory days of the Luftwaffe had passed and they were breathing their last gasp—or so it seemed.

Rammed at 15,000 Feet

In September 1944, ultimate defeat was staring the Nazis in the face and their leaders were scrambling for new ideas to turn the tide. According to former Luftwaffe fighter pilot Werner Zell, a thirty year-old *Oberst* (Group Captain) named Hans-Joachim "Hajo" Herrmann proposed a daring and desperate plan to Reichsmarschall Hermann Goering.

> *"With increasing production of our new Me-262 jet fighters, the day of the propeller-driven fighter is over," said Herrmann. "I propose that we gather 1,000 of our Me-109 fighters and in one massive attack, crash into the American bombers in midair. I believe that such an assault will so terrorize the B-17 and B-24 crews that they will refuse to fly more missions. At the very least, they will be forced to stop the bombings until more aircraft arrive from America to replace their losses. The respite will buy us time to improve our fuel supplies and build more Me-262 jet fighters with which to regain air superiority.*
>
> *"I believe that if an Me-109 crashes into a bomber amid-ship, the steel propeller will act as a saw, the sturdy wing with a steel beam running through it will snap the bomber's fuselage in two, and the long nose will protect the pilot well enough for him to bail out. I estimate that possibly half of our pilots may die in the crashes, but it's better to lose them this way than to have them gradually annihilated with nothing to show for it as is happening today."*

Goering agreed to consider the idea but doubted that sufficient numbers of pilots would volunteer for the Kamikaze-like mission. Further, given Hitler's dream of world domination, Goering had reservations about asking Hitler to approve a strategy that would clearly acknowledge the desperate nature of their situation. While Goering pondered, the vastly more powerful American air units were downing Luftwaffe fighters at an ever-increasing rate.

The German account of the battle and its preparations that follows was provided by former Luftwaffe pilot Werner Zell and partially confirmed to me by *Oberst* Hajo Herrmann.

In January 1945, Hitler finally approved the plan and on March 8, 1945, Goering sent the following message to all Luftwaffe day fighter and operational training units:

To Be Destroyed Upon Reading.

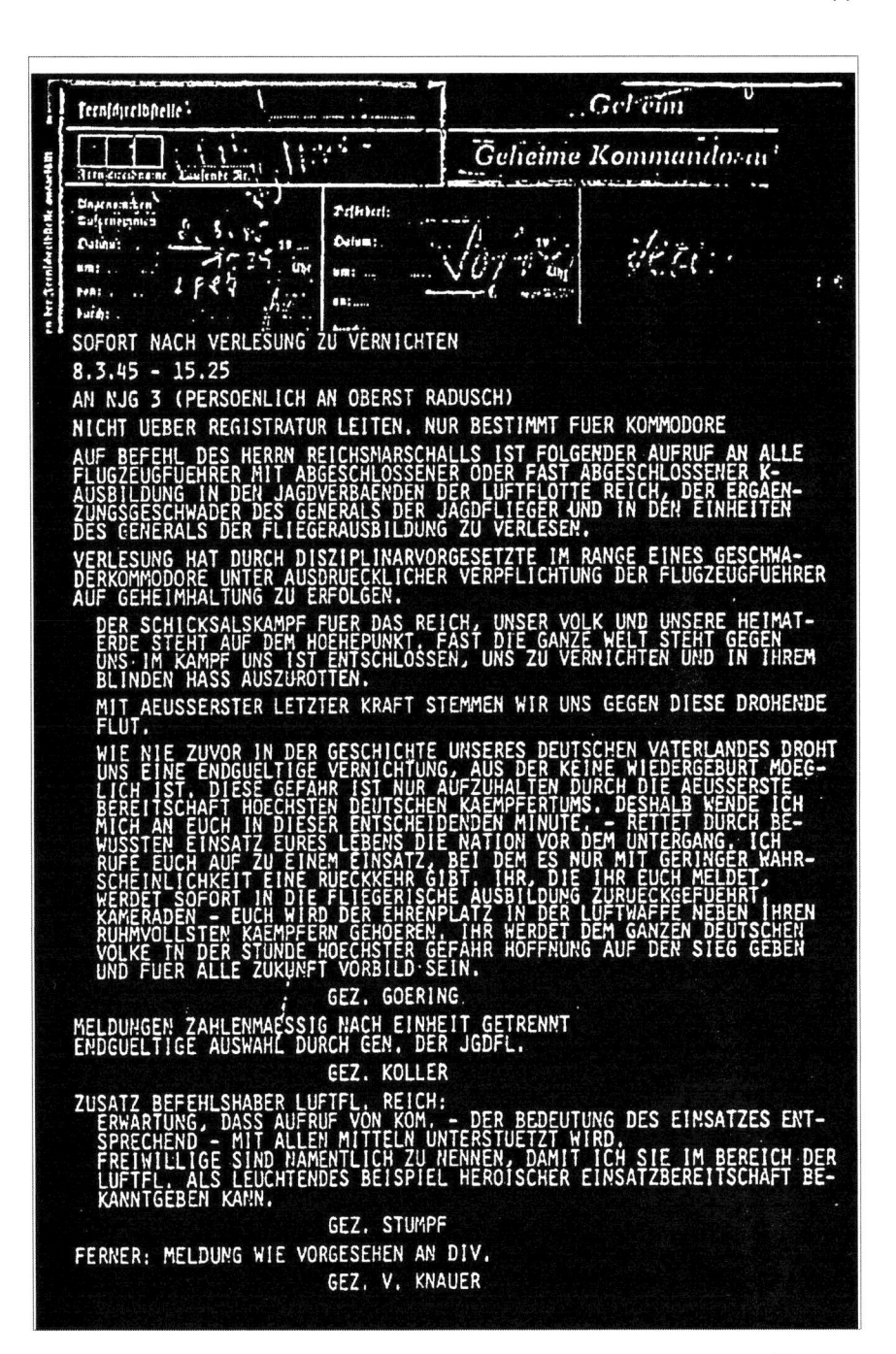

SOFORT NACH VERLESUNG ZU VERNICHTEN
8.3.45 - 15.25
AN NJG 3 (PERSOENLICH AN OBERST RADUSCH)
NICHT UEBER REGISTRATUR LEITEN. NUR BESTIMMT FUER KOMMODORE
   AUF BEFEHL DES HERRN REICHSMARSCHALLS IST FOLGENDER AUFRUF AN ALLE FLUGZEUGFUEHRER MIT ABGESCHLOSSENER ODER FAST ABGESCHLOSSENER K-AUSBILDUNG IN DEN JAGDVERBAENDEN DER LUFTFLOTTE REICH, DER ERGAEN-ZUNGSGESCHWADER DES GENERALS DER JAGDFLIEGER UND IN DEN EINHEITEN DES GENERALS DER FLIEGERAUSBILDUNG ZU VERLESEN.
   VERLESUNG HAT DURCH DISZIPLINARVORGESETZTE IM RANGE EINES GESCHWA-DERKOMMODORE UNTER AUSDRUECKLICHER VERPFLICHTUNG DER FLUGZEUGFUEHRER AUF GEHEIMHALTUNG ZU ERFOLGEN.
   DER SCHICKSALSKAMPF FUER DAS REICH, UNSER VOLK UND UNSERE HEIMAT-ERDE STEHT AUF DEM HOEHEPUNKT. FAST DIE GANZE WELT STEHT GEGEN UNS. IM KAMPF UNS IST ENTSCHLOSSEN, UNS ZU VERNICHTEN UND IN IHREM BLINDEN HASS AUSZUROTTEN.
   MIT AEUSSERSTER LETZTER KRAFT STEMMEN WIR UNS GEGEN DIESE DROHENDE FLUT.
   WIE NIE ZUVOR IN DER GESCHICHTE UNSERES DEUTSCHEN VATERLANDES DROHT UNS EINE ENDGUELTIGE VERNICHTUNG, AUS DER KEINE WIEDERGEBURT MOEG-LICH IST. DIESE GEFAHR IST NUR AUFZUHALTEN DURCH DIE AEUSSERSTE BEREITSCHAFT HOECHSTEN DEUTSCHEN KAEMPFERTUMS. DESHALB WENDE ICH MICH AN EUCH IN DIESER ENTSCHEIDENDEN MINUTE. - RETTET DURCH BE-WUSSTEN EINSATZ EURES LEBENS DIE NATION VOR DEM UNTERGANG. ICH RUFE EUCH AUF ZU EINEM EINSATZ, BEI DEM ES NUR MIT GERINGER WAHR-SCHEINLICHKEIT EINE RUECKKEHR GIBT. IHR, DIE IHR EUCH MELDET, WERDET SOFORT IN DIE FLIEGERISCHE AUSBILDUNG ZURUECKGEFUEHRT, KAMERADEN - EUCH WIRD DER EHRENPLATZ IN DER LUFTWAFFE NEBEN IHREN RUHMVOLLSTEN KAEMPFERN GEHOEREN. IHR WERDET DEM GANZEN DEUTSCHEN VOLKE IN DER STUNDE HOECHSTER GEFAHR HOFFNUNG AUF DEN SIEG GEBEN UND FUER ALLE ZUKUNFT VORBILD SEIN.
                             GEZ. GOERING.
MELDUNGEN ZAHLENMAESSIG NACH EINHEIT GETRENNT
ENDGUELTIGE AUSWAHL DURCH GEN. DER JGDFL.
                             GEZ. KOLLER
ZUSATZ BEFEHLSHABER LUFTFL. REICH:
   ERWARTUNG, DASS AUFRUF VON KOM. - DER BEDEUTUNG DES EINSATZES ENT-SPRECHEND - MIT ALLEN MITTELN UNTERSTUETZT WIRD.
   FREIWILLIGE SIND NAMENTLICH ZU NENNEN, DAMIT ICH SIE IM BEREICH DER LUFTFL. ALS LEUCHTENDES BEISPIEL HEROISCHER EINSATZBEREITSCHAFT BE-KANNTGEBEN KANN.
                             GEZ. STUMPF
FERNER: MELDUNG WIE VORGESEHEN AN DIV.
                             GEZ. V. KNAUER

March 8, 1945. Copy of Hermann Goering's original message asking Luftwaffe pilots to volunteer for a mission "from which your chance of return will be minimal"

Werner Zell Collection

3/8/45-15:25
To NJG: (Night Fighter Group 3. Trans. Note.)
(Personal message to Colonel Radusch.)
Not to be Routed via Records Office. For Wing Commanders' Eyes Only.

By order of the Reichsmarschall the following directive is to be read to all pilots who have completed or nearly completed training in the fighter units of Luftflotte Reich. Also included are the supplementary squadrons of the Chief of Fighter Aircraft and to units of the Chief of Pilot Training. Commanders of squadron leader's rank will give the reading, and pilots will be obligated to strictest secrecy.

The fateful struggle for our empire, our people and our native soil has reached a climax. Almost the entire world is arrayed against us, determined to annihilate us and to exterminate us in blind hatred.

With our utmost and ultimate strength we brace ourselves against the menacing flood tide. As never before in the history of our German fatherland we are threatened with absolute annihilation without any chance of rebirth. This danger can only be checked by the willingness to exercise the highest German fighting spirit. This is why I address myself to you in this decisive hour. Save our nation from its doom by deliberately putting your lives on the line. I summon you to a mission from which your chance of return will be minimal. Those of you who volunteer will be reassigned to pilot training immediately. Comrades, you will give hope for victory to the entire German people, and set an example for all to follow. Signed: Goering

Units will add up replies. Chief of Fighter Aircraft will make final selections. Signed: Koller

Addendum to Commander Luftflotte Reich: It is expected that this directive, in accordance with the importance of the mission, will have the full support of all squadron commanders. Volunteers will be mentioned by name so I can cite them throughout the Luftflotte as shining examples of heroic self-sacrifice. Signed: Stumpf

Furthermore, report as ordered to Division.

Signed: v Knauer

More than 2,000 German fliers volunteered for the undisclosed mission. Most were recent graduates from flying schools. The best and most experienced pilots, however, were ruled out for they were needed alive. Applicants deemed to be not brave enough to carry out the plan were also turned down. On March 20, a newly formed unit, *Rammkommando* (Ram Command) *Elbe* assembled the selected men at Stendal, an airfield west of Berlin. Here they were wined and dined on the best meats, sausages, cheese, chocolates, liqueurs, and cigarettes, then briefed on the mission.

Meanwhile, Me-109s were arriving at Stendal and at four other airfields where *Elbe* squadrons were to be assigned. Quickly, almost haphazardly the aircraft were stripped of nonessential equipment. On the Me-109's, this included removal of a cannon that fired through the propeller nose cone and one of two MG131 machine guns mounted in the wings. Only sixty rounds were left aboard for the remaining MG131.

The battle plan called for the stripped-down Me-109's to climb to 36,000 feet while, simultaneously, the Me-262s were to stay low and decoy the American fighters away from the bombers. This would free the *Elbe* pilots to dive down and crash into the unsuspecting bombers.

No one had experience ramming aircraft; so much of the training the *Elbe* pilots received was theoretical. In addition, because the objective was to dispirit the Americans, the pilots were discouraged from firing the one machine gun when on the offense against the bombers. The gun was purely a defensive weapon in case of an attack by an American fighter. The pilots were extended two options: they could either keep or eject the canopy before the crash. Most opted to leave it in place for added protection. Some of the men backed out; they had volunteered to attend a training course not to commit suicide.

At the final stages of preparation, the Germans found that rather than a shortage of volunteers, the overriding problem was a lack of aircraft and fuel. Combat losses together with operational and mechanical problems had whittled down the number of available propeller-driven fighters to no more than 200. In desperation and possibly against their better judgment, they forged ahead with the plan anyway. Under the cover of darkness, the *Elbe* pilots were trucked to their assigned airfields. Here, they were denied the heavier padded suits normally used for high altitude and winter flying. Instead, they were issued so called "bone-bag" lightweight summer flying suits. Some pilots wondered if they had not already been written-off.

On 6 April 1945, Eighth Air Force Headquarters sent out operational plans for the following day. The orders specified a maximum effort (M.E.) against sixteen targets in northern Germany. Of the Eighth's forty bomb groups, only two would stand-down and of the fourteen fighter groups, one would stay home. (At staff level, such missions were called M.E.s. Down in the trenches, tongue-in-cheek, they were "E.G.s"—everybody goes, including the colonels.)

The Luftwaffe had not substantially challenged the bombers for a month. Therefore, the mission planners had no reason to believe that the Germans would come up in significant numbers on the 7th. With this in mind, the 1,300 bombers, protected by 850 fighters, were directed to fly the mission at exceptionally low altitudes ranging from 14,000 to 21,500 feet. The planners reasoned that this would enable maximum bombing accuracy and also spare the air crews from the toe-numbing altitudes where we normally flew. The well-meaning blunder effectively increased the separation between the lower-flying bombers and the high-flying *Elbe* pilots. Hence, the fighters would be able to achieve faster, more lethal speeds before crashing into the bombers.

At dawn on April 7, the ceiling and visibility over most of England were zero-zero, typical springtime weather. There were no bike-riders that day; a wringing-wet fog had grounded everyone. As we groped our way to the combat mess, men could be heard muttering, "How the hell do they expect us to fly in this stuff? I can't see my hand in front of my face." Everyone homed-in on the greasy spoon aroma of brewing coffee and frying sausage. We had a standard breakfast of flapjacks drenched with hot rum-colored Karo syrup, ersatz scrambled eggs, greasy sausages, and black coffee—lots of black coffee.

In the mission briefing room, a colonel stepped to the podium and pulled back a frayed black curtain. A murmur of relief ran through the room when we saw that the string did not extend very far into Germany. He began, "Gentlemen, your target for today is an oil storage facility near Buchen." No one knew where that was but it hardly mattered; we judged our exposure to danger by the length of the string across the map. He continued, "The target is about 50 miles east of Hamburg. Expect light flak over the target. Take-off is at 0630, assembly altitude is 8,000 feet, and flight altitude is 15,200 feet." Silence was strictly enforced during briefing sessions but with mention of the low flight altitude, Tony Picone and I grinned at each other and mouthed, "milk run." Hey, we were veterans, we'd been around, knew the meaning of the word tough; we had twenty-four missions under our belt. He continued, "Estimated time of arrival back at the base for the first squadron is 1610. Expect weather conditions in the local area to be heavy cumulus clouds, with bases varying between 200 and 800 feet, and a mile visibility with fog and haze." Fog delayed our takeoffs until 1030.

At 1130, Luftwaffe air controllers in Central Germany alerted all fighter units that multiple spearheads of American bombers were crossing the channel. Green flares arched high and the last remnants of the German Air Force including 50 Me-262s and possibly 200 *Rammkommando Elbe* aircraft began their takeoffs.

At Delitzsch, an airfield near Leipzig, *Elbe* pilot *Unteroffizier* (Staff Sergeant) Werner Zell and his wingman *Obergefreiter* (Corporal) Horst Siedel were among the last to liftoff. Their lightweight fighters practically leaped into the air, the landing gear latched up-and-locked, and they turned west to meet the invaders. Immediately, Hajo Herrmann's plan began to unravel in a most unexpected manner. The pilots were unable to hear their flight controllers due to a woman's voice that was over-riding their radio transmissions. She aired patriotic songs such as "Horst Wessel," "Deutschland," and "Die Badenweiler March," interspersing the music with shouted slogans and catch phrases. "Remember the dead wives and children buried beneath the ruins of our cities;" "Save the Fatherland;" and "Think of Dresden!" In the confusion, some *Elbe* pilots were recalled and the remaining attackers were reduced to smaller less effective groups.

Meanwhile, *Elbe* pilots Zell and Siedel, while climbing to altitude, learned that the heaters had been stripped

1945. pilot (Sgt.) Werner Zell

1945. Me-109 German fighter (Werner Zell Collection)

from their Me-109s. With only their "bone-bag" flying suits as protection against the sub-freezing temperature, they had no need for patriotic stimulation to get on with the mission. Nearing Hanover, the two friends saw an approaching bomber stream. Their fighters were emitting contrails so they knew that it was only a matter of minutes before a roving band of Mustangs or Thunderbolts would arrive to harass them. They jettisoned the external fuel tanks, tightened their seat harness straps, got the sun at their backs, and prepared for battle. The radio transmitters had also been removed so they simply waved "good luck" to each other and began scanning the groups for likely targets.

The first B-17 groups were in tight formation, so Zell let them go by. Then along came a scattered B-17 unit. He selected a target, advanced the throttle full open and winged-over into a dive. He side-slipped to increase his speed, and with an overtaking velocity of plus 200 miles per hour crashed into the right side of the bomber's tail section.

Momentarily stunned, Zell regained his senses to find the cockpit dark. He thought he was dead until he realized that engine oil had sprayed back and obscured the canopy. He pulled the ignition switch to decrease the chance of fire, unsnapped the seat harness and pulled the canopy release handle to bail out. However, it would not move. Desperately he tried again, just then help came from a most unexpected source. A barrage of bullets slammed into the Me-109 and the shock dislodged the canopy. Sucked out of the seat by the slipstream, he hit the tail and fell away. Seriously injured, he painfully opened the parachute before lapsing into semi-consciousness. Suddenly, a P-51 zoomed by causing his parachute to oscillate, startling him back to reality. His ordeal was not over, however, for the Mustang pilot returned and fired a long burst at him. Whether the American meant to kill Zell or merely confirm his victory with the gun camera is unknown because as the Mustang roared away Zell passed out.

When consciousness returned, Zell found himself lying in an open field with an old farm couple cautiously observing him. He pleaded for help, but not knowing his nationality, they ignored him until Zell produced his flight cap and pay book. An ambulance transported Zell to nearby Schwarmstedt where other injured *Elbe* pilots were already being treated in the local hospital. While there, his parachute was brought in and nurses counted nineteen bullet holes in the canopy. He also learned that his plane had crashed into a barn, killing ten Russian prisoners of war working there. Wingman Horst Siedel was found crumpled on the ground in an unopened parachute. For them the war was over.

1945. Zell in "Bone-bag" flight suit

Aboard *E-Z Goin'*, nearing the Dummer Lake area at 1245, we began hearing groups ahead calling for fighter support and all thoughts of a "milk run" quickly disappeared. Suddenly, an FW-190 sliced in front of us firing at Lieutenant William Howard's B-17 forward and left of us. Immediately, bright orange flames engulfed the number three engine and wheel-well. Howard salvoed his bombs and shut down the engine. His navigator, Lieutenant D. R. Jones, was Tony's friend; and as they fell back, Tony shouted, "Hey look that plane's on fire. Oh hell, that's Jonesy's plane. Let's drop back and protect them."

"Can't do that Tony," Joe said. Silence. Their copilot, Lieutenant Genaro Delgado, was my friend, and as they began a 180-degree turn trailing thick black smoke, I thought, well, there goes half of the 100th's supply of Mexican pilots. (While in the service, Gerry was the only Latino military pilot I ever met. I am not saying there weren't more, I just didn't meet any.)

Howard leveled-off and the crew came tumbling out like sacks of dirty GI laundry. Later, we learned that three men died with the plane. Howard, Delgado, and Jones survived, although Jones got his front teeth knocked out by angry civilians.

The battle continued and the intercom was alive with gunners calling out enemy planes to each other. Gerling shouted, "Here comes one from five o'clock high!" I looked to my right just as an Me-109 swooshed by us so close that we bounced from the shock wave. Inexplicably, the pilot hadn't shot at us nor was he at his gun-sight aiming at some one below—he was looking at me. We stared at each other for a fleeting moment, and then he was gone. He rammed Lieutenant Arthur Calder's *Candy's Dandy* in the squadron below, the two planes exploded and everyone died.

Elsewhere, a Me-109 pilot crashed his right wing into the left side of a B-17 in the 490th Bomb Group. The fighter twisted under the fuselage, cart wheeled across the bomber's under-belly damaging the number three and four engines then fell away. The bomber turned back and landed on a friendly fighter strip. In the 452 Bomb Group, two B-17s were rammed by FW-190s and all four went down. Classmate Jim Smouse was the copilot of one of them. In the 389th a B-24 group, a Me-109 crashed into the nose of the lead bomber. The decapitated Liberator veered left into the right wing of the deputy lead's plane and all three went down. FW-190s also rammed two B-17s in the 388th, and the 550th lost *Van's Valiants* to a rammer, as did the 493rd when *Lady Helene* was rammed and crashed. In the 389th, *The Sky Scorpion* met the same fate. While over in the 487th, a B-24 lost its starboard fin and rudder to a Me-109 but was able to land on the continent along with other rammed planes from the 490th and 487th Bomb Groups. Twelve other bombers, including classmate Lieutenant Walter Center's *Happy Warrior*, also went down for one reason or another. Throughout the battle, our more experienced fighter pilots were having a field day with the unskilled Germans.

Caaarraash! E-Z Goin's nose yawed left, we skidded right and the fuselage shuddered like a dog shaking water off itself. Instinctively, Joe and I kicked hard right rudder, both pedals disappeared under the instrument panel then returned and dangled uselessly. The time was 1323.

The control columns were violently jerking back and forth, the number one engine was streaming smoke, and all the radios including the intercom were out. Lacking an intercom, we had no way to determine the crew's plight or to assess the damage. *E-Z Goin'* seemed to still want to fly, though, so we stabilized the rocking, rolling motion with the ailerons and hung on.

Five minutes later we arrived over the target. Ralph called "Bombs away" and the nose lurched up sharply as the bombs tumbled out. Joe rolled the elevator trim wheel forward to add nose-down trim but the wheel spun uselessly.

April 7, 1945. Inflight photo just after being rammed

We pushed with all our strength on the control columns but could not exert sufficient force to stop us from rapidly climbing toward another B-17 above us. At the last possible moment, Joe retarded the throttles and *E-Z Goin'* shuddered into a stall. The two B-17s slid by close enough to swap paint. By trial and error, we found that at 105–110 miles an hour, just above the stall speed at that altitude, we could maintain level flight. The number one engine appeared ready to catch on fire so we shut it down as strung-out remnants of the 100th disappeared into the haze and we remained behind to wallow through the sky alone.

The attacks finally tapered-off and Dude toured the ship to assess our condition. He reported back, "Everyone's OK. Paul says that a Me-109 crashed into us. There's two big slashes in the fuselage aft of the left gunner's window and the flight control cables and electric wire bundles are cut there too. What's left of the tail's flapping up and down so hard that it looks like the fuselage might break in two. The left elevator and the top half of the rudder are gone and there are bullet holes in the left side of the nose. We think a gunner in another B-17 was tracking the 109 that crashed into us and shot out our number one engine and the master radio control box. That's why the radios are dead. Tony was reaching down to pick up a map or they would have gotten him too."

On a B-17, the tips of the horizontal stabilizers are visible from the pilots' windows and I looked back to see what was causing the control wheels to jerk back and forth so forcefully.

"Joe," I said, "Dude's right. The tail's really bobbing up and down on my side. What's yours doing?

Joe checked his and asked, "Are you sure we're supposed to be able to see the tail from here?"

"Yeah, I'm sure."

"I don't have one."

Dude tapped me on the shoulder and asked, "Do you want to come back and take a closer look at the damage?"

"No, Dude, I'm needed here. (Truthfully, I was afraid of what I might see.) How's Paul doing? Is he still in the tail?"

"No, I ordered him out of there. He says that when parts from our plane went flying back, they knocked off the left horizontal stabilizer on another B-17 behind us. They're back there somewhere."

We later learned that Captain Joe King also nursed his damaged B-17 home to a safe landing.

Two P-51's came by. The pilots bracketed us and tried to establish radio contact. I signaled that our radios were dead so they looked us over, shook their heads hard, gave us a "thumbs up," and headed home. To us, their departure indicated that we were no longer vulnerable to enemy attacks. The crew jettisoned everything possible but the emergency equipment and with that, the airspeed increased by an encouraging blip or two on the dial. We breathed a bit easier.

An hour later, the coastline came into view and it was decision-time again. Should we attempt a landing on one of the many abandoned fighter airstrips below us? If so, we risked landing on a damaged runway or having the tail break off on touchdown with no medical help available. On the other hand, a decision to continue on to England required that *E-Z Goin'* hold together long enough to cross 150 miles of the North Sea. Further, we would then have to let down through the overcast without radio communications, locate an airfield, and land on instruments. We decided to chance it. I dialed-in the Thorpe-Abbotts frequency on the Instrument Landing System (ILS).

The system uses two fixed radio beams to guide a plane to a landing; one beam provides lateral guidance and the other establishes a glide path to the runway. The cockpit display on this instrument consists of two crossed needles. Stray off course left or right and the error is revealed in the movement of a vertical needle. Stray above or below the glide slope and a horizontal needle provides that indication.

Surprisingly, the ILS seemed to be operating properly. With the radios inoperative, however, we could not verify what station, if any, it had locked on to. We gambled that the instrument had acquired our home instrument landing system and would guide us there.

We began a long, slow descent into the clouds. Two hours later, as we neared the ground but still had not broken out, we knew that the morning fog had returned. I had a troubled feeling that we were about to die.

We broke out at 700 feet above the ground with a mile visibility and our home runway directly ahead. It was as if God had finally decided that we had been tested enough and intended to let us live—for now. As we made a sweeping turn into a long final approach to the runway, Norman Larsen began firing red-red flares and Joe signaled, "wheels down." I flipped the landing gear switch but nothing happened; the landing gear motor was inoperative. Quickly, Dude scurried back to the bomb bay where he manually cranked the gear down with the emergency system. The green indicator light came on.

April 7, 1945. View of the damage to B-17,   . Thirteen days and a few repairs later, Hank and crew flew the ship on the 100th's last mission of the war

We were nearing touchdown when another B-17 also firing red flares cut in front of us to land. We had no alternative but to go around. That, however, is quite impossible to do on only three engines, with the wheels down, and no rudder control. Dude laboriously cranked the gear up. Flight procedures called for us to waggle the wings at the control tower to indicate "Radio Failure." We disregarded the rule for fear the lateral air-pressures might further damage the tail—external damage would have to communicate the caliber of our problem. As we staggered over nearby villages at tree-top level, traffic stopped and people scrambled out of stores and cars to point at us. Given the number of damaged B-17s most of them had probably seen, the attention seemed a dubious honor.

We returned to the final approach. Dude cranked the gear down again, the crew assumed their crash-landing positions, and Joe brought us in for a

April 7, 1945. On the 25th mission, a Me-109 rammed the B-17, . The crew bombed the target then flew five hours to a safe landing at their home base in England. Standing, (L–R) : Sgt. Ralph E. Spada, togglier/nose guns; Sgt. Matthew Schipper, waist gun; Sgt. Alfred E. Collins, ball turret guns; Sgt. Paul R. Gerling, tail guns; Lt. Joe Carl Martin, pilot; Lt. Antonio Picone, navigator; Lt. Hank Cervantes, copilot. Kneeling, (L–R): Sgt. William Dudecz, engineer/top turret guns; Sgt. Norman E. Larsen, radioman/waist gun perfect two-point landing. I held my breath as we gently lowered the tailwheel to the runway. *E-Z Goin'* screeched, grated, and groaned like a giant beer can being scrunched on a sidewalk, but she held together. A plume of emergency vehicles trailed us to our hardstand where we shutdown the remaining three engines. Five hours had elapsed since the collision but no one cheered, embraced, or even shook Joe's hand. Perhaps we would have shown greater appreciation had we realized that the extraordinary feat of airmanship which Joe Martin performed that day has been rarely if ever equaled by a pilot with 800 hours of total flying time. But at that age, everyone thinks he is going to live forever and that death only claims others, not him.

When I was in flight school, our theory of flight instructors explained the rule in physics that governs why an airplane must have a tail to fly. I didn't question their wisdom then. But less than a year later, on 7 April 1945, God made an exception to the rule for nine very lucky airmen.

During debriefing, several pilots commented on the extraordinary aggressiveness of the German fighter attacks. The debriefers, however, pooh poohed our remarks and refused to give them any validity. During that last air battle of the war, escort fighter units collectively claimed 90 victories while bomber unit gunners made claims of 41 destroyed and 26 probables. The 100th's gunners claimed eight kills. I questioned the marksmen but none asked to be credited with shooting up our B-17.

Exaggerations about our flight persist to this day. One of the more popular tales alleges that, "Because the flight control cables to the tail were severed, the pilots made it back to Thorpe-Abbotts with the help of the crew, who moved to the rear of the plane to raise the nose and to the front to lower it." Whenever asked to confirm the story, I facetiously reply, "Certainly it's true. You should have seen me directing traffic when we came in to land, then had to go-around." They forget that our right elevator remained operational throughout the flight.

On April 8, Third Air Division Headquarters issued the following Confidential Assessment of the Battle:

> Thirteen bombers are known or suspected of being lost to collisions with enemy aircraft. These were not suicidal ramming attacks but in each case were aircraft clearly out of control either through injury to the pilot or structural failure of the attacking aircraft. Closeness of the attacks has given rise to rumors of rammings, but a review of complete Division experience fails to substantiate the ramming theory.

Almost simultaneously, Eighth Air Force Headquarters issued this report:

> The command lost twenty-three bombers and three fighters in yesterday's operations. The Luftwaffe lost 133 fighters.

Three days later, on April 11, the German High Command issued this supplemental report:

> As already mentioned in the Wermacht report of April 8, German fighter units displayed exceptional fighting spirit in warding off American terror-bombing attacks on north Germany on April 7. The German fighters engaged in bitter dogfights in which they broke through the enemy fighter barricade. And disregarding violent defensive fire from countless aerial guns sacrificed their lives by crashing into the four-engine enemy bombers. The American forces suffered heavy losses and the encounters also took a heavy toll of Germans. More than 60 four-engine bombers were destroyed by rammings alone. Some German fighter pilots were able to save their lives by bailing out.

Near Calle, Germany, stands a monument dedicated to the pilots who died performing the Kamikaze-like mission

More than forty-five years would pass before the German account of the battle gained acceptance in the United States. Three books, all written in the late 1990's, address the encounter: Ulrich Saft's *Das Bittere Ende Der Luftwaffe*, Adrian Weir's *The Last Flight of The Luftwaffe*, and Martin W. Bowman and Theo Boiten's *Raiders of the Reich*. The saga of *E-Z Goin'* is well known among German veterans of the battle.

In 1996, Herr Zell contacted me to confirm that he rammed us. Our exchanges led us to the conclusion that he crashed into another B-17 and convinced me of the existence of *Rammkommando Elbe* and its unique mis-

Hans-Joachim   Lt. Henry Cervantes   Walter Schuck
"Hajo" Herrmann

November 1998, Long Beach, California. Three old adversaries come together at a "Gathering of Eagles." (L–R) (Col.) Hans-Joachim "Hajo" Herrmann, Lt. Col. Henry Cervantes, (Lt.) Walter Schuck. Herrmann had 9 victories and was the architect of RammKommando Elbe. Walter Schuck, the world's 3rd-highest ranking, living Ace, had 206 victories, 17 in the west, including 8 while flying Me-262 jet fighters. He got misty-eyed when Hank said to him, "Had you been on our side we would have made you a general and given you the Congressional Medal of Honor to boot"

sion. Although they were the enemy, I remain in awe of the courage and daring exhibited by *Elbe* pilots on that fateful day. They, however, did no more or no less than was done by many others on both sides.

* * * *

On April 8th, our crew received a seven-day "flak leave" and most of us went to the seaside resort, Brighton-By-The-Sea. There, the hotel manager recommended The Dome for entertainment. The old red brick building had once served as the King George IV's royal stables, so we arrived there not knowing what to expect. The ceiling of the huge rococo hall resembled the top-half of a circus carousel. The longest bar I have ever seen took up one entire side, a full orchestra was on an elevated stage playing loud enough to rattle your teeth, and the monstrous floor was alive with dancing couples. We got drinks then drifted apart to find dance partners.

One petite, dark-haired girl was hard to miss. She was in a black and white polka-dot dress that made her look like a Spanish fandango dancer. I smiled and nodded and she pretended bored aloofness. So I acted as if I had not been turned down and headed toward a tall redhead seated nearby. Immediately, the little one intercepted me. We danced for one number but my adrenaline was still pumping from having cheated death the day before and, grateful to be alive, all I wanted was to hold Gabriella close. I began my plan to seduce "Gabby" by inviting her to get drunk and celebrate. With a shy smile and a Spanish accent, Gabby let me know that she did not drink and only cared to dance. Fine, her green eyes, pale skin, and wasp waist would do for now. We danced well together but if I held her too close she would freeze then resume dancing. I was getting nowhere fast and regretted that I had not gone for the redhead instead.

Closing time came and the other fellows and their dance partners invited us to join them for fish 'n chips. I begged off. The night was warm, a full moon was so bright that it cast shadows, and I was more interested in romance than food. I invited Gabby to walk the large formal garden that surrounded the building. She nodded and took my hand, more as a means of keeping track of it than as a sign of togetherness. The crunch of gravel beneath our feet made a good home-like sound, and I asked Gabby to tell me about herself. Born in Madrid to a Spanish father and an English mother, she had run away from an overly strict household and made her way to England. She lived alone, worked in a neighborhood shop, and enjoyed going to The Dome. We came upon a secluded elm tree that seemed like a good spot to make my move.

I took Gabby in my arms and gently explored her closed mouth with my lips. When she didn't respond I drew back and murmured, "Can't you kiss back?"

"No."

"Why not?"

"I don't even know you."

"Well, why don't you kiss me and we'll start to know each other better."

"That's a new one. No."

"Shh, don't say that honey, I want us to spend the night together. We don't have to do anything if you don't want to. I just want to hold you close."

Gabby's shyness retracted like a roll-up window shade, "Whatever you want to do, it will cost you Yank."

"Huh? Are you crazy? What do you mean it'll cost me? Why didn't you say so earlier?"

"Because we were having a good time. Why, don't you want to be with me?"

"Sure I do, but I don't want you to be with me because I pay you. I want you to be with me because you want to. I like you."

She smiled, "Oh, that's right you're Mexican. Well all right, you don't have to pay. But we'll have to be very careful and not make noise going up the stairs to my flat. My landlady's rooms are in front and she charges me extra if I bring anyone up."

We took off our shoes and with childlike whispers and tiny giggles she led me up the stairs of her rooming house. Suddenly, there was a blinding flash and a deafening explosion shattered the darkness. The building rocked and a powerful air blast seemed to lift it off its foundation and plop it down again. Plaster, paint, and dust rained down as we stampeded down the stairs.

The landlady stood on the landing, arms crossed, less worried about the explosion than the rent. She screamed, "You little whore, I knew you had a man up there." Her tirade trailed us out the door. On the street terrified people wrapped in bedclothes and blankets were all looking and pointing in one direction.

Word came that a V-2 rocket had hit four blocks away. I drew Gabby to me and said, "Honey, I'm going to see if I can help. But before I do, let me give you some pounds to pay the landlady. How much do you need?"

She pushed my hand away and pleaded, "Oh no, please don't do that, I don't want anything from you. But do you think we could meet tomorrow night and pretend that tonight never happened?"

"Sure, Gabby, I'd like that."

She flung her arms around my neck, went up on tiptoes and whispered in my ear, "*Yo te amo*, Enrique. I'll see you at The Dome tomorrow night."

I joined a stream of people running in the direction of the blast. Two elderly air raid wardens in gas masks and World War I battle helmets were blowing their police whistles in an effort to control the crowd but most ran by them. I did not. I returned to the hotel, for death and destruction had ceased to be a novelty.

I went to the dance hall four nights in a row but never saw Gabby again.

* * * *

While we were away, Lieutenant Delbert Reeve and his crew joined with the 100th. On their first mission, a Me-262 attacked their B-17. The bomber burst into flames, did a vertical roll and spun to earth. Three men were seen to bail out but only the bombardier, Flight Officer George Woodham, survived.

George landed in dense woods and remained in a tree for two days while armed German teenagers searched for him. When they gave up, George climbed down and made his way to a road where he eventually hailed a fast-moving column of General Patton's forces. The unit commander refused George's request for transportation back to the coast. He said, "We're not going in that direction, we're headed east and can't spare the fuel." He handed George a rifle and continued, "Here, have one of the men show you how to use this and earn your keep the old-fashioned way, as an infantryman." George fought along side the trigger-pullers until a sufficient number of

M. Sgt. Alfred T. Conte, E-Z Goin's crew chief

downed fliers were collected to make the trip back worthwhile. George returned to the 100th. As an escapee, he had earned the right to rotate back to the States but refused the offer. He said, "I haven't written home to tell my girl or my folks that I'm over here. And I haven't been here long enough (sixty days) to wear the ETO (European Theater of Operations) ribbon. Without proof, nobody's going to believe that since I was last home I flew a combat mission with the 'Bloody 100th,' got shot down by jets, bailed out, evaded the Germans, and fought in Patton's army. They'll laugh me out of town. I'd rather stay here." George was assigned to our crew.

We returned to flying status. In the interim, Major Rovigno had ordered Master Sergeant Alfred T. Conte, *E-Z Goin'*s crew chief, to fit the bomber with a new tail and repair the other battle damage. Conte and his team of experts completed the job in seven days, and on April 20, we flew her on a combat mission to Oranienburg. She flew like a wounded duck, but it was great to have her back. The following morning we were briefed to bomb an airport near Munich but the mission was canceled before takeoff. Then on the 23rd, we prepared to hit the Buchen railroad station and again the flight was canceled. It suddenly dawned on everyone that there was no place left to bomb.

For the 100th the war was over. Between June 12, 1943, and April 20, 1945, the group had flown 306 combat missions with 351 B-17s. Of them, 204 went down due to enemy action, 61 were salvaged at the field, and 25 were returned to the States, with *E-Z Goin'* among them.

The group lost 1,772 crewmembers for all causes, 732 were killed in action, 901 were captured, and 81 evaded the enemy. Our crew flew 228 combat hours on 26 missions. During our flights, the 100th lost fourteen B-17s and the group's gunners shot down fifteen enemy fighters including several jets.

In 1987, Joe Martin, Tony Picone, Norman Larsen, Paul Gerling, and their spouses, joined me in Long Beach, California, for a reunion of the 100th Bomb Group Association. More than 2,000 people were at a gala held on the final evening of the event. Yet, it is doubtful that few if any took notice of a situation that is a norm at this as well as other bomb group reunions I customarily attend. A strolling mariachi group came by and after performing a song for us, asked to have their picture taken with me. We were posing for the photo, when one of the men whispered in my ear, "*Señor*, you are the only man of color in this entire room." And that's the way it was.

May 1945, Amsterdam. Dropping ten-in-one rations during Operation Manna

May 1945, Amsterdam. Civilians used bedsheets to mark the drop site

Expressions of gratitude were everywhere.

Louisa, the Bar Room Contortionist

The ground war continued. Eisenhower had bypassed strong German forces in the Netherlands for fear they might blow up the dikes in retribution for a ground attack. Dutch civilians, however, were starving to death at a rate approaching 1,000 a day and after some maneuvering the German commander allowed us to make food drops to provide a measure of relief. The agreement required that we stay under 500 feet, remain within strictly mandated corridors, and not carry gunners aboard. No one felt better when the briefer added, "Anyone fired upon will receive credit for a combat mission."

The modified bomb bays were loaded with boxes of ten-in-one rations and on May 3rd we flew on the first of several "Operation Manna" missions. We went in at wave-top level, hopped over the dikes, and skimmed by telephone poles in an effort to stay as low as possible. German flak batteries where everywhere and we kept a wary eye at the gunners who squinted at us like duck hunters waiting for the season to open. Early May is tulip time in Holland and despite the ugly scars of war, carpets of blazing colors dotted the countryside. Joyful women and children were everywhere. Some waved American and Dutch flags at us while others pointed to messages in open fields that read, "Thank You Boys," and the like. Near Amsterdam we "bombed" an open field centered with a white cross that appeared to be fashioned from bed sheets. Below us it was a free-for-all as civilians with German soldiers among them could be seen scrambling for boxes as even more of the 50-pound missiles showered down.

May 1945, Linz, Austria. The author posing with French Lt. Col. Eugene Cassignol (R)

On May 5th, we repeated our performance over Bergen and were again treated to the heartwarming sight of mothers hugging their kids as they pointed at the big grins on our happy faces.

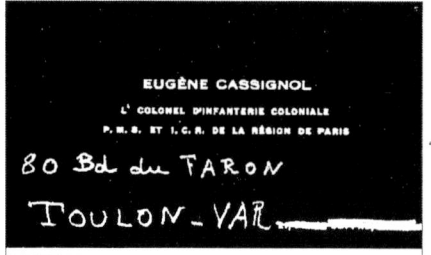

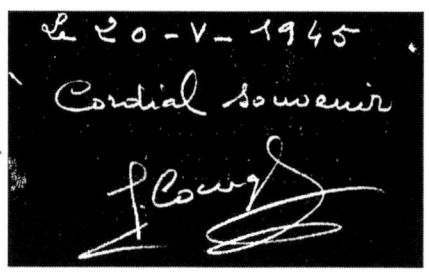

The war ended on May 9th and the following day our adjutant, Major Horace Varian, swore me in as a second lieutenant.

Next we were called upon to repatriate French soldiers and civilians from the German prisons back to airfields near their homes. The bomb bays were modified with wood palettes and on May 20th, we landed at a fighter strip at Linz, Austria. B-17s were parked everywhere and we had time to burn, so I strolled over to a hangar in hopes of seeing a German plane. Instead, I found an enterprising young GI selling souvenirs from a small mountain of Nazi uniforms and equipment. I rummaged through the stack, came up with an officer's Beretta pistol, and handed him a pound note. Carl and Tony could not believe that I had paid for it. After a long wait, two well-dressed French colonels and twenty-seven soldiers approached us. I had a camera and asked the friendlier of the two colonels to pose for a photograph with me. He complied then removed a business card from his wallet, wrote on it and handed it to me. It read:

> EUGENE CASSIGNOL, L' COLONEL D' INFANTERIE COLONIAL, P. M. S. ET I. C. R. DE LA RÉGION DE PARIS. He added his address and a greeting: *80 Bd du FARON, TOULON-VAR. Le 20-5-1945, Cordial Souvenir.*

I don't mean to make light of the horrendous suffering that occurred at the prison camps, but who can imagine a just-released prisoner of war handing out calling cards? Ah, those Frenchmen always ready to socialize. Relying on Tony's Italian and my Spanish, we placed the two colonels behind the pilot seats, distributed the men throughout the plane, and took-off. Our destination was Chartres, a Paris suburb. As we neared the area, I headed for the Eiffel Tower. The men went bananas! They climbed all over the colonels, cheered, cried, and kissed one another and us. It was undoubtedly one of the happiest moments of their lives. The sensation I best recall, however, was a creepy-crawly feeling that their cooties were taking advantage of the situation to jump ship to my clean brown body.

To land on the steel-matted runway, aircraft were required to skim by the tall Gothic spires of the Chartres Cathedral. The two officers crossed themselves as we flew past. I didn't ask if they were paying homage to their religion or just thankful we missed the church. The men deplaned, one of them pulled out a homemade French flag and they proudly marched off singing "La Marseilles."

Several belligerent-looking B-26 twin-engine fighter-bombers were practicing touch-and-go landings while we waited in line to take off for our return to England. As we jealously watched them, Joe and I agreed that it was appropriate to demonstrate what a four-engine bomber could do in the hands of expert airmen. We took the runway with the engines roaring and the brakes screeching in protest. I set the turbo-supercharger regulator at full-blast, and we were off. Unfortunately, we forgot to lock the tail wheel and the power was more than Joe could control with the brakes. His turn

June 1945. 100th Bomb Group: 349th Squadron airmen waiting to go home. Standing (L–R): James Toomey, New York; Wilford Murray, Utah; Ralph Smith, Kentucky; James Crighton, Kentucky; Billy Hurst, Texas; George Woodham, Alabama; Robert Dornan*. Kneeling (L–R): George Timms, Washington DC; Joe Martin, Texas; Joe Bohrer, Minnesota; Dusty*; Jim Mack, Illinois   * home state unknown

continued beyond the runway heading and he quickly overcorrected to the opposite side. Back and forth we went, wildly careening across the strip desperately trying to gain take-off speed. We finally left the matting on an angle and went bounding through weeds and trash before barely lifting over a couple of parked planes. I'll bet those B-26 pilots are still laughing at us. There was no small talk on our way home, we had just dodged a bullet and we knew it. We ferried soldiers for several days then repatriated civilians. Pretty girls were always assigned to stand behind the pilot seats. It made it more convenient for them to express their gratitude when I buzzed the tower.

During the war the best protection against losing a friend had been not to have any. Now all that had changed and we had time to relax and get to know one another better—but not me. Barracks bull sessions invariably reverted to discussing the two subjects all armies talk about, home and family. There was no way I was going to admit that my father was a laborer and my mother was in a mental hospital. When pushed, I claimed that Father was a metallurgist and Mother a nurse. It helped my fellow pilots to rationalize, in situational terms they understood, how a Mexican could logically reach their level of attainment.

We also reminisced about wacky crewmembers. For example, whenever a combat mission was scheduled the next day, the barracks had a ritual. At 2200, Will Murray would wind-up an old portable phonograph and play our one American record, "I'll Walk Alone." With that, the lights were turned off and quiet prevailed. One night, a new crew failed to douse its light promptly. A shot rang out, the bulb shattered and the bullet ricocheted around the room. The sharpshooter was the fellow we had been warned about when we arrived, Lieutenant Tom O'Neill.

Tom acquired his squirrely reputation after several run-ins with the MPs. Our barracks was equipped with three inefficient coke-burning space heaters that were rationed a bucket of coke a day. On some nights, this was simply not enough and we froze. One exceptionally cold night, Tom signaled his distress by firing a red-red flare at the guardhouse. Within minutes, two MPs entered the barracks peering through the smoke for a perpetrator. Tom readily confessed but he was no fool. From past experience, Tom knew that the MPs guarded the base coke pile and thus kept their offices toasty-warm. He spent many a night comfortably sleeping in a jail cell. The French had a saying that fit Tom's lighthearted antics: "The incredible frivolity of the dying." Tom was Larson's copilot and died trying to reach Russia.

On June 4, the B-17s were loaded with homeward bound GIs and we took-off on a marathon flight to the only uncongested seaport in the area, Casablanca. As a crow flies the trip was a nine-hour jaunt. Spain refused to allow combat aircraft to over-fly the country, however, and this forced us to take a circuitous route; southeast to Marseilles, across the Mediterranean to Oran, then reverse course along the Atlas Mountains to Casablanca. Sixteen hours later, the weary men deplaned and we took-off again on a ninety-mile hop up the coast to the U.S. Navy base at Rabat, the capital city of Morocco.

June 6, 1945, Rabat, Morocco. Lt. Robert G. Clark

Upon landing, I met classmate Lieutenant Bob (Robert G.) Clark. Bob had come in from Italy with a load of men and we agreed to go into town and see the sights. The fact that the Navy commander had restricted all B-17 crews to the base never entered our minds. Behind the hospital, we found a corpsman loading a pickup with dirty bed sheets for transport to a civilian laundry in Rabat. He sandwiched us in between the sheets and we departed. The long trip was akin to being trapped in a dirty port-a-john during a heat wave in Florida—broiling hot, humid, and malodorous. Seeking relief, we conducted a process of elimination, determined to throw the most offense piece of laundry overboard. Unfortunately, we found that the biggest problem was our sweat-soaked flight suits. I didn't know anyone could smell so bad.

The sailor dropped us off at the old walled part of the city. The *souk* (market) was a jungle of colors, textures, and noises. Merchants were yelling, Bedouins haggling, dogs barking, camels braying, and Arabic music blaring. Tenacious hawkers tugged at us to buy hookahs, camel saddles, and potions they graphically illustrated would increase our sexual powers.

Along the way, we picked-up a retinue of street urchins begging for cigarettes and chewing gum. One of them spoke Spanish and nearing nightfall, I asked him where we might get a drink. He charged two cigarettes for his secret then led us through a maze of medieval alleys to an unmarked door. He hid us nearby and waited until a Navy officer came, unlocked the door, and went in. Quickly, one of the kids ran to keep it from closing and our guide pushed us inside.

A long path led to an intimate courtyard centered by a fountain complete with pink cupids and exotic water plants. The building appeared to be a mansion converted into a private club. Some French and American officers were at the bar and we were making our way there when three nubile waitresses pounced on us and led us to an obscure table. Flirty and overly solicitous, they rubbed against us for no reason and plied us with green wine, spicy olives, and hot roasted almonds. Suddenly, a manager-type appeared and spoke sharply to them. Away went the food trays, their swaying hips became more disciplined, and they assumed a more business-like attitude. I wish it were possible to say that along with a dinner of lamb piled high with *cous-cous* and topped with a sheep's eye we were entertained by an Edith Piaf crooning sad torch songs of faded youth and lost love. Or, as he did in the movie *Casablanca,* Dooley Wilson tickling an ancient piano while singing, "You must remember this, a kiss is just a kiss ...." No, we had to settle for a parade of full-figured women in clinging dresses and veiled smiles silently promenading around our table hinting romance. But we weren't buying, uppermost on our minds was what the Navy would say when we get back to the base.

We hailed a rumbling old Mercedes

June 6, 1945, Paris, France. While flying back to England, the crew recalled a rumor that a P-47 pilot had flown through the Arc de Triomphe. They contemplated celebrating the 1st anniversary of D-Day by flying their B-17 through it taxi for the ride home. Rail-thin and stripped to the waist, the driver nodded vigorously as I gave him directions in Spanish. He must have been seven feet tall for he reached back and without stretching, opened the back door. He hunched over the wheel like a race driver, floor-boarded the accelerator, and off we went. Windows open, hair flying, exhaust roaring, gears slipping, and a clear view of the blacktop through cracked wooden floorboards. Nearing the airfield, roadside signs in four languages warned drivers to, "Slow down and prepare to stop." Instead he speeded up and began flashing the lights and blowing the horn. The gate guard retreated into his cubicle for protection and offered us a half-hearted salute as we thundered by. Four blocks into the camp we skidded to a stop, the driver jumped out, and with a big toothy grin held our door open. He could not have done better. We tipped him very well.

Overnight, the Spaniards lifted their restriction and we were allowed to fly a direct route back to England. Approaching the Cherbourg Peninsula, Joe recalled the significance of the date June 6th, 1945, the first anniversary of D-Day. Down we went to sightsee remnant tank traps and a long semi-circle of Navy ships intentionally sunk to form an artificial harbor for some of the landings. Off in the distance, the top of the Eiffel Tower was barely visible, reminding me of a long-standing rumor that an American had flown his P-47 Thunderbolt through the Arc de Triomphe. Unaware of its dimensions, but determined not to be outdone, we considered it an opportune time to find out if a B-17 would fit through the Arch. A low-level flight up the Champs-Elysees led us to the monument. There, a huge French tricolor gently waving in the gateway informed us that no one would carve a niche in French history that day.

As we continued our low-level tour of the city, a P-38 Lightning appeared off our wing and got in close formation with us. I cocked my camera and motioned the fighter pilot to come in for a better shot. Instead, he gave me a thumb-up motion indicating that we should gain altitude. We immediately headed for home and along the way Tony threw his navigation log overboard in case someone asked where we had been. He could have saved himself the trouble. As our tires skidded on the Thorpe-Abbots runway, we could see a reception committee by our hardstand—it was decidedly unpleasant. The incident ended my career as an "aerial-photographer" but not my curiosity about the rumor. The question remained unresolved in my mind until 1998, when during a ski trip to Germany, I stopped in Paris to measure the arch's dimensions. The wingspan of a P-47 is 40-feet

June 1945, 100th Bomb Group, England. (L–R) Hank Cervantes, George Woodham, Claire Hanson

9-inches and I estimated the passageway to be 60 feet wide at the base. A tight fit but no doubt some hot rock could have managed that part of the problem. It is highly improbable, however, that the huge four-bladed propeller would have cleared the inner curvature of the arch.

* * * *

Our return to the States began at an Army personnel depot near Blackpool. We checked-in and within an hour, George Woodham and I were at the front gate hitchhiking to town, any town. George stood about six-feet tall and had a thin frame, a boyish face, brown curly hair, and an "ahh-shucks" attitude. He hailed from Opp (The City of Opportunity), Alabama, and unless you were from that area of the country, his thick southern accent required one to lip-read and watch for facial expressions in order to grasp his meaning. We were having one of those conversations when two frowzy bottle-blondes in a tiny Austin stopped for us. They coached us on how to accordion ourselves in, and took-off.

They too were in a party mood and invited us to join them at their favorite pub. Nowadays people are required to get shots and wear hard hats when they enter the sort of place where they took us. Upon seeing them, a frumpy barmaid drew two pints of bitter then asked George and me what we were having. The women downed the syrupy drinks like a pair of parched camels. After allowing a dainty little burp to escape, my "date," Louisa, boasted that she was a circus contortionist. She seemed a bit plump for that career field so I asked her to prove it. She summoned the barmaid and after gabbing for a bit, the bleary-eyed woman awkwardly climbed atop a beer keg, rang an old sea bell, and in a boozy, Cockney accent shouted, "Gather roun' so's you can watch Louisa show this Yank she can put both legs behine er ead."

I tossed a large coin on the bar, and we elbowed our way by some big-bellied stevedores to the front row. Louisa grabbed her beer, went to a central area, drained the mug, turned her back to us and carefully tucked the hem of her loose skirt under her panties. She then sat on a chair and deftly lifted one then the other leg and locked them behind her head. She gave them a reassuring pat and with a big "tah-dah" and a smile extended her arms to gather in the applause. Hardly anyone clapped. Obviously disappointed by our lack of appreciation, Louisa's smile faded although she continued to hold the grotesque pose. Embarrassed because we were together, I motioned her to come on. She didn't respond, so I sidled over to her and whispered, "The show's over. Get your legs down and let's get out of here." "I can't," she groaned, "it hurts too much." It may not have been the courteous thing to do, but I ordered her another pint of beer and we left.

* * * *

Thirty soldiers of all ranks boarded a C-46 twin-engine transport and after an over-night stay in Iceland, we flew to Bluie-West 1, an emergency landing field in southern Greenland. The all-thrills, no-frills strip was carved into the end of a long, steep-sided fjord that ended at the ice cap. Pilots had one chance to make a safe landing; there was no room for error or for going around again. On the ground, the pilot advised us to settle in. The next leg was an 800-mile hop to Goose Bay, Labrador, and good weather had to prevail over the entire route before he could takeoff.

That afternoon, several of us visited a nearby Inuit (Eskimo) village where we bought small sealskin dolls as souvenirs. The next morning the entire barracks smelled like a dirty latrine. When informed that the doll-skins had been cured with urine, we pitched them out into a snow bank. Later that morning, a big Russian freighter docked for repairs and its all-female crew trooped into the officers club for lunch. Rough and tough, most were built like stevedores, a few had metal front teeth, and a couple looked like they had been hit on the oblique by a freight train. But desperate times call for desperate measures and although no one spoke the other's language, we were soon chug-a-lugging vodka together. The club closed and the party adjourned to the barracks where it deteriorated into an orgy. Two days later when the repairs were completed, one of their officers got on the base loudspeaker system and called the crew to re-board the ship. Only a few responded and their captain angrily accused the base commander of holding the missing crew members against their will. The harried colonel ordered an "officers call" and delivered a message that was as short as his temper, "Give them up or face a lengthy stay and a court-martial." We all got together and arm-in-arm, escorted the beaming, gratified women back to the dock. As they boarded the ship, some turned and waved their going-away presents, cute little sealskin dolls.

The weather broke and we went on to Camp Beale, California. As we neared the base, there were no shouts of, "There she is," or "Home at last." Nor were there bands, parades, "Welcome Home" signs, or heroic posturing when we landed. We had made it. We were tired and only wanted to see our families.

After a quick medical evaluation, everyone's records were stamped with a standard entry: "Moderate stress is exhibited by the following symptoms: slight inefficiency, startle reactions, depression, reclusive tendencies, excessive drinking, and excessive smoking. Only a small degree of impairment of efficiency suffered, with prognosis for further combat flying best determined after prolonged rest in the Zone of Interior." Most of us disagreed with the diagnosis but who cared; it justified a 45-day leave of absence. Yet years later, some seemingly unrelated sight or sound will take me back in time and I will flinch. Perhaps those doctors knew more about post-traumatic stress disorder than we realized.

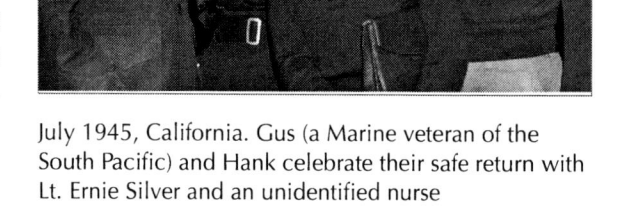

* * * *

July 1945, California. Gus (a Marine veteran of the South Pacific) and Hank celebrate their safe return with Lt. Ernie Silver and an unidentified nurse

A short, boxy, fast-talking infantry captain named Frank Colosuano and I boarded a Greyhound bus that passed through Oakley on its way to his destination, Stockton. He was a fellow passenger on the C-46 and we had hardly settled down when I said to him, "Damn Frank, you smell worse than the sealskin dolls." He cackled, "You're not the first one who's said that.

July 1945, California. Hank and an unidentified friend couldn't find any girls willing to have their pictures taken with them, so they did the next best thing

I've been wearing the same clothes since I left Europe. Here, let me show you." He opened his B-4 bag on the back seat of the bus and out popped a huge Nazi flag protecting dozens of optical lenses. Frank said, "I worked in a lab before the war and know good microscope lenses when I see them. We were the first guys to go into the precision glass factories in Zeitz, Germany. And when I saw these babies, I dumped all my clothes and liberated as many as I could. They're going to set me up." (In the late 1940s, I landed a B-25 at Stockton Airport and on the road into town, noticed several road signs advertising a car agency owned by someone named Colosuano.)

Within a week of my arrival in Oakley, Gus received his discharge from the Marine Corps. During the war, his letters were more censored than mine, so I had no idea that he had fought in the deadly battles for Rendova and Guam. We had a lot of catching up to do and celebrated our safe return in Antioch's landmark bar, Marchetti's. The joint had free-swinging doors with frosted, windows etched with tipped cocktail glasses. If one entered in broad daylight, it was akin to stepping into a skid row theater after the movie started. Your eyes had to adjust to the darkness and your senses had to adapt to an overpowering odor of dead fish, old cigarette smoke, and stale beer.

Gus and I were there, telling each other war stories when he nudged me and nodded toward two zootsuiters with slicked-back hair, long sideburns, and droopy mustaches. One of them eyed me and said to the other, "*Carnal, estoy watchando ese vato* (Pal, I'm watching that jerk) with the wings and fancy ribbons." "*Chale mano*" (Yeah, dude), replied the other, "I'll bet they're not his." Gus handed me his beer, grabbed the nearest one by the lapels and shook hard. Only the outsized drapes swished back and forth while the fellow remained stationary. Frustrated, Gus said, "I know you're in there somewhere you sonavabitch, take that back or I'll wipe the floor with you." I said, "I'll take the other one, Gus." "No," he said, "you're an officer, stand back. I'll take both of them." They fled. I was home at last—my big brother was still taking care of me.

Chapter 4

Post War Years
(1945–1950)

America, Land of the Big PX

Oh, I'm going to a better land.
They jazz there every night.
The cocktails grow on bushes,
So everyone stays tight.
They've torn up the calendars.
They've busted all the clocks.
And little drops of whiskey
Come trickling down the rocks.
  "The Passing Pilot"

My orders required that I report back to duty at Santa Ana Army Air Field. Gus and I had outgrown Oakley and when my leave was about to end, he accompanied me to Los Angeles. We checked in at the Hill Hotel and took a room overlooking the Angels Flight tramway. Most of our evenings were spent in two nightclubs near Olvera Street. The upscale Club Brazil showcased Miguelito Valdez singing his hit song "Babalu," while La Bamba, with its black padded entrance door and fake palm trees, featured an unknown performer, Lalo Guerrero. His first night there remains ingrained in my mind. A flesh-colored spotlight flashed on. A small combo struck a note and a tall, thick-featured Mestizo in black trousers and an orange-ruffled

August 1945, Los Angeles, California. Hank and Gus met Esther Soto. They asked her to decide between them; she chose Gus

shirt began to mystically swirl a pair of maracas. He tilted his head toward an overhead mike and time stood still as his golden-voice began belting out the Mexican hit songs of the day, "Hilos de Plata," "Palabras de Mujer," and "Angelitos Negros." The room was crowded with returned Mexican GIs, and we would not let him stop; the music reassured us that we were truly home.

At that point, I had every intention of leaving the service and getting back in lockstep with Gus. However, he wisely urged me to stay in. I received an assignment to Minter Field located in the flatlands north of Bakersfield. Nearly 200 pilots were assigned there with nothing to do but attend roll call twice a day and fly four hours a month for pay. We embodied the old saying: "There is nothing more useless than a pilot in peace time."

To break the monotony, I volunteered to ferry war-weary B-17s from Plains Field at Lubbock, Texas, to Kingman Field, Arizona. Thousands of bomber crewmen had trained at the former gunnery school but it was now a collection point for Air Corps aircraft on their way to auction, a smelter, or the scrap heap.

At one time more than 7,000 planes, most of them flyable, were parked on the desert floor southeast of the airfield. The armada included 1,832 B-17s, 2,562 B-24s, 478 P-38s and hundreds of P-47s. B-17s sold for $13,750, although some sold for as little as $750. Most Mustangs and Thunderbolts went for $3,500, P-40 Warhawks for $1,250. One fellow bought 5,437 planes for less than $3 million.

The B-17s we delivered sold particularly well. From force of habit or possibly for profit, the Plains Field ground crews fueled the planes to capacity with 2,800 gallons of 100-octane gasoline. With Kingman only 600 miles away, our tanks were still brimming when we landed. High-octane gasoline was still in short supply commercially and it took a while for Ferry Command officials to realize that people were buying the planes, siphoning the fuel, and abandoning them where they stood. When they finally caught on, fueling operations were controlled so closely that we were forced to check the "fuel remaining" over Albuquerque to assure we could reach Kingman.

One day I borrowed a jeep and, determined to find *E-Z Goin',* went to the B-17 parking area. From a distance, the fleet appeared to be seaplanes floating on shimmering heat waves. Up close, they no longer bore any semblance to the powerful juggernauts that had beaten the Luftwaffe's best in vicious air battles, proven the case for daylight bombing, and brought Germany to its knees. Gone were the air crews with their flight-kits, yellow Mae-Wests, and parachutes. Gone were the ground crewmen in greasy sheepskin jackets, dirty fatigues, and floppy caps. And gone were the fuel or oil trucks, tugs, bomb trailers, hard stands, and maintenance tents. All that remained was an armada of old war-horses silently living out their last days hunched against a fiery wind. Many were cannibalized or half-deconstructed with nothing more to manifest their days of glory than a faded array of designs, circles, stripes, bars, insignias, and catchy names. Once badges of honor, the markings now seemed no more meaningful than a child's art displayed on a refrigerator door.

After an hour of bouncing in and out of gopher holes, I spotted the 100th's black combat markings and *E-Z Goin*'s nose art. Her paint had peeled, a tire was flat, the engine nacelles were clogged with tumbleweeds, and the flight control surfaces were flapping in the breeze. I greeted her as one would a sick friend. "Hi," I said, "they're not treating you very well here." I circled her slowly like a mother inspecting a child, patting her here and wiping a smudge there. Inside, the fuselage was like an abandoned roaster oven. Dust, dirt, and cobwebs were everywhere. I squeezed through the bomb bay to the flight deck. My two long, emergency yellow, USAAF, back-cushions were still in place and a cloud of dust arose when I sat down. Rather than months, it seemed like years since I had sat in my confessional and prayed the fervent prayers that all airmen pray at one time or another.

Time came to leave. I closed my eyes and thanked *E-Z Goin'* for all the times she brought me home, even when I had little faith she could. I locked the flight controls, returned the levers, switches, and knobs to off, and closed the windows and doors. Although she had fallen on hard times, to me she was still a battle-tested friend and a proud member of the Bloody 100th. As I drove away, I avoided looking into the rearview mirror; I wanted to remember her as she had been in her glory days as a mighty Flying Fortress.

Back at Minter Field, I along with several others, volunteered to perform an annual officers inventory of the PX. The job entailed counting goods and merchandise and seemed to be a perfect opportunity to meet the sales clerks. Instead, the PX Officer assigned me to audit the service station. Disappointed, I found my way there and to my surprise, a lovely young woman introduced herself as the manager. Friendly, almost intimately, she asked that I call her Chickie and I asked that she call me Hank. I audited quickly, anticipating the opportunity to play kneezies with her when it came time to reconcile the books. The inspection revealed a shortage of more than $1,600 in gasoline and accessory sales. Aware that any bad news would surely chill my chances with Chickie, I double-checked the numbers, but they were accurate. I went to see her. Without a blink Chickie said, "You're just like the rest of them. None of you know what you're doing. Just leave the forms with me. I'll do them right, then you can come by and sign the certificate. I'll run them back to the office. I have to go there every night anyway." No way. I reviewed the figures and returned to see to her. Chickie gave me a dismissive look and said, "Lieutenant, I'm busy and you're bothering me." The PX Officer fired her and put me in charge of the station. What a letdown. Instead of improving my social life, I had become a pump jockey.

Three months later, Minter Field closed and all the pilots were transferred to Lowry Army Air Base in Denver, Colorado. There, a harried personnel officer reviewed my civilian employment records to determine where to assign me. Exasperated by my lack of relevant experience he said, "We don't have a war for you to fight and we don't need gardeners or farm workers. What did you do at Minter before you came here?" Sarcastically, I replied, "Pumped gas." End of discussion. He assigned me to be the Assistant PX Officer.

Upon my arrival at the PX office, a chubby, pugnacious, redheaded captain named Richard Davis appraised me, then asked, "What was the volume of the Minter Field PX?" I replied, "Volume, what's that?" He leaned back in his chair like a general, lit a cigar, blew a smoke ring, and said, "This is the biggest PX operation in the Air Training Command. I service over 20,000 GI's and 1,800 officers. I do three million dollars a year with 175 employees and have two large retail stores, two cafeterias, two service stations, a guest house, and several concessions including barber and beauty shops, cleaning and laundry service, watch repair, photo services, and more." He stood up and said, "Come with me. I'm going to teach you the retail business the way I learned it, as a stock boy at Woolworth's. What do your friends call you, Pancho?"

"No," I said, "people call me Hank. What do they call you?" He sucked in his belly and said, "Butch." I thought, Pal, it's going to be a cold day in hell when I call you Butch.

We entered a warehouse, where without bothering to introduce me to anyone, he handed me a brush and said, "I want you to clean and rearrange the merchandise in every bin. It's the best way to learn what we carry." The warehouse was large and the task demeaning, nevertheless I donned an old flying suit and went to work. Three months later I returned to his office. He seemed surprised to see me.

"Sir," I said, "the job is done."

"That's fine," he said. "Let's go back and have them teach you some other things you need to know."

I stopped him. "Captain, I already know how to drive a truck, price merchandise, fill requisitions, and do stock record cards. I'm not here to be a janitor. If you can't use me in the job I'm supposed to be doing, tell me. I can always be a full-time flight instructor."

"Don't get huffy," he said. "I just thought you'd be more comfortable working among your own people."

It had not escaped me that everyone in the warehouse but the manager was Mexican and that he treated them as if they were invisible. Nevertheless I said, "Captain, the people who wear this uniform are my people and, if that bothers you, I say again, send me back to personnel."

He gave me a thin-lipped grin, "Boy you're touchy. Tell you what we'll do. Why don't I let you supervise the day-to-day activities of my operations in Area Two. They include a store, restaurant, beer bar, service station, and barbershop. I'll even set you up with an office there, that way you'll be closer to your work. How's that sound?"

"Fine," I said, but his narrow-minded intentions were obvious. The north-south runway sliced through Lowry Field like a razor. Area One included the administrative offices, schools, morale activities, and most of the barracks. Area Two housed three thousand African-American soldiers with their "separate but equal facilities."

When I wasn't supervising at the PX, the flight line was my second home and I quickly qualified as first pilot in the B-25 Mitchell bomber, the C-47 Sky Train, and the C-45 Expediter, all twin-engine aircraft. Soon I was flying with two legendary pilots, Colonels John R. ("Killer") Kane and Stanley J. Umstead. Colonel Kane was a brusque, burly, hard-liner who earned the Medal of Honor by leading the Ploesti raid during World War II. He was my group commander but I was closer to Colonel Umstead. The portly veteran had a shock of gray hair, a handlebar mustache, and when in the cockpit wore granny glasses perched on the tip of his nose Santa-style. Colonel Umstead also drew his share of attention by wearing Command Pilot and Balloonist wings. Once when I asked about his experiences, he replied, "Never look back son. Look to the future and prepare for it. You have yet to do things I can only dream about." Then I learned that he was the test pilot on the maiden flight of the Douglas B-19 experimental bomber. With that information as a pry bar, my questions became more persistent and we grew closer.

1946. Colonel John R. ("Killer") Kane

Early one morning I called Colonel Kane, "Sir, I need an emergency leave. My sister just called. My mother was hit by a car last night and I'd like to go home."

The gravelly voiced hero said, "I'm sorry to hear that Hank. How is she?"

"Sir, all I know is that she has a broken leg and internal injuries. I'd like to leave right away if I may."

"Sure Hank, but how are you getting home? You're from California, aren't you?"

"Yes, Sir, I'll just go out to Stapleton Field and catch the first plane headed to the Bay Area."

"Slow down son. Go pack some clothes and by the time you get to base operations, a B-25 will be ready for you to take home. Stay as long as you have to. Don't worry about the copilot and the engineer; we'll put them on orders to cover their expenses. Good luck."

"Thank you, Sir."

My younger siblings were waiting for me when I landed at the Stockton airport. During our drive home, they briefed me on Mother's status. On rare occasions the hospital staff would grant her short furloughs home to attend a special event or to re-bond with the family. Mother was crossing a street on her way to church when a car hit her a glancing blow. Although serious, her injuries were not life threatening. Gus was already there from Los Angeles when I arrived and she was overjoyed to see us together. Later in the day, as is predictable in such circumstances, Gus and I began reminiscing but that seemed to disarrange her thought processes, so the doctor sedated her and recommended that we leave. My brother and I were never closer than we were leaving her that day.

Taking unauthorized people up in military aircraft was prohibited but I had waited too long and wished too hard to pass up the opportunity. Upon our return to the airfield, I invited my brothers and sisters aboard and thoroughly buzzed the Brentwood-Oakley area. Down below were fields, where I had once crawled in the dirt, as well as the people who had segregated my family, called me "Rochester," and ridiculed my clown shoes. However, my wounds were minuscule compared to what my siblings had to endure as a result of Mother's illness. Now they could at least say to their detractors, "My big brother is an Army pilot, and he took me for a ride in his bomber. Maybe you saw us."

* * * *

Mary Maxine Scott and I met on a flight aboard one of Continental Airlines' three DC-3s. We bonded instantly and she was my first true love. Scottie had ash-brown hair, big brown eyes, a beautiful smile, and a body made for the figure-hugging uniforms flight attendants wore then. The rebellious daughter of a wealthy farmer in Rifle, Colorado, she had come out of the Women's Army Corps (WAC) to become the third stewardess on the start-up regional airline's seniority list. Scottie was not the type of girl who said, "I'll have what he's having," or, "Whatever you want to do is fine." She had learned assertiveness as a WAC and did not have a shy bone in her body.

We were at an airline party one night when she buttonholed the company president, Bob Six, and said, "Bob, I want the 'snap test' stopped."

Puzzled, Six replied, "What are you talking about, Mary?"

"Chris, Chris Imboden. Whenever she gives us a check-ride, she snaps our girdles to make sure we're wearing one. My fanny's black-and-blue from her inspections." Soon thereafter, the chief stewardess deleted the item from her checklist.

Scottie traveled in Denver's social circles and whenever she risked inviting me to one of her affairs I was as petrified as an eighth-grader on his first day in high school. I did not know which fork to use, ate like I was late for takeoff, and floundered on the dance floor. She tactfully honed my social skills and for Christmas gave me a gift certificate for three lessons at the local Arthur Murray Dance Studio. I was head over heels in love.

Due in part to Scottie's positive influence, I received a promotion to first lieutenant and used the extra cash to buy my dream car, a black 1941 Ford convertible. Oddly and quite suddenly thereafter, Butch Davis became my bosom-buddy. What had changed? Had I forced him to deal with his conscience? Or had a bigot simply altered his stripes because there was something to be gained by being my friend?

* * * *

One Sunday morning the telephone rang and Captain Glenn Leatherman, a flight operations officer, said, "Sorry to wake you Hank, but a little girl is dying of polio on a farm out near Hays, Kansas. We need you to go bring her to a hospital here in Denver."

"I'll be right down Glenn," I said, "but please have someone find me a cup of black coffee. I need it bad."

In base operations, Glenn pointed to a spot on a flight chart and said, "There's a small airstrip right about here. It's the closest one we can find to the farm where she's at. I talked to the farmer who owns it. His son used to use it a while back. He says that it's partially gravel and thinks it's about a 1,000-feet long. Do you think you can land on it?"

"Hell, I don't know, Glenn," I said, "but I'm willing to try."

"Fine, go for it." A group of medical technicians finished moving their equipment aboard a C-47 and we departed.

Cows were feeding on the "runway" when we arrived. I buzzed the field to chase them off then went out to prepare for a short-field landing. The strip was perpendicular to an adjacent two-lane highway and I planned to skim the road just high enough to clear a barbed wire fence and touchdown on the first few feet of runway. We were nearing the strip when a black sedan came racing down the road and stopped under my intended flight path. The driver got out, apparently intent on seeing us going off the far end of the strip. He ducked as we over-flew him but unfortunately the car could not and we heard a loud *thud*. I touched down and with a heavy foot on the brakes stopped with pasture to spare.

The medics were moving the child and her parents into the plane when a Kansas State Trooper in a Smoky-the-Bear hat drove up. Trailing him was a black sedan being driven by a man who had his head stuck out the side window. The reason became clear as they neared. The car had a deep skid mark on the top and a shattered windshield. The trooper listened to our accounts of the incident then issued me a citation for having caused a collision on a Kansas highway. The medics helped me plead my case but he said, "I was just doing my job."

Regulations required that accidents be reported to the commanding officer within twenty-four hours. Early the next morning, I entered Wing Commander, Brigadier General Tom Lowe's office. Every step was a mile, my knees were shaking uncontrollably, and my fingers were trembling as I saluted and said, "Sir, in accordance with regulations, I'm here to report an aircraft accident."

He took off his reading glasses, leaned back in the chair and said, "Oh, I haven't heard about it. What happened Hank?"

"Sir, I hit a car."

"Oh, I see. That's not an aircraft accident, that's a taxi accident. When did it happen?"

"Yesterday morning, Sir. But it didn't happen on the ramp, I was going in to land."

"Let me see, you were coming in to land and you hit an automobile. What the hell was a car doing on the live runway?"

"He wasn't on the runway, Sir. He parked on a road in front of me and I got a ticket for hitting him."

"A traffic ticket! When did military policemen start issuing citations to pilots on my airfield? Linda, call Colonel Hewitt, get him in here. On the double!"

"No, Sir. You don't understand. I hit the car in Kansas and a highway patrol officer gave me the ticket. Here it is."

He read the citation, heaved a sigh of relief, wadded it into a spitball and tossed it in a wastebasket. "Well, Hank," he said, "I guess we can't send you back to Kansas."

The child survived.

* * * *

The Area Two PX facilities were of the duct tape and Naugahide variety. No signs or policy letters barred African-American soldiers from the larger better-stocked stores in Area One, but whites used all the time-worn insults, coded language, and mannerisms to make them feel unwelcome. The most serious problems occurred in the barbershops. Whereas Area One had a shop for officers and another for enlisted men, Area Two had but a single shop for everyone. Any African-American officer bold enough to patronize the officers' shop risked receiving a bad haircut, an insult, or both.

The guilty barbers were fired but this hardly mollified the victims who had been humiliated while their peers wink-nudged each other, looked out the window, or stared at their magazines.

Relying on the authority Davis granted me, I developed a plan to improve the Area Two facilities. Word got around and it may have been coincidental but unexpected orders arrived sending me to the PX Management Training School at Fort Monmouth, New Jersey.

While there, students who were also pilots flew planes based at Mitchell Field, Long Island. We went there on weekends. Not far from Mitchell's main gate was a dying little airfield where I occasionally stopped. I would stand at the head of the runway, imagine it to be a gray morning in May 1927, and mentally throttle-up Charles Lindbergh's fuel-heavy *Spirit of St. Louis*. Then while appraising some power lines near the end of the strip, I would ask myself, "Would you release the brakes or shut it down?" The decision was always, "Shut it down." Roosevelt Field should have been preserved as a shrine. Instead, they turned it into a shopping mall.

Upon my return, I found the modernization plans scrapped and, equally disturbing, Davis had hired a sexy blond with a Veronica Lake hairdo to cashier in the beer hall. Against a backdrop of segregation, this was a blueprint for trouble. Despite my protests, he refused to replace her with an African-American and soon white soldiers were coming over to check her out. Confrontations became a common occurrence and after one violent fight, word went out that whites would no longer be allowed in the bar. One night, Lowry Two had a race riot and the next morning Davis was found under the PX building badly beaten. With that, all military personnel not residing off-base were restricted to their areas and a few officers were issued side arms. They rioted again the following night. During the melee, General Lowe was struck by a rock while boarding a fire truck. Warning shots were fired and the crowd dispersed.

In the days that followed, all enlisted men in Area Two were transferred elsewhere and the area closed. Soon thereafter, General Lowe retired, Davis and the blond bombshell shipped out, and I became the PX officer.

* * * *

In 1947, the "brown-shoe Air Corps" became the "black-shoe Air Force." In formal terms, the United States Army Air Corps became the United States Air Force. And in 1948, President Harry Truman signed an executive order ending segregation in the military. Although widely acclaimed, in the viewpoint of one minority member, all the proclamation did was drive the rednecks undercover.

In the end, perhaps the troubles in Area Two foreshadowed better days to come. For the area was modernized and in 1950, it reopened as the Air Force Academy's interim home pending completion of the campus at Colorado Springs. (Lowry eventually closed and in 1998, I visited the Wings Over the Rockies Museum that historically-minded veterans established in one of the hangars. In addition to many photos of on-base scenes and events, the display dwelled on the reconstruction of Lowry Two and the Academy's Cadet Corps. I failed, however, to find one photograph of the African-American soldiers who were stationed there for so long a time. I guess old attitudes die hard.)

Our new commander was Colonel Rosenham Beam. His reputation preceded his arrival. He topped the colonel's seniority list with twenty-six years of service in that grade, wore strange ribbons that no one recognized, and was a stickler for military protocol. Soon after his arrival, he announced that he had noted a lack of basic service etiquette among his junior officers and intended to hold something called a "Dining In" to improve it. *The Daily Bulletin* disseminated the bare facts:

A Dining In will be held at the officers club.
The affair is formal.
Attendance is mandatory.
Wine will be served.
Seating is by date of rank.

Wine was considered a sissy drink and we junior officers arrived early to knock down a few martinis before the formalities began. Promptly at seven, chimes rang out and everyone found his place. We lieutenants were seated far from the head table and immediately got into the wine. More carafes arrived for the requisite toasts to God, motherhood and apple-pie, and yet another round accompanied the entré. After a huge steak dinner, the craggy-faced colonel rose to deliver his hail-to-the-chief address. It went like this: "In 1916, when I was a lieutenant serving as a company commander on Brigadier General John J. Pershing's staff, he formed an expeditionary force to go out and capture a Mexican bandit named Pancho Villa. Pancho and his gang of ruffians had raided Columbus, New Mexico and we were determined to punish them for it.

"To mount this operation, General Pershing directed that I establish an advance headquarters at a place called Culbertson's Ranch, some 100 miles east of El Paso, Texas. My company of 200 men and I boarded a train and two days later it stopped in the middle of nowhere. There wasn't a town, a building or a tree in sight. Nevertheless, the conductor informed me that we had arrived at our destination. I unloaded my troops and we pitched our tents in that god-awful barren desert. The following morning, I called in the youngest officer in my command, he was only a year out of West Point, and said to him, 'Lieutenant, come 1700, the day-after-tomorrow, I want to hold a formal retreat ceremony here. I want a flagpole in place with our nation's colors flying high. And I want our mess tent as well as my office to have a wood floor. Is that understood?'

"I don't know where that young man found a thirty-foot pole, or the lumber to frame and floor the two tents, but he got the job done. That officer's flawless performance of duty exemplifies the initiative and resourcefulness that enabled him to become what he is today, Chief of Staff of the United States Air Force, Four Star General Carl A. ("Tooey") Spaatz!"

A drunk lieutenant at our table yelled out, "What happened to you, colonel?" Colonel Beam's face flushed blood red. He turned to his adjutant Major Donald Andre and sputtered, "Major, arrest that man. That's an order." We were all leaning away from the culprit when Don staggered to our table and ordered the lieutenant to stand. He placed the officer under arrest and together they marched unsteadily out the door.

Later that night, the MPs stopped one officer who claimed to be driving home on a well-lit street; it happened to be the live runway. The incident served as an alert and officers were found passed out in the latrine, on the lawn, behind bushes, and against the perimeter fence.

The lieutenant left the service and Colonel Beam was promoted to brigadier general, which I suppose vindicated him somewhat. Higher rank usually means reassignment, however, and he received transfer orders to the Panama Canal Zone. Possibly a little drunk with power, the general ordered that two C-47s transport his furniture down to Howard Field. The flight enabled five other pilots and me to visit Panama, Guatemala, and Mexico. Unfortunately, regulations prohibited the shipment of personal belongings by air and the general was also drummed out.

"This Flag Is Presented to You"

In 1948, families who lost loved ones during the war were given the option of having them returned to the States for reburial. Many requested this courtesy and I was among a group of soldiers of all ranks detailed to act as "escorts."

Remains of soldiers from the Midwest were sent to a quartermaster warehouse on Chicago's South Side. There they were re-identified, prepared for reburial, and placed in a new casket. Our indoctrination required that we visit the processing area. Rather than a forensics laboratory, it looked like someone had dug up a graveyard. Bones and body parts were everywhere, the scent was stifling, and the procedures were gruesome beyond description. Most of us lasted but a few minutes.

Every four days, an escort accompanied the remains of a soldier of equal or lower rank to his hometown. For nearby destinations, the flag-draped coffin was delivered by GI ambulance and distant locations were serviced by railway. In those instances, the casket was sealed in a heavy wood case, one of the soldier's dog tags was nailed to it, and a flag strapped over it.

My first destination was a hamlet in a remote corner of Michigan's Upper Peninsula. I had never attended a funeral and wondered if the deaths I had seen in the 100th would come back to haunt me. No, I decided, they hadn't affected me then, why now? I didn't even know these people. I decided to do my job in a soldierly manner.

A blustering north wind was blowing off Lake Superior as the four-car milk train pulled into a tiny station. On the platform, about fifty farm people were peering at one car then another not knowing which might disgorge the grim cargo they had come to mourn. I double-checked the black armband on my left sleeve and went to the baggage car. Rail workers had already removed the casket from the shipping case and helped me transfer the flag. An anguished wail of distress greeted us when the casket appeared. I looked for a hearse, there wasn't one. Instead, an old fellow in blue overalls and a fur-lined cap with flaps positioned his horse-drawn farm wagon next to the baggage car. We made the transfer and I stepped down to the platform where a stocky woman who appeared to be in her early forties came forward and introduced herself to me in a thick Irish brogue. She had a ruddy complexion, faded copper-colored hair, tired blue eyes, and held a brown plaid mackinaw close to her body. I expected to see other family members but there were none, she was a widow and the war had taken her only child.

We formed into a cortege. Two American Legionnaires led the procession with their flags ruffling and snapping in the wind. The mother and I trailed the wagon and the others followed, crowded together for warmth and support. Marching at half-step, we shuffled down a deserted main street to a well-maintained farmhouse at the far end of town.

They held a wake that evening. Escorts were not required to attend such events but the thought of my mother having to endure such a tragedy compelled me to go. It was eerie. A large color photograph of a young pilot with red hair, freckles, and blue eyes was centered over the flag-draped coffin. Votive candles cast flickering shadows on the walls. Old men in work clothes sat in back whispering, while teenage girls cried and old ladies knelt, counting their beads and praying. Remote and lost in her thoughts, the mother sat alone, her tear-swollen eyes on the portrait and her hands on her lap, palms up. Ramrod straight, I marched stiffly to a chair next to her and sat down. Determined to remain aloof from the suffering in the room, I kept my eyes forward, fists clenched, jaw tight. She reached over and patted my hand as if to thank me for being there. All went well for about two minutes. Then she reached over, tenderly took my face in her hands, looked deep into my eyes and with huge tears coursing down her cheeks half-whispered, "You look just like my boy." I gasped! I knew all she could see was the uniform, but the pain was more than I could bear and fell into her arms crying. The wailing swelled to a crescendo as she contained her own grief to mother and console me.

Later, when most of the people had left, a doctor and I were in the kitchen chatting when she came and drew me to the casket. "Henry," she said, "please open it. I want to see if it's really my boy." We had been briefed to "expect anything," but this was unbelievable. Rather than comply, I assured her that a soldier's remains had to pass fourteen different tests before they were certified for return to the family. Quietly but firmly she said, "My son broke the little finger of his left hand playing football in high school. It didn't heal right and that kept him from being accepted at West Point. I want to see his finger then I'll know that it's him for sure." Earlier, others had shown me newspaper clippings stating that her son had died in a fiery B-24 crash. Furthermore, my visit to the warehouse and a scorched dog tag nailed on the shipping case left me with no illusions as to what was in the box. Gently, I held her hands to hinder her attempts to open it. The doctor had been watching us and I gestured that she needed a shot. He gave her a sedative and the casket remained closed. She and I remained on Christmas-card terms until her death nineteen years later.

* * * *

I was stepping down to the train platform at a whistle-stop near Frankfort, Kentucky, when an angry voice behind me said, "Git back on that cah. We don' need yoah heah!"

The voice belonged to a man with pinched facial features and close-cropped black hair, clad in stripped overalls, a frayed white shirt, and a black pre-tied bow tie. I assumed him to be the boy's father and said, "Sir, I'm only here to help you."

"I doan need your elp. You guys ev elped me enou aready."

"All right, Sir. If you'll just sign some papers, I'll leave."

"Goddamit, I ain't signin nothin. You brown bastard, I wish it was yoah in that box 'stead my boy. Now git outta heah!"

I reboarded the train and watched as he and others moved the casket to a hearse. His worker's body and gnarled hands reminded me of my father and I hid my face against the windowpane. A woman who had witnessed the outburst embraced me and in a teary voice said, "Please forgive him, everybody behaves badly in these circumstances."

Another order sent me to a mortuary in a blue-collar neighborhood in nearby Wheaton, Illinois. The next of kin was alone and did not share the deceased officer's surname. He appeared to be in a rush and the mortician confirmed that the fellow had taken time off from work and they were going directly to the cemetery. We were in the mortuary office completing the paperwork when the ambulance driver pulled a lace curtain aside, pointed out the window and said, "Sir, look."

Instead of lifting the heavy, flag-draped casket out of the ambulance, the next of kin and two mortuary assistants had lowered one end to the ground and were about to tip the other end into the hearse.

I rushed out and stopped them.

The next of kin exploded, "Listen, you friggin half-breed, you don't have anything to say about this. The papers I signed say so, and you're making me run late."

"You listen to me, mister," I said. "I don't know who you are, but no one is going to desecrate that flag or that officer's body in front of me. Either you do it right, or by God I'll take him back and we'll bury him ourselves. Here let us help you."

He continued to curse.

Back in the office I said to the mortician, "I can take that stuff all day but let me tell you something, I'm going to follow you to the cemetery. And if I see one wrong move that you could have prevented, I'll blackball you and guarantee that you'll never see another government contract in this place again."

In the ambulance, the driver, an African-American GI, said, "Hell, lieutenant, you don't have to put up with the crap that guy laid on you. I would've co-cocked him."

"No," I said. "That's not what we're here to do."

At the cemetery, we watched from beyond a long row of marble slabs as the next of kin stood before the casket for a moment then turned to leave. He took a few steps, hesitated, rushed back and threw himself bodily on the flag-draped coffin. I tapped the driver, "Let's go home, pal."

Perhaps the most moving episode occurred at a mansion in nearby Cicero, Illinois. We arrived there in an ambulance and a little, paunchy, pasty-faced priest met us at the door. We introduced ourselves then he said, "Lieutenant, my sister is the next of kin. I will preside at a wake to be held here tonight and at the funeral tomorrow morning. We've made reservations for you in a hotel downtown but would rather you stay here with us. A nice room has been prepared for you, and it would be much more convenient for everyone if you did."

As he spoke, I noticed a patch of brown hair and one big brown eye peeking out from behind his pants leg. He introduced me to Jason, his six-year-old nephew. As I leaned down to shake the boy's hand, he opened his arms wide and we embraced.

"Did you know my daddy?" he asked.

"No, Jason, I didn't. But I know he was a very brave man."

"Yeah I know, my mom tells me about him all the time. Are you going to stay with us?"

"I will, if you want me to."

"Yeah. Was my daddy's uniform the same as yours?"

"Yes, only his had a lot more ribbons."

"Really? Wow, wait till I tell my mom." He ran off.

We placed the casket in a large side-room where it almost looked insignificant under a grand chandelier. I was admiring the rich furnishings when a woman entered the room. She appeared to be about twenty-five, small, black hair, olive complexion, doe eyes, and from what I could see, a curvy body. We introduced ourselves then she said, "Let me show you to your room." I grabbed my overnighter, she took my arm, and we went up a richly carpeted staircase to the second floor. At the landing she pointed to a doorway and said, "Make yourself at home. We'll be going to a restaurant for dinner. Please be ready in an hour."

We had a nice dinner, came home, and Jason was put to bed. Meanwhile, the area surrounding the casket had been adorned with dozens of arrangements and bouquets of cut flowers—long-stemmed roses, gerberas, snapdragons, calla lilies, birds-of-paradise, and orchids of every hue. The room looked as if someone had raided a greenhouse in an effort to disguise the fact that we three were the only people there. The priest said mass, then we drank coffee for two hours without anyone saying much.

I was in a canopied rosewood bed trying to fall asleep when I heard a soft rap on the door. It opened slightly and the woman whispered, "Are you awake?" Startled, I sat up, turned on a small bed lamp and said, "Yes."

"May I come in?"

"Yes." She entered and quietly shut the door, "Are you sure that I'm not bothering you?"

"No, of course not."

"Good." She pulled a chair close to the bed, tucked her legs under her robe, smoothed it around her body, gave her pinned-up hair a reassuring pat and said, "I can't sleep. Tell me about the Army." We chatted with only passing mention of how my experiences may have pertained to her husband. After a while, her topknot loosened, and tendrils and wisps of hair began falling seductively around her face. The dim light made it impossible to be sure, but it seemed that her eyes, once passive, were now flirting with me. I was tempted but the price for an error in judgment was astronomical, so rather than chance it I said, "Give me a moment, I'm going to get up." She started to leave, but I quickly slipped into my pants and caught her at the door.

We went down to the living room where I sat across from her and said, "Tell me about your husband." That opened the floodgates. Everything poured out: his mannerisms, their courtship, their dreams, the pain of raising a son without his father, and her loneliness. Throughout our long conversation, there was no mention of other family members beyond her son and brother so I avoided the subject. A sliver of daylight was shining through a crack in the drapes when we finally stood up to share what I thought would be a warm embrace. Instead, she molded herself into my body like a baby, as if expecting me to make a more intimate move. A long moment passed with neither of us willing to initiate the next step. Finally, she backed away and took my hand. As we silently climbed the stairs, I resolved that if upon reaching the landing, she took one step toward the bedroom, come what may, I would not cross the line. Suddenly, we heard the sound of muffled steps and a door click shut. She stopped, blew me an air-kiss, gave me a small push toward my door, and disappeared down a hall.

We buried her husband in the shade of a massive oak. My chin began to quiver as I meticulously folded the flag. I dreaded the next step but there was no escape. In a ragged voice I uttered the most difficult words I have ever had to say:

"On behalf of the President of the United States and a grateful nation, this flag is presented to you in honor of the supreme sacrifice your husband . . . ."

I choked, fell to my knees and placed the flag on her lap. She was no distant stranger. I knew all about her, we were friends. She clutched the flag to her breast. I embraced her and her trembling child, and we wept. The hum of the lowering straps blended with the mournful sound of a distant bugler blowing "Taps."

On the trip back to Chicago I felt like an emotional basket case and thought, I can't keep doing this. It's like I'm burying members of my own family over and over again. But how could I not? Other families were waiting for my comrades to come home.

The experience taught me that it is easier to lose a friend in combat than to bury a stranger. During the war, a fellow may have slept next to you but when he went down, there were no cards, flowers, wakes, or funerals. He disappeared to some nebulous place you did not care to think about, another guy replaced him, and you carried on. It was not until I helped all those bereaved families and friends that I began to truly understand the enormity of war.

I also concluded that Latinos are too emotional to be good escort officers. Ritual is important when dealing with grief and my feelings often get the best of me. I hope that the families I served remembered me as a compassionate soldier who came to share their sorrow, rather than an automaton there to do a job. The detail lasted four months. It was the toughest duty I performed in the service.

"Given That You're Mexican . . . ."

The African-Americans were not the only ones experiencing racial problems at Lowry. In one incident, which ultimately changed the course of my military career, I too felt the sting of blatant prejudice.

During the war, a great majority of officers had received reserve commissions. Now the Air Force wanted to realign its ranks by selecting the cream of the crop into the regular component, and all reserve officers were urged to apply. However, there was an unspoken disadvantage buried in the invitation. Whereas regular officers were only allowed to leave the service "at the convenience of the government," a reserve could simply say, "I quit," and walk away. Given the restriction, many reserve officers, I among them, had mixed feelings about giving up this freedom of choice. Nevertheless, ingrained competitiveness compelled me to apply.

Six colonels from other bases formed the augmentation board that interviewed the local candidates. When called, I marched in, saluted and was invited to sit. Proud of my combat record, job experience, and performance appraisals, I let those items ride and delivered a forthright but optimistic statement about my weakest credential, education.

All went well until a non-rated colonel, who according to his ribbons lacked overseas experience, asked, "Given that you're Mexican, what leads you to believe that junior officers, non-commissioned officers, and enlisted men will follow you in a stressful situation?"

I would never admit it but I secretly liked the war. It had afforded me an opportunity to demonstrate bravery and competence. Now after having done so, here was a desk-bound, paddle-foot trying to shoot me down with an irrelevant question. Reverting to an ancestral trait, I assumed a stoic face and struggled to maintain my composure. But my reservoir of pain and rage overflowed and in a voice quavering with anger I lashed out, "Sir, senior as well as junior officers and enlisted men have followed my orders in battle without hesitation. I believe my commendations speak for themselves, which is more than I can say for others present. I withdraw my application."

The colonel reddened, "Listen here you ...."

The senior colonel interrupted him, "Why is that, lieutenant?"

"Sir, I just would."

"Why? You must have a reason."

"Because I resent the question."

"I see. Well, all right, you're excused."

Back in the reception area, I grabbed my cap and blurted, "God damn it. Here too? Where the hell does one have to go to get away from this crap?" The secretary and waiting candidates were all friends of mine but no one said a word.

The incident killed my chances of being selected into the regular component and in turn may have adversely affected my being considered for promotion ahead of my peers who were regulars. But for the most part, I think my supervisors were able to overlook it due to my unstinting loyalty, honesty, and willingness to work—the most prized attributes a supervisor looks for in a subordinate—and I had certainly given a full measure of those. In fact, following the incident I seemed to sense a more paternalistic air in my supervisors' attitudes toward me.

The Great Schnozzola

Jackie Kennedy's second husband, billionaire Ari Onassis' advice for living the good life was, "Dress impeccably, have a good address, and show a tan all year around." Salesman Art Kovary followed his guidance to the letter. Tall and not unhandsome, Art sauntered into my office unannounced. Perfectly tanned and coiffed, he was in a perfectly matched glen-plaid suit, pale blue French-cuffed shirt, a dark silk tie, Italian made shoes, and a tiger-eye pinky ring. He was just in from the Big Apple and during a rambling dissertation boasted that he had inherited a million dollars and spent it on good whiskey, fast women, and slow horses. To back the claim he spread out several wrinkled newspaper clippings from Walter Winchell and Earl Wilson's columns that mentioned him being seen here or there with a Latin Quarter or Copacabana showgirl.

The schlock in his sample cases didn't interest me but his stories of glamour and glitzy girls did, so I accepted his invitation to dinner that night. I picked him up at the Brown Palace Hotel and we went to a swank supper club owned by two ex-vaudevillians, Willie and Jerry. Nearing midnight, Jimmy Durante and other celebrities in town for a March of Dimes Benefit came in for dinner. Willie introduced them and invited Durante to do a number. Durante gave the crowd a warm wave and graciously declined. But Willie persisted and ultimately resorted to pleading. Finally weary of the bother, the Great Schnozzola consented. Jubilant, Willie launched into a lavish introduction that included crowing that Durante's performance would christen their new baby grand piano.

Durante took the stage, told a few jokes, then carefully examined the piano. He lovingly ran his hand over its elegant lines, blew his breath at a couple of spots, polished them with his coat sleeve, and sat down. He scrunched his fedora down around his ears, pulled his sleeves halfway up his arms, raised his hands high, played a rousing introduction, and began singing "The Lost Chord." In keeping with the title, Durante was searching for a specific note. He crooned a couple of gravely voiced choruses, stopped, clinked an "A," checked his tone, and trilled the scale. It was not there. He played the white keys, no, the black keys, no again. Different combinations still no luck. Exasperated, Durante inspected the piano, the piano bench, and the surrounding area. He simply could not find the lost chord. With that, Durante lost all patience; he threw his hat on the floor, stomped on it, broke a leg off the bench, opened the piano and as he continued to sing, battered the soundboards until the strings were twanging off in all directions. He stopped, ran his elbow across the keyboard, and listened to the few that responded. Did it again. None was the lost chord. Disgusted, he threw the bludgeon inside, slammed the lid shut, stacked the broken bench on top, retrieved his Fedora, punched it once to extend the crown and stalked off. The customers were rolling in the aisles but Willie didn't ask for an encore.

Art had Jimmy Durante's table and ours joined and insisted that their charges be included on our tab. This sobered me instantly because the only condition I placed on our having dinner together was that we share the bill equally. One by one, the great entertainer's friends departed until just Art, Durante, and I were left. Our waitress was cleaning after them when Art lifted her mini-skirt and patted her behind. She erupted with a string of profanity and although Art quickly apologized, she continued to verbally batter him. Finally, in desperation, Art reached into his pocket, opened a suede pouch and spilled a dozen or so gold rings on the table. Each was set with a ruby, opal or pearl, and he said to her, "Darlin', you can have anyone you want. But on one condition, you gotta promise me you won't tell anyone where you got it." Her wrath turned to smiles, she promised and demurely settled on a ruby. Within two minutes, we were inundated with waitresses, cashiers, and female customers. Some of the less prissy ones also received rings.

Although Willie generously picked up the tab, he did not stay around to see us off and the bartenders helped me load the two wasted men into the car. On our way back to the hotel I said, "Art, I know most of the waitresses that you gave rings to. I told them that they are company-owned samples and asked that they be considerate and return them tomorrow night. I'm sure they'll bring them back. We'll stop by and pick them up." Art said, "Forget it Hank. Those rings aren't worth two dollars apiece, their fingers will turn green in a week." Durante said, "Lemme see 'em." Art handed him the pouch containing a few remaining trinkets. Durante threw it out the window and said, "Serves 'em right. The lousy piano was outta tune anyway."

Several years after leaving Lowry, I read a newspaper article that caused me to wonder if the item had been written about a salesman I once met there. The story stated that a fellow who claimed to be an Arabian oil sheik got drunk in Hollywood's Trocadero nightclub and amused himself by insulting several movie stars in the room. The manager was about to throw him out when he opened a suede pouch and scattered some expensive rings on the floor. He wanted to see if any stars would demean themselves by getting on hands and knees to gather the baubles. The article named two famous women seen scrambling under the tables and chairs.

Wolf, the Pilot's Seeing-Eye Dog

One had to see Colonel Everett Majeski to believe he existed. He stood about six feet four, with wispy sandy-colored hair, a bloated face and a beer belly that stretched the imagination. He wore aviation sunglasses regardless of the hour, his uniform looked like he slept on a bench, he walked like Charlie Chaplin, and his constant companion was a huge police dog named Wolf.

Majeski headed the Civil Air Patrol (CAP) in the area and had me appointed as his instructor pilot. On one occasion, He, Wolf, and I were flying in a C-45 to Olathe Naval Station near Kansas City. The weather was tailor-made for thunderstorms and nearing the field, we were startled by a loud flash-crack. The nose-clearing odor of a lightning strike invaded the cabin and we entered a furious hailstorm. The clatter sounded like a thousand machine guns, the updrafts were tossing us about like the teacup ride at a carnival, and Wolf began barking non-stop. Majeski coaxed, threatened, and then began screaming red-faced at the terrified dog to shut-the-hell-up.

I was on-instruments, working to keep us right side up, and to get a radio clearance for an instrument approach to the field. It is doubtful that the ground controller had ever heard a pilot, a wild man, and a dog simultaneously transmitting in a hailstorm. For rather than heed my requests that he broadcast the clearance "in the blind," he kept repeating, "State the type of emergency, type of aircraft, amount of fuel, number of souls aboard . . . ."

Exasperated, I let Wolf yap into the mike a few times to help the fellow get the hang of it. He went off the air, probably to get a hearing aid, and we assumed that he had cleared us to land.

We rocked and rolled in, landed, and taxied to the ramp. Quickly, I shut down the engines and scrambled out to check for hail or lightning damage. Two young sailors were standing by when Majeski exited the plane with the now-leashed Wolf. With his cap askew, tie-knot under collar, shirttail out, bedraggled pants at half-mast, and rivulets of rainwater dripping off his sunglasses, he looked like a blind man following a seeing-eye dog as he waddled off behind Wolf. One sailor double-checked him, eyed me, and then said to the other one, "Man, the Air Force must really be hard-up for pilots these days."

General Ike and Mrs. Eisenhower

Lowry was built on the site of a former sanitarium. The main building became the headquarters and an adjoining wing was converted into a Bachelor Officers Quarters (BOQ). I lived in one of those rooms. One day I received an urgent phone call. "Hank, this is Larry Paquette at the base housing office."

"Sure, Larry, what can I do for you?"

"Pal, I can't tell you why, but you're going to have to vacate your quarters and move into the BOQ behind the officers club. Can you be out by close of business today?"

"Sure, Larry I'll move during the noon hour."

A few days later, the world knew the reason for my eviction. Five Star General Dwight D. Eisenhower had retired from the Army and had been appointed President of Columbia University. Mrs. Eisenhower's parents lived in Denver and his office had announced that they planned to visit there often. Offices were needed on the base to accommodate his needs and my quarters were among those confiscated for that purpose.

My image of General Eisenhower had been that of an older man with the famous boyish, gap-toothed grin on a moon-shaped face. In fact, he had intense deep blue eyes, a stern countenance, wore severe black suits, and articulated in the crisp, precise manner of one not given to being questioned.

When on base, he normally had a light lunch at a permanently reserved table in the Officers Club dining room. He seldom spoke to anyone and ,other than his waiter, no one dared approach him. We junior officers also lunched there and our bantering usually centered on whose turn it was to play Gin Rummy against the "pigeon." My incompetence with cards had earned me the title.

One day several games were in progress when the general stopped by to kibitz. He looked around and said, "I want to know. Who is the pigeon?" Everyone laughed and pointed at me. He got the familiar "Ike" grin on his face and in a mellow voice said, "I'm a pretty good poker player. Let's see what we can do to help you." He pulled up a chair beside me and the others gathered around to watch.

My opponent dealt a new hand and Ike's first pearl of wisdom was that I align the cards by suit and ascending order. Overwhelmed by his presence, I awkwardly spilled the cards on the floor. Without a word, he patiently helped me retrieve them then gently taught me the proper way to hold a hand of cards. With that, he moved his chair closer, smacked his lips, adjusted his bifocals and pointed to my first discard. I snapped it down and my opponent said, "Are you sure that's the one you want to discard?" Ike replied, "Certainly, we're sure." The fellow snatched the card and whooped, "Gin!"

Gales of laughter erupted and when I finally regained control I asked him, "General, are you sure you know how to play this game better than I do?" He laughed so hard his pate turned pink and tears welled in his eyes. At last, he cleared his throat, wiped his glasses, looked at his watch and said, "Well, I really do have to go." I stood up, shook his hand and said, "Thank you, Sir. I really appreciated all the help." He burst out again and continued laughing all the way out the door. After that, he occasionally stopped by to help me. However, if disinclined, he usually said, "Go ahead, you're gettin' it." I never did learn what I was gettin', other than beat.

Later, when the general became president of the United States, he selected one of our better Gin Rummy players, tall, handsome, Second Lieutenant Keith Christiansen, to copilot his plane *The Columbine.* Keith was an excellent pilot but we always wondered which skill earned him the job.

Mrs. Eisenhower also frequented the base and this led to the general's aide becoming a thorn in my side. He called one day, "Lieutenant, this is Colonel Schutt in General Eisenhower's office. Mrs. Eisenhower and three of her friends will visit the PX tomorrow morning at ten o'clock. I want everything in the store to be in order, and I want you to assure that she receives the best possible service by waiting on her."

"No problem, Sir," I replied. "We'll be ready for her and better yet, I'll have our store manager Mrs. Johnson at her side."

"Apparently, you didn't hear me, lieutenant, I want you to take care of her needs."

"Yes, Sir."

The next morning, Mrs. Eisenhower's black limousine arrived at the front door and I greeted her and her friends. They listened attentively as I described the store layout then, like a compass needle points to North, they headed for the women's department. I trailed along and as they entered the lingerie area, slipped behind the counter. Mrs. Eisenhower stopped, nailed me with a withering look, and hissed, "Lieutenant."

Without a word, I motioned to Mrs. Johnson to replace me and disappeared. Later when Mrs. Eisenhower and I became better acquainted, I confided my reason for trying to help her buy a foundation garment. She laughed and in a stage whisper said, "He always does that. I won't tell if you don't. Let's just keep it our little secret."

Mrs. Eisenhower loved to shop. It became common for her to call and tell me that she had found this-or-that item in a downtown store, then ask if I could arrange for her to buy it at the PX.

"Certainly, Ma'am," I'd reply. "It should be ready for you by tomorrow afternoon. I'll let Colonel Schutt know." I'd then call the store in question and arrange for a distributor with whom we both did business to transfer the item between us, so I could sell it to her at a lower price. I would not say she was tight, just frugal.

* * * *

In March 1951, I landed a C-47 at Burbank airport. My orders were to fly Les Brown and his Band of Renown to Lowry where they would back *The Bob Hope Show* the following evening.

The group came aboard and we took off on the five-hour jaunt flying at 11,000 feet. Low altitude summer flying can be a hell on earth and it was a turbulent ride. The passengers were in bucket seats and the cabin lacked air-conditioning so it was not long before several men turned green and others became airsick. In an effort to relieve their boredom and discomfort, I took over the copilot's seat and invited anyone who wished, to come and take a turn flying the plane. Only Les' brother, drummer Stumpy Brown, came forward. We stacked cushions on the seat for him to see out and he took over. It would be good-hearted to say that Stumpy did a great job. In fact, he was so uncoordinated that a couple of the sickest men aboard stumbled to the cockpit and begged that he be relieved of pilot duties.

At Lowry, a huge hangar had been converted into an auditorium with hundreds of chairs and a stage. GI's and their families began filing in hours before the broadcast was scheduled to start. By show time, other than the front row, all chairs were taken and hundreds of disgruntled soldiers were milling about behind the seating area.

Bob stepped onstage to thunderous applause and as he was about to open the show, noticed the long row of empty chairs. Off mike, he pointed to them and asked a major standing by why they were not occupied. They were reserved for the "brass." Bob got on the mike and said, "This show will not go on until the chairs here in front are filled by you guys standing in back. Seats for my shows are not reserved for officers." The GI's went wild. It was a great show, headlined by two great entertainers.

* * * *

I had been at Lowry for more than five years when the Wing Commander, Brigadier General Warren R. Carter, called me to his office and said, "Hank, you're doing a good job and we've kept you here a long time, too long in fact. During my time, we have kept you from going to the Berlin Airlift and to a bad assignment in Turkey. I've also turned down numerous requests to send you to fight the war in Korea. You have more multi-engine time than any one in the Training Command who hasn't been there and you're ripe for picking. I'm being transferred to Waco, Texas, where I will head the new Flying Training Command. And one of the first things I have to do is activate a base in Wichita, Kansas. I need you to go there and set up the PXs for me. If you do a good job, I'll let you fly a new jet bomber that's being built there at the Boeing plant. What do you say?"

"I'm ready, Sir. When do we go?"

He laughed, "I knew you'd say that. Keep it under your hat. We have to get a replacement in here, then I'll get you some orders."

"Wow, I'm going to be a jet jockey!"

Chapter 5

The Jet Age
(1951–1955)

Wichita, Air Capital of the World

Wichita is 367 air miles southeast of Denver and lags by an equivalent number of years in development of cultural and recreational activities. Three aircraft plants, Boeing, Beech, and Cessna, provided a basis for its slogan, "The Air Capital of the World." "The Used Car Lot Capital of the World" would have also fit nicely.

Scottie and I drove into town on a hot sticky day in April 1951—she had an unlimited airline pass and had agreed to accompany me down then fly right back to Denver. Despite her pleas, I was too proud to stop and ask a mere civilian for directions. Instead, I toured the city's perimeter for an hour craning for a glimpse of the usual indicators of a military airfield—a boldly checkered water tank or a spindly-legged aircraft control tower. Finally, the Continental flight schedule required that I take Scottie to the tiny civilian airline terminal that I had previously bypassed.

While we were there, in response to Scottie's question, the ticket agent pointed across the main runway to an old yellow brick hangar and said, "They're running tests on a new plane over there. Maybe that's what you two have been looking for, but I don't know how to get there from here."

I watched Scottie board the plane then followed a gravel road to the isolated building. Parked halfway into the small hangar, was a sleek, new, swept wing, six-engine jet bomber. Its nose was stenciled:

U.S. AIR FORCE - MODEL B-47A
AIR FORCE SERIAL NO. 49-1909
CREW WEIGHT: 750 LBS.

No one was around so I closely examined the silvery monster then went to the lobby. The office directory had two columns. One read: "Project WIBAC (Wichita-Boeing Aircraft Company), Commander Paul W. Tibbets, Jr., Colonel USAF." The other: "Wichita AFB, Commander Henry R. Spicer, Colonel USAF."

The base adjutant welcomed me and was reviewing my orders when a deep voice called out from within the commander's office, "*Enrique, ven aqui* (come here)." Surprised to hear Spanish being spoken in that setting, I looked in. Leaning back in a chair with his boots propped on the desk was a tall, handsome, deeply tanned, balding colonel with a huge mustache and a smile to match.

Speaking fluent "Mexican" around his pipe, Colonel Henry "Russ" Spicer cheerfully related how he learned to speak *el idioma* (the idiom) while living on the wrong side of the tracks to attend college in Phoenix, Arizona. We chatted for a while then he said, "Come on, let's take a ride and get you acquainted with the base." As we drove off in his staff car, I asked, "Colonel, how many men do you have stationed here?" "Well, Kiki (a Spanish nickname for Enrique), you're my sixth officer and I have 200 airmen. How's that for a command?"

June 1951, Wichita, Kansas. Legendary fighter pilot Col. (Later, Maj. Gen.) Henry "Russ" Spicer, first commander of McConnell AFB

We arrived at a sun-baked encampment that appeared to be an Army reserve unit on a field training exercise. He pointed to the sea of tents and disgustedly said, "Look at this place. Can you believe it? My men are maintaining the most advanced bomber in the world and living in damn tents." We returned to the airline terminal building where he jerked a thumb toward the basement and said, "That area is being converted into flying training ready rooms. That's all there is. End of tour."

Only the prospect of flying the stunning B-47 kept me from feeling that it was pay back time for all the good years I'd spent in Denver. He saw the dejection in my face and said, "Let's go up to the coffee shop and let you see the upside of this assignment." We sat at the counter and a lone waitress came flouncing toward us; mid-20s, good looking, bold brown eyes, blond pony-tail, breasts spilling out of a flimsy white blouse, and everything bobbing in unison.

Spicer smiled a greeting and introduced us, "Kiki meet Sherri Blum. Sherri say, *Gracias a Dios.*"

Sherri said, "Whaat? What's that?"

"Never mind, say, *Gracias a Dios.*"

"Alright, grash a dio, why?"

"Sherri my dear, you're always after me to introduce you to a pilot. Well thank God because your prayers have been answered. Kiki here is one. On top of that, he's single, drives a convertible, and just got in town."

Sherri reddened, laughed nervously, and slapped his hand, "You liar, I never said that. What do you want?"

We ordered Cokes and she left to make them. The colonel reached in his pocket pulled out a handful of bills and whispered, "Get some money out and tip her whenever she leans over."

Sherri was well on her way to becoming independently wealthy before we got back to business.

He asked, "Kiki, how long will it be before you can have some kind of a PX operation for my men? They're living in atrocious conditions and I have to improve their situation."

"Do you have any support aircraft assigned here?" I asked.

"Well yes, we have a B-25, a C-47, and a C-45. Why?"

"Well, Sir, I happen to be current in all three of them. Give me the Gooney Bird and a tent, and in a few days I'll have you a store with the basic items the men need."

Whap! He slapped my back and a big grin spread the mustache across his face. "General Carter told me you were a go'er. Have at it, Kiki." He dropped me off at my car and left. I checked my watch; Sherri would be getting off soon.

The next day, I found a copilot who had never been in a C-47 and a flight engineer who said he had, and we took off for Lowry. I signed a receipt for an assortment of basic merchandise, borrowed $250, three old showcases, two cash registers, and a tiny safe, and returned to Wichita. Three days later, with a sergeant's wife at the helm, we had a PX ready for business.

Colonel Spicer had promised to "cut the ribbon" for the grand opening and I stopped by the hangar to take him over. He and Colonel Tibbets, the Project WIBC commander, were together when I arrived. Whereas Spicer was irreverent, gregarious, and a celebrated World War II fighter pilot, Colonel Tibbets was deliberate, soft-spoken, and deadly serious. His personality fit what one would expect in the pilot who dropped the first atom bomb on Hiroshima. Talk about legends.

One day when I was in his restricted area, Colonel Tibbets stopped me, "Lieutenant I want to thank you for the mobile snack bar you brought in for my men. We really appreciate it. I know you're busy and I don't want to inconvenience you but would it be too much to ask that you get a security clearance?"

I submitted an application for a "secret" clearance and the next time I was home, Father took me out to the backyard for a private chat. With worry etched in his face he said, "Two men from the FBI were here the other day and asked questions about you. They also went to the neighbors and asked questions about us. What's going on?"

"Papa," I said, "they have to investigate me because of the work I do. Don't worry. I haven't done anything wrong and I'm not in trouble, OK?" He kissed me but his concern remained evident.

My frequent trips to Lowry for merchandise continued until we became so large that it was no longer feasible. However, that did not curtail my trips there. Training Command flying units were allocated resources based on the number of flying hours they expended. Thus, pilots were encouraged to fly wherever they wished on weekends so long as they had the plane back in time to meet the flight schedule on Monday morning. Accordingly, four days a week, Scottie would fly through Wichita on her scheduled trip to Tulsa, and I would spend most weekends with her in Denver. Our romance was alive and well.

Fort Leavenworth housed a Federal penitentiary, an infantry division, and an airfield. I flew there for a meeting and the local PX officer came out to meet me at the plane. He had the top down on his convertible and as we headed toward the base, I asked that he drive by the prison for me to see it. The menacing gray walls were surrounded by an expanse of lawn and as we slowly made our way through the area, someone called out, "Hank, Hank." The driver stopped. The only visible person was a prisoner in blue fatigues with a large white "P" stenciled on the jacket and pants. The fellow looked familiar and I kneeled on the seat for a better look. The driver warned me, "Whatever you do, don't get out." The prisoner was Richard "Butch" Davis, my old boss at Lowry. He smiled, waved and went back to spearing wind-blown trash with a stick. Baffled by the sight of a former officer in prison blues, we discussed all the possibilities that came to mind. We never did learn the reason he traded a pair of oak leaves for the privilege of idling his engine there.

The next day, while at a merchandise show in Kansas City, I met Captain Orville Smiley, the PX Officer at Forbes AFB, Kansas. We had been classmates in flying school and agreed to meet for dinner that evening at a steak house across the street from the Mulebach Hotel.

Orville came in with Colonel C. F. Necrason, his wing commander, in tow. We were all in civilian clothes and were seated in a booth near the restrooms. The Strategic Air Command (SAC) had a worldwide reputation as a tough, straight arrow outfit. So, I felt honored to be in the company of one of its leaders, particularly one wearing a West Point ring.

The place was crowded and we were patiently waiting for service when the Maitre-d' led a lone mobster-looking guy to a nearby table and took his meal order. Minutes later, while we were still waiting for service, he was served a steak with all the trimmings. The fellow grabbed a handful of french-fries, stuffed them in his mouth, and went to the restroom. Without a word, the colonel followed him in and almost immediately reappeared. As he passed by the mobster's table, he picked up the platter, brought it over, and placed it under our table, concealing it with the tablecloth. The mobster returned, found the meal missing, and whistled at the waiter. Together, they went around scrutinizing every table in the room and by the time they got to us, the fellow was cussing a blue storm. Meanwhile, we were kicking the platter back and forth to distance ourselves from it in case he questioned us. Fortunately, we passed inspection and they served him another meal.

Seeing a wing commander perform a schoolboy antic was incredulous to me. I mentally excused it as the unthinking reaction of a senior officer unaccustomed to being ignored. After dinner, we left the money on the table, and rushed out and into a cab. Once away from the restaurant, Orville asked that we be taken to a gambling club outside of town. It was raining and the streets deserted when we stopped at the first red light. While waiting for it to change, our driver exchanged pleasantries with a cabby who stopped beside us. Their conversation continued well after the light turned green and they did it again at the next light. When they continued visiting at the third light, the colonel lowered his window, pulled out a water pistol and squirted the other driver in the face. The fellow jumped out ready to fight one or all of us. Fortunately the light changed and our driver took off. That did it for me. When we arrived at the club I excused myself and returned to the hotel. Colonel C. F. Necrason went on to attain the rank of major general and head the Alaskan Air Command.

* * * *

One broiling hot September afternoon in 1951, Colonel Spicer called and requested that I meet him in the rotunda of the airline terminal. I thought nothing of it. One of our flight training groups operated from the basement of the building and thought that he might have secured space for a PX snack bar there. Several Air Force office employees and curious airline passengers where standing by when I arrived. He summoned me to the central area then called out. Scottie stepped forward in her flight uniform and together they pinned captain's bars on my shirt collar. Immediately, Scottie kissed my cheek and ran to re-board her flight, continuing back to Denver.

The promotion rather cemented my status as a "rare bird." Although the Air Force did not begin to keep such records until much later, they have estimated that over the years no more than two hundred Latino pilots have been on its roles at any one time.

Our PX sales were increasing rapidly and I advertised for a bookkeeper. A thirtyish, statuesque, six-foot blonde named Mary Kay Ash came in to apply for the job. She looked familiar and during a break in the interview I asked, "Haven't we met before?"

She laughed, "Are you trying to pick me up?"

"No," I said, "but I feel that I know you."

"I doubt it," she replied, and we changed the subject. I hired Mary Kay and after studying her face for a few days, it came to me. Back with the 100th, she was the girl in a framed photograph we all admired whenever

Merrill Jensen's navigator, Dick Ayesh, was not around. Mary Kay and Dick divorced, and she changed her name from Ayesh to Ash.

Mary Kay had a lusty laugh and exuded a brand of sexuality that attracts men like flies. The Base Legal Officer, Major Bill Mika, was her most ardent admirer and although she tried to discourage him, he became an unwelcome fixture in the office. Drawing on all the courage a new captain needs to correct a senior officer, I drew him aside and said, "Sir, please stop bothering Mary Kay in the office. If you want to see her after duty hours that's your business. But here it's mine." With his displeasure evident, he stared hard at me then silently departed.

Increased sales invited increased pilferage and to assure our losses did not exceed the regulatory limit, I asked for an "officers inventory." Major Mika volunteered to head the team and I knew that it was payback time. The losses were found to be well within the allowable limits. However, in writing the report, Mika ignored the regulation, attributed the losses to my personal negligence, and recommended that I be held liable. Perhaps due to Mika's key position, the group commander approved the findings and the case was routinely reported to Flying Training Command Headquarters in Waco, Texas. A week later, we were informed that (now Major General) Carter was due in to inspect "tent city." On the date of his visit, our group commander gathered all of his officers with duties in the tent area and aligned us in three rows. Embarrassed to be the subject of an investigation, I hid in the rear rank behind the tallest officer in the unit.

General Carter stepped out of his staff car, returned the colonel's salute in an off-handed manner then stood back and studied us. He saw me, broke through the ranks and threw his arm over my shoulder. Flustered, I tried to salute him but he held my arm down to prevent it and said, "Hi, Hank, how are you doing? Show me your operation." The startled officers parted and we toured the PX activities with the colonel trailing us. When we finished the general smiled, shook my hand and said, "Fine, Hank. You did exactly what I sent you here to do. Good job." He turned and spoke to the colonel for the first time, "I want you to relieve Captain Cervantes of this assignment and see to it that he is entered in the next B-47 transition class. Is that understood?"

"Yessir, General Carter."

"Very well. Show me around." The charge disappeared, Major Mika shipped out, and I requested a thirty-day leave to visit Mexico before entering the school.

[In 1934, then Captain Warren R. Carter and 34 other U.S. Army pilots formed The Order of Daedalians. The society seeks to honor the memory of the first American pilots to fly in time of war and is the most prestigious group of its kind in the world. Members must be, or have been, commissioned military pilots. I am proud to be a life member of the order as a small tribute to General Carter.]

Fiesta Time!

Whenever old military pilots meet, usually the first question asked is, "What did you fly, bombers or fighters?" If a fellow claims to have flown fighters he will probably have bragged about it earlier. But if in doubt, knowing veterans will check the fellow's left wrist. It's common knowledge that fighter pilots wear oversize wristwatches to divert attention from their anatomical shortcomings elsewhere.

In my case, the test goes beyond that. As an anomaly in the tight fraternity of Caucasian military pilots, the first reactions when I say, "I'm a pilot," are who-in-the-hell-is-this? stares, as if I am some kind of lowlife, usually followed by sly smiles, caustic skepticism, a turning of backs, or an attempt to discredit. "(Smirk) What did you fly, transports?"

"Yes, I flew them," I say. "I also flew fighters and bombers." The assertion is normally accepted at face value when it comes from others. But with me, it's grounds for a quiz, and the results can vary. At one end of the scale are those who refuse to accept that a Mexican matched or, God forbid, surpassed their accomplishments. And at the far end are the closet racists who when finally convinced that it's true, attempt to tenderize the facts to ease their discomfort. A typical exchange goes like this:

"You're so brown. Are you a golfer?"

"No, I'm Mexican."

(Hilarious laughter) "No really, what are you?"

"I'm Mexican."

"No way, you can't be. Where were your parents born?"

"In Mexico."

"But they're from Spain, right?"

"No, they're from Mexico."

"Well, yeah, but they came from Spain, right?"

I won't allow them to go there to get off the hook. "No, one was born in a place called Ojo Caliente and the other in a village named Jalpa."

"But you don't look Mexican." It's meant to be a compliment.

"Thanks, but I assure you I am."

The wheels in their heads start to spin. Their faces contort with confusion, they get doe-eyed, and mumble an "Excuse me" or "Well, if you're not going to be serious, I'll drop it."

"OK."

Sadly, the issue is not limited to close-minded fliers. Latinos have been fighting the scourge of racism since year one, and societal reminders that they are among the unwashed exist everywhere. Insults abound and however veiled they may be, finely tuned antennae pick them up and we go back to lamenting past inequities. This prompted the Mexico trip. I needed to confront my genealogical roots and establish a clear picture in my mind of who I am: Mexican, Mexican-American, or American?

In Mexico City, I checked into the Ritz Hotel then went out to admire the modern skyscrapers and grand monuments that line El Paseo de la Reforma. I had only gone a block or two when a strange sense of physical freedom washed over me. The feeling was so tangible that I sat down at a bus stop to ponder the reason. Suddenly I knew; it was stress. The question always came up. But rather than risk loss of status by admitting my heritage outright, I evaluated each new contact to decide if I should lie. No need to hide it here. Angered by the realization, I wanted to climb atop the highest monument, face north and shout, "God damn you! You've given me all those medals. If I'm so good, why is it that I have to come all the way down here to feel like a man?"

Scottie joined me for a long weekend. I wanted to see her reaction to a part of me she hardly knew. The brown component that can become as emotional over the Mexican national anthem as "The Star Spangled Banner," that enjoys mariachi music as much as Gershwin's "Rhapsody in Blue," and that relishes *chorizo con huevos* (Mexican sausage and eggs) more than lobster thermidor. I also wanted to see if she would be dismissive or rude to anyone. If so, I knew the day might come when it would be my turn in the barrel. I should have known better. It didn't happen. We had a fun time and she returned to Denver.

The next day I joined a planeload of snowbirds in suits and furs bound for Acapulco. There, waiting to board the DC-3, were an equal number of sunburned bodies in green palmetto hats, *guayabera* (loose, lightweight outer garment worn in the Tropics) shirts, and new *huaraches* (sandals).

Acapulco was far from the neon-lit, go-go dancing jungle it is today. Back then, it was a quiet fishing village centered round a picturesque church plaza with a raised bandstand. On one side were narrow cobblestone streets, crumbling commercial buildings, and an open-air *Mercado* (market) with its mesmerizing sounds, scenes, and smells. On the other, there were old adobe houses, sun-baked kids, black-clad women, and *paleta* (Popsicle) salesmen pushing jingle-carts.

I rented a rusty old convertible Volkswagen and checked into The Americana, one of the three hotels that advertised in English. Built on the summit of a spectacular bluff, the gleaming white structure had a panoramic view of the bay, the largest *alberca* (pool) in town, and gave special rates to American Airline stewardesses. I changed into a bathing suit and tracked the sound of a shrieking parrot to a bougainvillea-draped bar. Some of my fellow passengers were already there, laughing and backslapping one another as they watched their complimentary margaritas being Osterized. Two big guys and I sat opposite from them and were soon joined by a striking blond and her girlfriend. The sexy one had a perfect tan, long blond hair, deep blue eyes, and a body encased in a tight white jumpsuit. As is usually the case, her friend was a tall skinny freckled-faced woman with hair the color of a ragged windsock and a sun-suit that hung from her shoulders like a wet flag.

Freckles suggested that we all introduce ourselves. It seemed out of character for a female so wanting of breasts or hips to be that forward, but the men across the bar jumped on the idea. They were Philco salesmen on a three-day vacation for having won area sales competitions. The two big guys were Dick Stanfel and Joe Schmidt of the Detroit Lions. They had played in the All-Pro football game in Los Angeles and were down enjoying their $1,000 checks. The blonde was a schoolteacher and Freckles airily informed us that she was Thelma Anderson, a columnist for Oklahoma City's *The Oklahoman*.

Rather than invite doubt or admit to being a PX officer, I said, "My name is Hank Cervantes and I'm also in sales. My territory extends from Ohio to Oklahoma and I only carry one line, personal sewing kits." Everyone laughed and with mock disdain I said to the salesmen, "I don't know why you guys think it's so funny. You're only here for three days while I'm here for thirty."

They looked at me with newfound respect, but Thelma used the remark as an opportunity to impress. She snickered and in a voice dripping with condescension said, "You certainly have an exciting job. Next time you're in Oklahoma City look me up. I have a lot of bachelor-friends who need your kits something awful."

I smiled and replied, "Hey that's a great idea, Thelma. I promise you I'll do that. I'll even give them a good price on a special travel kit we have with extra needles and thread."

With an offhanded wave she said, "Oh, don't worry about the price, they can afford it."

Ernest (Teddy) Stauffer stood about 6'1", had a slightly stooped frame, a Teutonic accent, and wore his graying hair shoulder-length a decade before it became popular here. Years before, while on a world tour, his orchestra went broke in Acapulco and Teddy elected to settle there.

Local kids had long tested their *cojones* (courage) by diving 135 feet into the surf at a narrow cove called La Quebrada. Teddy built a gravity-defying nightclub overlooking the site and converted their game of *gallina* (chicken) into La Perla's twice-a-night featured attraction. Along the way, he married an Austrian actress named Hedy Lamarr. Teddy was the fourth of six husbands, so you know it didn't last long. Nevertheless, the resultant publicity sparked an invasion of Hollywood celebrities and the club became a Mexican edition of the forecourt at Hollywood's Grauman's Chinese Theater. Hardly a night went by that an actor was not photographed next to his or her autograph etched in the club walls.

The bar was the town's social center. Across the street was Teddy's well-preserved small hotel where he maintained a harem of mostly tall Scandinavian blonds. I cultivated Teddy's friendship and he invited one of them to leave, renting her place to me for $8 a day. The small rooftop apartment had thick adobe walls, an ocean view, a palm-frond roof, and iron chandeliers. So what if they turned off the power at 2200? By then, one of Teddy's bored friends had usually knocked on my bright blue door.

I was in the club one night and a striking blond with a seductive strut kept passing by. The combo played a sensuous Cha-Cha and she invited me to dance. I was doing my stuff when she exerted two-hand pressure on my shoulders to downshift me out of overdrive and said, "You do a very scientific Cha-Cha. Where did you learn it, Arthur Murray's?" Embarrassed, I replied, "Don't make fun. I happen to be a proud graduate of their accelerated one-week course. Let's sit down. I'll buy you a drink if you'll tell me your name." Over margaritas she said, "I'm Chili Williams." [In the late 40s, Chili gained her fifteen minutes of fame by being the first bikini-clad woman to appear on the cover of *Life* magazine.] "I came to Acapulco for a weekend of fun and ended up marrying the head cliff-diver, Raul Garcia. I work next door at the El Mirador Hotel. That's my story. Now tell me about you."

One night Chili invited me to a "wrap" party for a Hollywood film crew that had just finished a movie titled *A Woman's Devotion*. We drove on a narrow mountain road to a pair of huge carved wood gates where a guard allowed us entry into a serene, palm-swathed estate. Two long rows of whitewashed rocks led to a Spanish-style oceanfront house with a breathtaking view and a swimming pool on the roof. The affair was in full swing, and Chili introduced me to the important members of the crew: producer John Bash, director-actor Paul Henreid, and stars Janice Ruhl and Ralph Meeker. We had a fun evening but through it all, the men puzzled me. For rather than dance to a hot mambo combo, or watch sexy girls fin the surface of the pool above, they stayed close to me and seemed fascinated by my every word. Nearing the end of the evening, Ralph admitted the reason. Their driver had left them stranded and they needed a ride back to town. We all piled into the "bug" and returned to the hotel with the corrugated fenders scraping the tires at every bump.

* * * *

It was one of those soft tropical nights people dream about—a full moon, a star-drenched sky, silver light dancing off the water, and the seductive beat of bongo drums in a distant bar. A TWA stewardess named Betty Barker and I spent the night on Playa Caleta, and when a brilliant sunrise ended our diversion, I walked her to El Club de Pesca. We kissed

1951, Acapulco, Mexico. Chili Williams

good night and she went upstairs. Rather than catch a quick taxi home, I went to the hotel pool for a swim. Except for a youngster setting out towels and lining up chaise lounges, the area was deserted. I was practicing dives when a tall prematurely gray man arrived and carefully lowered himself to one of the padded chairs.

Touched by his appearance, I swam to his end of the pool, got out and asked, "Hi, are you OK?"

He grunted.

I was about to jump back in but something about his eyes stopped me. Despite the pallor and bleak expression, the once boyish face was still evident. He was General Hoyt S. Vandenberg, the recently retired Air Force Chief of Staff.

I said, "Hi, General, I'm in the Air Force too."

He looked me up and down and said, "Oh, whose?"

"You're the boss," I said.

He grinned and I introduced myself.

He said, "You're so dark I would have never thought that you were from the States much less in the Air Force."

I pulled up a chair beside him. He did not seem to be in a mood to chat or mutter platitudes. Instead, we mutually allowed the morning solitude and our common bond to draw us together, and we silently contemplated the pool.

Mrs. Vandenberg's arrival broke the spell and I invited them to meet me for dinner at La Perla. Raul and Chili joined us and had not been there long when the general asked Raul if he had seen *Life*'s [then] risqué photographs of Chili. Raul admitted that he had not. So, while Mrs. Vandenberg squirmed with embarrassment, Chili jiggled with delight, and Raul and I roared with laughter, the general launched into a racy description of Chili's physical assets. The combo was playing a slow rumba and to help Mrs. Vandenberg get over the moment, I invited her to dance. She laughed, waved me away and said, "I can't do that. I have no idea how to dance like that." Chili encouraged her, "Oh go ahead. Hank's a good dancer. Just walk the way your mother told you not to." Mrs. Vandenberg stood up, shifted her weight stiff legged a couple of times then said, "No, I don't think Acapulco is ready to see me do this," and sat down.

The general soon tired, and I escorted them back to the hotel where they invited me to come over for breakfast. When I arrived, the desk clerk asked, "*Señor, es su nombre*, Hank?" "Yes." "*Si señor*, the general checked out early and left you a message." The note read: "Hank—sorry. Give us a rain check. Have one for us. Van & Gladys." Within a few weeks, in April 1954, at age 55, General Vandenberg was dead of cancer.

* * * *

Jim Dolan was an eighteen-year old Californian, well-built with spiked blond hair and a wispy mustache. He had diving gear and I had a car, so we went diving out by Playa Revolcadero near where the Princess Hotel stands today. We were down on the ocean floor in a dreamy world of warm water and weightlessness when I suddenly felt as if someone had jammed an ice pick into my left foot. The pain was so intense that I thought a shark had attacked me. I looked back to see how much of my foot was gone but no wounds were visible. I forgot the spear gun and made it to shore where I flopped on the sand gasping, unable to catch my breath. Other than some red welts in my instep, there seemed to be no reason for the excruciating pain.

I was probing my foot when Jim arrived writhing in agony from fiery welts on his body and legs.

He saw me and wailed, "Don't touch 'em, you'll only make 'em go deeper."

"What are you talking about?"

"Sea urchins, God damn sea urchins stung us."

"OK, but why does it hurt so much?"

"Cause their spines are hollow and they shoot poison through 'em."

"That's all," I said, "come on pal, let's go see a doctor."

"Not me, I'm not going to let anybody cut me up. I'm going to the Indians."

"The Indians? Are you crazy? Come on."

Jim refused and hobbled off toward two huts a hundred yards down the beach. I shouted at him to come back but he waved over his shoulder and continued.

Back at the Mirador, the hotel doctor gave me a local anesthetic and with his trusty scalpel, removed about twenty tiny harpoons from my foot. He wrapped it to the ankle, loaned me a cane and charged $12.00. Three days later, I was in the hotel lobby with my sore foot propped on a table and curing a case of *la cruda* (hangover) with a Bloody Mary.

Jim appeared accompanied by a shapely blonde in an all-but-transparent, fuzzy, white mohair swimsuit. He slapped the bandage and said, "See, I told you."

No man passes an opportunity to enjoy a sight he only dreams of and without prying my eyes from her I said, "OK, so it looks like I made a mistake. What did you do?"

"You know, I went to see the Indians. Look at me. You shoulda come along. They know all about this stuff."

"I'm sure they do, but what'd they do for you?"

"Well, two guys came out, laid me down under a *palapa* (palm-frond-covered shelter) and pissed all over the stickers. Then they ..."

I abandoned the feast to address him, "They did whaat?"

"They pissed all over me."

"Why? Because you're a white guy or because they learned it in medical school?"

"Hell, I don't know, I just covered my face with my hands."

"You did the right thing, that stuff burns like hell when it gets in your eyes."

"How do you know?"

"You don't want to hear it. What happened next? Don't tell me they crapped on the stings."

"No, they packed hot lard on 'em."

"This is getting good. Then what?"

"They lit a couple of candles and let the wax drip on the lard. It burned like hell. Anyway they covered the stickers real good and told me to stay there overnight. Man, I couldn't sleep. Have you ever tried using a lousy diving fin for a pillow?"

"No"

"Well don't."

"Don't change the subject, what then?"

"Well, the next morning they came out and peeled the wax off real slow and the damn stickers came right out. It felt so good that I gave 'em my diving gear. Come on baby, let's go. This ole bastard's not too sick. He's staring holes through you."

* * * *

John Bash finished the details of filming *A Woman's Devotion* and we returned to Mexico City together. He wanted me to meet his friend Carmen Lopez Figueroa. John and Carmen met during a time when her brother, Pancho, owned the Beverly Wilshire Hotel in Beverly Hills and she was having a riotous affair with Errol Flynn. No one can be as irritating as a beautiful Latina when she doesn't have her way and John had his hands full trying to satisfy her whims. Her sister-in-law owned a prestigious art gallery that stayed open late, but Carmen demanded that she close early and be a dinner date for "*Este gran aviador de Los Estados Unidos.*" (This grand aviator from the United States).

We arrived at a sumptuous nightclub fronted by a waterfall and foot-high lights blinking its name, Uno, Dos, Tres. Adjacent to the futuristic pink building was an open-air taco stand. A hissing gas lantern provided illumination and boldly scrawled on a plank beneath it was the taco stand's name, Quatro, Cinco, Seis. Few Mexicans can resist the tempting smell of hot tamales, corn tortillas, and refried beans, and the spotless, white oil-cloth counter was crowded with well-dressed customers. At Carmen's insistence, we got in line with them. Suddenly the crowd parted and reverently ushered an older couple forward. They knew Carmen and after a flurry of *abrazos* (hugs) and air-kisses, she introduced us to Mexico's great composer, Augustin Lara and his wife Petrita. [In a cover story about him, *Time* magazine once described El Maestro's music as better known in the Americas than that of any other songwriter. His songs—all about love, heartbreak, and betrayal—are classics in English and Spanish. Jimmy Dorsey, Glenn Miller, and several vocalists recorded such hits as "You Belong To My Heart," "Amapola," "Granada," and many others.] Later, in the Uno, Dos, Tres, Augustin was introduced to riotous applause while I was acknowledged by decidedly less acclaim and possibly a boo or two. Petrita invited us to come over for brunch the next day.

Their elegant home was in the El Pedregal area where one is more apt to see a tennis court over the garage than a spare bedroom. During the visit, Augustin invited me into his den for a chat and we traded backgrounds. As an infant, he was abandoned on the doorstep of a whorehouse. The women raised him to be the janitor and he eventually learned to play an old piano they had there. He fell in love with one of the girls and wrote a song for her that he titled, "Rosa." The lyrics were so poignant that the first time he sang it to her, Rosa thought that she was being demeaned. Furious, she pulled a knife and slashed his face from his eye to his throat. A livid scar and a soft raspy voice, the result of a partially severed vocal chord, became his life-long trademark.

We commended each other's accomplishments, but the last exchange captured the essence of our meeting. I said, "All I've done is help to kill people who will be grieved for years to come. While you will always be remembered for the love, joy, and happiness you have brought to millions. When we are both standing before Saint Peter, who do you think he will let in first, me or you?" He chuckled softly, gave me a big *abrazo* and in his whispery voice said, "*Tu eres un heroe pero no lo sabes.*" (You are a hero but you don't know it.) "No," I said, "you're the only hero here and I think you know it." Arm in arm, we joined the others.

* * * *

I returned to Wichita bursting with stories to tell Scottie, and she agreed to fly down the next day. The plane landed and I waited for her at our usual meeting place, the building rotunda. She entered and I opened my arms wide to welcome her but she stopped short. Her Samsonite overnighter banged on the marble floor and she demanded, "When are we getting married?" Though I loved Scottie, as I had so many times before, I tried to tap dance, "Scottie honey, you know …" Her eyes reddened and she slapped me, hard. With tears rolling down her cheeks, she cried, "You don't want to marry me. You'd be happy having me come down here on weekends forever. You think you're so brave because you fly those airplanes, but you're a coward. You don't even have enough confidence in yourself to settle down and be the good husband and father you could be. You're a liar and a cheat. I never want to see you again. Good-bye!"

The vault echoed her words as she picked up her bag and ran to reboard the Convair. Despite my repeated efforts to see her, Scottie remained true to her word and eventually married a colonel.

Jet Jockey

In 1952, America was still five years away from its first jetliner when I began flying the B-47 Stratojet. My classmates were civilian test pilots at aircraft plants that, in addition to Boeing, built the 1,800-plane fleet.

A mouthy little sergeant in the personal equipment section indoctrinated me into the program. He was carefully adjusting a gleaming new

1951, McConnell Air Force Base, Kansas. Hank went from selling hot dogs and hamburgers to flying the most advanced bomber in the world, the B-47 Stratojet

white helmet to my head when I jokingly asked, "Is this thing really going to help me if I crash?"

"No, Sir," he said, "these helmets aren't called brain-buckets for nothing. They just help keep things together, if you do crash."

He fitted my flight combat boots then handed me a ballpoint pen, "Sir, print your name and rank in the helmet and inside the tongue of each boot."

"Hey, that's a good idea," I said. "Do you have much of a problem with people stealing these things?"

"No, not really, Sir. We have you do that in case you crash and we only find one end of you. It helps us know who you were."

A five-month ground school on the Lockheed T-33 and the B-47 included courses on High Speed Aerodynamics, High Altitude Weather, Instruments, High Speed Navigation, Aircraft Systems, and Performance Characteristics. Flight training began with 30 hours in the T-33, a tandem-seated version of our first operational jet fighter, the F-80 Shooting Star. The plane weighed about 15,000 pounds, had a top speed of 525 miles per

Boeing's B-47 Stratojet

hour, could be nursed up to 42,000 feet, and came in "over the fence" at 115 miles an hour.

Fully loaded, the B-47 weighed about 220,000 pounds, could attain 50,000 feet, had a top speed of 600 miles per hour and normally touched down at about 125 miles per hour.

Upon graduating, I became the only pilot qualified in every plane on the base—the B-47, T-33, B-25, C-47, and C-45. The school had me slated to be a B-47 flight instructor, but the perception that General Carter and I were buddies gained me an assignment to the T-33 section. I loved the sense of physical freedom and exultation of flying alone.

The majority of the T-33 instructors were a cocky, clannish group of young lieutenants who left a trail of bloody fingernails when they were dragged from the Fighter School at Williams AFB, Arizona, to Wichita. They treasured their fighter jock status and a graying Mexican captain whose claim to fame had to do with flying bombers and selling bras hardly enhanced their self-conceived image. Perhaps the most disdainful of me was John Whitehead, a ninety-nine pound, African-American fighter pilot whose skeletal facial features had earned him the handle "Doctor Death." John called me Pappy once; no one did again.

Our students were older, higher-ranking SAC pilots who resisted the idea of some kid with an attitude teaching them something they thought

Lockheed's F-80 Shooting Star was the single-seated version of the T-33

they knew how to do well. Their most troublesome task was staying ahead of the plane. Gone were the days of lengthy preparations, crew briefings, pre-take-off tests, and checklists required to get a reciprocating engine bomber aloft; no more power checks, magneto checks, propeller checks, carburetor heat tests, and cowl flap settings. Here, we expected them to start the engine and by the time we got to the runway, be ready to blast off.

At cruise altitude, the T-33's true airspeed was better than 400 knots. While that speed is mundane now, to the bomber pilots of those days, it was remarkable. Learning to land the T-bird may have been the most troublesome part of their indoctrination. Bringing a bomber in for a landing is normally done in a minutes-long series of responses to a checklist. In contrast, we required an approach that melded an unbroken sequence of rapid-fire actions into a smooth procedure that began upon arrival over the runway at 1,000 feet. At that point we expected them to: retard the throttle to idle, open the dive brakes, slam the stick left—instantly standing the plane on one wing. Then, while reefing back on the stick to maintain a tight, descending 360-degree turn, it was landing gear down, wing flaps down, gear indicator lights green, check for conflicting traffic, get final clearance to land, roll-out slightly above landing speed, and touchdown on the numbers. Piece of cake. Initially, many complained that the maneuver was hot-dogging, but as they shed their humdrum habits and became more tigerish most, but not all, enjoyed it.

Colonel George Y. Jumper, Commander of the 40th Bomb Wing at Schilling AFB, Kansas, had fallen behind his class. Due to my advanced age and bomber experience, the West Pointer was reassigned to me. We went up for an evaluation flight, and then I gave him some homework to check his study habits. Minutes into our second flight it became obvious that he had not studied. I said, "I've got it. Tighten your safety harness." I then turned off the intercom and did a few aileron rolls, a loop, and a split-S, then landed. I parked, climbed out, and waited for him by the wing. Sweat was pouring down his pate, his wire-rim glasses were fogged-up, and he was red-faced mad. He sputtered, "Why did you turn off the intercom? Why did we come down? Who do you think you are anyway?"

I smiled and said, "Colonel Jumper, you may be the wing commander back home but here you're my student, and when I give you homework I expect you to do it. You're behind your classmates, but with your cooperation I think we can play catch-up. But I promise you one thing: You're either going to be a good jet-instrument pilot or the best acrobatics pilot in the 40th Bomb Wing." He folded his hands on the wing like a bad boy and said, "Sir, I'm going to do anything you say." He made it through and we parted fast friends. After that, colonels and generals were routinely assigned to me.

* * * *

Harvest season was a special time in the Midwest. Farmers overflowed their silos with wheat and for want of storage facilities, hauled the surplus into town, dumped it in the main street, and sold from there. Annually, during this time of the year, the Wichita Chamber of Commerce chartered a passenger train and made a good-will trip through the surrounding wheat-belt. At every whistle-stop, an Oom-Pah-Pah band played while the merchants glad-handed farm families and did whatever possible to entice them to shop in Wichita. Our first year there, Colonel Spicer joined the boondoggle. He saw it as a community-relations event but quickly realized that his Air Force presence was being overshadowed by the gross commercialism.

He called the T-33 Section Commander, Major Gene McGuire, and in turn, Gene called two other instructors and me. Gene said, "Colonel Spicer's train will arrive in Clay Center, Kansas, at twelve sharp. Fly with your students, then meet the train there and put on a little air show. Don't be late and keep the show going until the train leaves. Hank, you lead, you're older and less likely to break any flying regulations."

We arrived over the town at the appointed hour at 500 feet and put on an impromptu air show. Upon landing back at the base, the other instructors disappeared and I went into the major's office to report "mission accomplished." Gene interrupted his telephone conversation, handed me the instrument like a dead mouse, and said, "Here. He wants to talk to you." Colonel Spicer asked, "Where were you, Kiki?"

"Sir," I said, "we were there at twelve sharp as you requested."

"Hell, I saw three airplanes in the area but that's not what I wanted. I want you to cut the smoke on that engine. I want people to know I'm there."

"Yes, Sir." He hung up.

Next stop Blair, Kansas. We tightened our safety harnesses, set the throttles at 100 percent, hit the deck and followed the railroad tracks. No question that we cut the smoke on the engine then twisted and turned at terrain-hugging altitudes until we were low on fuel and returned home.

Our students were former B-36 pilots and as the six of us were hiking back to the operations office one said, "Hank, from that bald-headed colonel down to the very last one of you, you're all crazy."

"Major," I replied, "setting up housekeeping in your aluminum clubhouse for three days complete with a KP roster and a latrine detail isn't flying. This is flying. When's the last time you landed from a three-hour flight feeling mentally and physically exhausted instead of sleepy?"

He shook his head, "Well, I just hope your insurance is paid up."

"Yes, Sir, and I hope you have ended your membership in the Book of the Month Club because you won't have time to read here."

Colonel Spicer quit complaining and I continued to lead the missions.

* * * *

One Sunday morning in early spring, I was asked to put on a show at Kinsley, Kansas, at one o'clock sharp. If it were not that the Arkansas River and a railroad cross there, mapmakers would not have wasted ink to put the hamlet on the map. The town appeared to be asleep except for a park where a number of cars were parked under trees surrounding a doddering old baseball stadium. It was opening day of the baseball season. I went out a few miles, waited for 1300, accelerated, skimmed the outfield fence, and whizzed by the second baseman before he knew I was there. The players took refuge in the dugouts, and I gave them a show. Nowadays, when Kinsley's old timers are sitting around the cracker barrel spittin' and ruminatin' about the old days, I'll bet no one tops that second sacker's baseball story. We responded to many similar invitations. Jets were the newest wonder of flight, we were the modern-day daredevils and barnstormers, and like the originals, were eager to please.

* * * *

Before clearing a student to fly solo, we required that they accomplish a night cross-country flight. The standard plan required that they fly 120 miles south to Oklahoma City, turn left, ninety miles to Tulsa, return to the base, and shoot three touch-and-go landings. Any experienced pilot would consider this a simple test.

Bomber pilots, however, were long accustomed to having a copilot and a navigator as well as other crew members at their disposal. Here, we did not assist them as they controlled an unfamiliar, far more maneuverable plane at a greater speed than they were accustomed to. The feeling is akin to the first time one drives a new car at night—except that every error can have much more dire consequences.

An arrogant major had twice reprimanded young instructors for not saluting him while on the flight line. The courtesy is usually set aside in that environment and we resented his stuffiness. Time came for his night flight and Gene scheduled me to fly with him. We took off. Twelve minutes later, as we neared 24,000 feet, Enid, Oklahoma, was visible off the right wing, and Oklahoma City was dead ahead. Seven minutes later we arrived over the city as planned. Despite the glaring sea of lights beneath and the radio magnetic indicator's wild gyrations, the major continued on a southerly heading.

"How are we doing?" I asked.

"OK," he replied, but there was an edge of doubt in his voice.

"Are we just about there?"

"Yeah, I can see it up ahead."

Rather than accept the obvious, he thought that Norman, a town of about 20,000, was Oklahoma City. I zipped my flying suit up tight, said "I've got it," and rolled the T-33 belly-side-up. He was no lightweight and hanging from those straps is not only uncomfortable but also scary. I held us there until a rat's nest of dust, dirt, and old chewing gum wrappers stopped raining from the floor above then said, "Look up. See that rotating beacon on the left flashing a double green light?"

No reply.

"Well, do you?"

"Yeah."

"That's Tinker Field. And do you see that beacon on the right flashing a single green light?"

"Yessir."

"That's Will Rogers Field and everything in between is Oklahoma City. Now that we solved that problem, let me tell you something. The next time you hard-time one of my lieutenants for not saluting you on the flight line, you and I are gonna take another one of these little rides." I righted the plane and said, "You've got it. Now turn this thing toward Tulsa before you get to Texas and give Ok' City a position report before we get out of radio range."

The Yoga exercise did wonders for his disposition.

* * * *

McConnell AFB, Kansas. Memorial dedicated to the men who died during test or training accidents between 1951 and 1958

One of our B-47s crashed during a training mission and all aboard died. The student-pilot was a major from a small town in Maryland and I was asked to fly his remains home for the funeral scheduled to be held the next day. The casket was loaded into a C-47 and Major Charlie Bell and I took off. Nighttime fell and we were over Ohio in the low-flying transport when word came in that a line of violent thunderstorms had developed between our position and the destination. We landed at Lockbourne AFB, Columbus, Ohio, where the meteorologist advised that we postpone our takeoff until morning. We agreed; Charlie called the grieving family to advise them of the delay and I took charge of the casket. The base was on standby status and deserted except for a reserve fighter squadron. A call to the squadron commander's home quickly established that neither of us knew anything about embalming. We also agreed that my schedule would best be served if we had the major remain over night (RON) in the officers club's walk-in refrigerator.

We placed the flag-draped coffin in a pickup truck and drove through the all-but-abandoned base to the front door of the club. A Friday night party was in progress and some of the revelers thought that we were playing some kind of sick joke on them. Understandable or not, I was in no mood for nonsense and pulled the plug on the jukebox. After a few well-chosen words, everyone quietly went home. We departed early the next morning. Our delay had caused the distraught family to alter their plans and given the unfortunate circumstances, we stayed over for the funeral. On our flight home, Charlie and I got into a rhetorical discussion and he asked, "At what age do we begin to realize that we are not immortal and start being more careful?" We agreed that awareness begins to sink in at about age thirty. I was right on schedule. Unfortunately others were not and during my five years at the base, we lost nineteen pilots due to testing and training accidents.

∞

Chuck Yeager

Nothing is more useless to a pilot than:
The ground-checks he didn't make.
The fuel he didn't take on.
The runway he didn't use.
The altitude he didn't gain.
     Pilot's proverb

Flight attendants have always been one of my many weaknesses and one weekend I made a date with Pat Clinton, a Wichita girl stationed in New York with TWA. I was in base operations preparing for a T-33 flight to a strip at the Brooklyn Navy Yard when the operations officer approached me. Major Arthur Pitts said, "Hank, would you mind dropping a passenger off at the airport in Charleston, West Virginia? I've checked the map and it's not far off your flight path. You won't even have to refuel." The request irked me because in all likelihood, it meant a delay in order to brief some tenderfoot on all the "don't touch this" and "don't touch that's." I said, "Art, you know I'm running late. I'll only take him if he's checked out on the oxygen system and ejection seats. If not, no go."

As he walked away Art said, "Oh, I think he can handle it. We're having a cup of coffee. He'll be ready whenever you are." I got a weather briefing then returned to the operations counter to complete the flight plan. The dispatcher was standing by and I said, "Sergeant, what's the passenger's name? I need to enter it in the plan." Over my shoulder a twangy voice said, "Major Charles Yeager."

I thought, Dammit, that does it. Pitts told the hitchhiker that I don't want to take him and now the smart-ass is being a comedian. Spoiling for a confrontation, I spun around to find Chuck Yeager and Pitts grinning from ear to ear over their "gotcha." Chuck was the hottest test pilot in the Air Force; I guess he knew about ejection seats and oxygen masks. Chuck was on his way home to visit family.

As with most fighter planes, preparing for a trip in a T-33 is decidedly different than for one in say a 747. Fighters do not have luggage compartments, overhead bins or coat-racks. We squashed our civilian clothes into the gun-bays next to the batteries, squeezed our overnight kits into the map cases, and shoes went wherever. Only my rayon tie that flaunted every color in the rainbow received special consideration. I draped it on the rear view mirror.

Chuck isn't exactly talkative but he is amiable and we chatted our way to Charleston. Upon our arrival, I flew the landing pattern exceptionally fast and tight in an effort to impress him, but Chuck never said a word. A mechanic parked us and as we were climbing out Chuck said, "I'll tie the parachute and hard hat down with the seat harness so you won't have to worry about them coming loose in flight, OK?" "Great, thanks Chuck." I waited for him and we went to base operations where we parted.

I filed a new flight plan, returned to the plane where I made a cursory walk-around check, and climbed in. I saw no need to check the back seat, the great Chuck Yeager had just been there. I took the runway and began the takeoff. Halfway down the strip, I sensed that the T-33 was not accelerating properly. Despite my increasingly demanding efforts, the plane refused to fly so I traveled the length of the strip then literally pulled it off the ground, raised the landing gear, and nosed down into a ravine formed by the Elk River that flows nearby. A few telephone poles and church steeples went by before the airspeed increased sufficiently to establish a slow climb back to the runway elevation. A quick glance at the flight instruments indicated that all was normal except for low airspeed. But something had to be wrong so I forced myself to study the entire instrument panel.

Off to the side, hardly visible in the bright sunlight, an illuminated yellow warning light announced that I had taken-off with the speed brakes down. But that was impossible; my switch was "Up." The corresponding switch in the back seat had to be "Down." An override system (which I should have also checked before takeoff) closed the brakes and the airspeed increased immediately. In retrospect, it is obvious that Chuck became concerned by my excessive speed in the landing pattern and actuated the switch. Unfortunately, he failed to return it to the "Up" position after landing.

Chuck has done so many great things in supersonic aircraft that they renamed the Charleston airport after him. But admiration and respect aside, I want the world to know why I damn near crashed into his backyard and what I think of his competence in a rinkydink trainer.

Thelma

Lieutenant Hal Heber, a handsome blond flight instructor, and I were directed to deliver two T-33s to Tinker Field near Oklahoma City. Upon landing, we were advised that due to severe weather in the area, we would not be picked up for return to Wichita until the following day. We checked into the BOQ, changed into Class-A uniforms and caught a ride into Oklahoma City. We were wandering around and happened by *The Oklahoman* newspaper office building. I remembered the columnist, Thelma Anderson, and related the Acapulco incident to Hal. "Let's go see her," he said, "maybe she'll introduce me to the good-looking schoolteacher. Or better yet, maybe she knows where we can get a drink in this dumb dry town."

In the lobby, I asked the receptionist, "May we go in to see one of your columnists, Thelma Anderson?" She scanned us with an interested eye and replied, "We don't have a writer by that name."

"Do you have any one named Thelma Anderson?"

She checked and said, "Yes, take an elevator to the fifth floor. But remember, if you have a problem, come back and see me."

The elevator door opened and we stepped out into a large room occupied by long rows of women furiously typing away. Intimidated by the clatter and their concentration, I hit the button to re-board the elevator but it had gone on. As we watched the floor indicators, the pounding gradually stopped, and we turned to see a hundred pair of eyes staring at us.

A supervisor appeared and she asked, "Can I help you?"

"Yes, ma'am, this is Lieutenant Heber and I'm Captain Cervantes. We just flew into town and thought we'd stop by and say hello to a friend, but we don't want to bother you."

"Oh, that's all right. Who did you want to see?"

"Thelma Anderson."

She pointed toward the back of the room. Thelma was hunched over with her elbows on the table, idly twisting a strand of hair and watching us. I could feel every eye fixed on me as I walked up the long aisle toward her. Suddenly she gasped, wrapped her arms around her head, and lowered it to the keyboard.

I held out my hand and said, "Hi, Thelma. Boy, this paper sure has a lot of columnists. I just stopped by to drop off the sewing kits you ordered from me in Acapulco. You remember, the ones you wanted for all the rich bachelors you know."

She shook her head slowly, and in an agonized voice said, "Go away. Please, go away."

I persisted, "Would you like me to leave some of our special travel kits, the ones with extra needles and thread? I'm sure they'd really like them. Oh, I should tell you, we've also added a larger supply of buttons."

Wearily, her head rocked back and forth.

"Well, OK. But I'll come by the next time I'm in town. Remember, you said that you know a lot of guys and promised to help me make some sales."

As we waited for the elevator the supervisor smiled and said, "When Thelma told us about her trip to Acapulco, she didn't mention that she'd met a handsome pilot. We'd better ask her what you two did that requires her to need a sewing kit."

"That's OK by me, but please also mention that I promised to come back if she doesn't tell the truth."

Flight Testing

During the early years of jet aviation, the life of an engineering test pilot was not for the faint of heart. The B-47 had stretched the limits of aerodynamic design and everyone involved with the weapon system knew that added exposure to danger was a given. However, being at the cutting edge of Air Force aviation is exciting, and the sense of achievement more than made up for the attendant risks.

By late 1954, the hurly-burly expansion years at Wichita (later McConnell) Air Force Base had ended. More than seventy B-47s, forty-five T-33s, various base flight aircraft, plus a heavy flow of transient traffic, clogged the traffic pattern and our maintenance people were constantly busy. To expedite their work, an engineering flight-test section was formed to check aircraft after heavy or critical maintenance and to fly them elsewhere as required.

As a rule, pilots selected into the section came from engineering or aircraft maintenance backgrounds and had a high degree of proficiency in various types of aircraft; be they fighters, bombers, or transports. Skills gained selling hot dogs, cold beer, and foundation garments were not considered qualifying experience. The section-head, Major Charlie Bell, and I were friends, however, and he had me transferred to the group. The job fit perfectly into my overall scheme of life. For I never wanted to acquire things, I wanted to do things.

Women did not exactly consider Charlie the best catch in town. A reclusive bachelor, he had a slight pot, thinning blond hair, bad skin and lived in a trailer home with his mom.

On the day Wichita opened Midcontinent Airport, Charlie and I took a B-47 over and made some low altitude speed runs, then landed to display the bomber. While there, Charlie met a very attractive woman that some of us knew. They began dating and despite veiled warnings, he married her. Marital problems began immediately and Charlie became so stressed that the flight surgeon temporarily grounded him. Days later, Charlie unexplainably collided with a tree. Although he had no major injuries, in view of his other problems, he was returned to instructor duties and I was put in charge of the unit.

Perhaps because we were a small unit not directly connected to the training activity, our flight credentials had not been scrutinized as closely as those of the flight instructors. I asked that this be corrected and we were immediately sent to a refresher course at the physiological training school at Chanute AFB, Illinois. The purpose was to re-train us on the dangers of anoxia. To illustrate how insidiously anoxia can creep up on a pilot, the highlight of the process was a demonstration conducted in a large steel tank that resembled a land-locked submarine with portholes. While the class watched through the windows, volunteers sat inside and performed simple tasks while the oxygen supply was depleted. The subjects gradually, but unknowingly, lost their ability to coordinate and think logically until they lapsed into semi-consciousness and were revived. I always volunteered; I felt it important to know the symptoms first-hand, not have someone tell me about them.

* * * *

Second Lieutenant Smith ("Smitty") Swords III reminded me of a teenager in a Norman Rockwell painting; gangly, tousle-headed, handsome boyish face, innocent brown eyes, and polite to a fault. Smitty came to the unit as a new copilot but was so adept that he gained the distinction of being the youngest, lowest ranking pilot to command a B-47.

One day Smitty and I were at 38,000 feet testing the cabin pressurization on a new B-47. The system had a two-position master switch. In Normal, the pressure held at about 6,000 feet, equal to that of a commercial airliner at altitude. In Combat, the pressure decreased in order to diminish the explosive decompression that would follow if a bullet pierced the cabin. I had just switched the system to Normal when *Boom!* A large hole suddenly appeared ahead of the windshield followed by a heart-stopping roar. Confusion reigned; my ears popped, I felt a sharp chest pain, the temperature plunged, dirt, maps, manuals, and equipment *whooshed* out through the hole, a thick fog formed and the canopy iced over. Wits are not easily gathered at such a moment and it took me a while to conclude that I was alive and that we were in controlled flight. In a voice that sounded squeaky and high-pitched over the intercom I asked, "Smitty, are you OK?"

Smitty's voice was equally distorted, "Well I've got a nosebleed and a heck of an earache. But yeah, I'm OK. What happened?"

"The forward emergency ground escape hatch blew off. Let's go to 100 percent oxygen. Are you sure you're OK?"

McConnell AFB, Kansas. Col. Christopher O. Moffett (L) and ground crew greet the author (center) and Maj. Charles Bell (3rd from right) after final test flight to demonstrate B-47 engines' capability to fly 1,000 hours without overhaul

"Yessir. But when those guys were teaching us about explosive decompression, they should've emphasized the explosion part more. Man!"

"I'll go with that; hold on Smitty, I'm going to make a high-speed letdown." Upon landing, we found the hatch deeply embedded in the leading edge of the vertical fin; it had been improperly installed.

Smitty transferred elsewhere shortly after the incident and I lost track of him. He was a frustrated fighter pilot, so in the last performance appraisal I completed on him, I recommended him for that type of assignment. I later learned that he flew F-4s in Vietnam. When in Hawaii, I never fail to visit Punch Bowl Cemetery where, engraved in one of the white granite columns that honor the Vietnam War's Missing in Action, is the name Colonel Smith Swords III.

* * * *

Early models of the B-47A had automatic forward-extending wing slats to improve its swept wing stalling characteristics. Concern that they might extend asymmetrically (unevenly) led to the system being disarmed in that model and discontinued in later models.

My copilot, Lieutenant Daniel (D.K.) Barton, and I were about to touchdown after flight checking an "A" model's left outboard engine. Suddenly, a loud "bang" sounded, the plane shuddered, and we rolled to the right. During the low-level acrobatics that followed, I managed to scrape both outboard engines on the runway before we settled on the main landing gear and stopped.

D.K. immediately spotted the problem; the left wing slat had extended and the right one not. Subsequent investigation determined that the left slat actuating assembly had not been disarmed as part of the engine installation procedure.

* * * *

I took off in a T-33 that required a flight-check following an engine change. The wheels and flaps were retracting when a row of circuit breakers popped, several warning lights flashed and the nauseous odor of an electrical fire filled the cockpit. Quickly, I released the external fuel tanks and hauled back on the stick to buy time and consider my options. I had two, land straight-ahead or turn back to the runway. The engine was running so I elected to turn back. Blinding smoke forced me to eject the canopy and with that, fire erupted from the electrical panel. The wheels came down but the flaps would not and I touched-down at 160 miles an hour near the takeoff end of the runway going the wrong way. Jackrabbits scampered in every direction as I went bounding across the field and came to a jarring stop on the edge of a drainage ditch.

Later one of the control tower operators said, "I had you with the field glasses. You were holding the stick with one hand, swatting at flames with the other and stomping you're feet like a bronco rider coming out of Chute Number One." My only injuries were a tender shoulder and a hotfoot. Nevertheless, as medics will, they weighed me, measured my height, took my temperature, had me say aah, X-rayed the shoulder, applied Unguentine on my foot, and sent me back to work. Investigation determined that the aircraft starter and generator had been improperly wired which overloaded the electrical system.

Following the incident, I stopped by the personal equipment section for a new pair of flight boots. The airman checked the charred boot with a critical eye and asked, "Sir, did this damage occur on the job?" "It certainly did," I replied. He remained skeptical, "Sir, we've never issued a second pair of combat boots to anyone. Are you sure this happened on the job?" I showed him the half-used tube of Unguentine and said, "Would you like to see my foot?" He fetched a new pair, handed them and a ball point pen to me, and said, "Sir, I'm not going to ask you for a written statement but ...," I interrupted him, "Tell you what pal, I'm going up later today, why don't you come along for the ride. I think you could use a little re-indoctrination on what we're all doing here." "Not me," he said, "they don't pay me enough to do that."

* * * *

"Charlie, this is Hank. There's an old B-47 at Amarillo that they've been using as a training aid for new mechanics. They're through with it and they want it flown to Lowry. Want to go with me?"

"Sure, Hank" he said, "When are you going?"

"Whenever you're ready, pal. There's a B-25 standing by ready to take us over."

"Thanks for nothing. I'll be right there."

It took us a day to get the B-47 off the ground and as we neared, I called Lowry, "Tower, this is Air Force Jet 2713, twenty miles south east, request landing instructions."

"Roger, 2713, altimeter setting 29.87, wind calm, clear to land, call on initial." ("Call on initial" was a standard landing instruction given to fighters. Bombers were given long coal-chute approaches.)

I made a fighter approach and when the tower operator saw a six-engine bomber making a steep turn at low altitude, he became flustered.

"Air Force Jet 2713, I, I'm sorry, Sir, I thought you were a fighter. C-c-clear to break off and re-enter traffic on down-wind."

"That's awright," I replied, "we'll do it your way." We landed and the Transient Alert driver parked us in front of the base operations building; a spot normally reserved for dignitaries. A crowd was on-hand, and I assumed that they were there to welcome some big-shot landing behind us.

We never wore rank insignia on our flight suits and my flight-cap was still in my pocket when I exited the plane. At that moment the wing commander, Brigadier General Charles Caldwell, and his public information officer (PIO) drove up in a staff car. The PIO stuck his head out and shouted, "Hey, where's the pilot?" "Will I do?" I replied. The general jumped out, slammed his door shut, and said, "No, no, Sergeant, we need the pilot. This is the first B-47 to land here, and we want to take pictures."

To avoid embarrassing him I said, "Sir, Major Bell will be down in a minute." In the meantime the PIO recognized me and said, "Say, weren't you the PX officer here at one time? Are you the pilot?" "Yes," I said and put my cap on. The red-faced general apologized and they got their pictures. Life's simple pleasures are the best.

* * * *

The T-33 could be difficult to get out of a spin and the manufacturer, Lockheed, issued a fix to improve its performance in this area. The modification required that foot-long triangular pieces of metal be riveted on the leading edge of the wings. Our first plane was modified and the operations people requested that it be tested prior using it for student training.

It was a routine matter. However, to be sure all the bases were covered, I said to the Maintenance Line Chief, "Sergeant, please do a weight-and-balance check on this bird before I fly it tomorrow."

"Yes, Sir," he replied.

I had spun T-33s before but as a precaution thought it best to review the spin recovery procedure in the pilots' flight handbook. One paragraph in particular got my eye. In bold letters it stated:

Warning: If a definite recovery from a spin has not been established and a pull up initiated prior to the aircraft reaching a ground clearance of 10,000 feet—eject.

The next day the Line Chief greeted my chase pilot D.K. and me, and I said, "Good morning, Sarge, is she ready to go?" "Yes, Sir." We took off in the two planes, leveled off at 21,000 feet and I radioed D.K., "Here we go D.K., three turns and recover. Keep an eye on me." I retarded the throttle, pulled the nose up, held it until the airspeed bled-off to zero, kicked full right rudder, and entered the spin. I counted the turns over the radio, "There's one, there's two. Whoops!" The nose pitched up to near vertical, then down again, and the spin resumed. It did it again, then again. Each time I applied the "book solution" which was:

"Throttle-Idle, Ailerons-Neutral, Control Stick-Full Aft, Rudder-Against the spin until rotation stops then neutral."

Several applications of the procedure were unsuccessful. Meanwhile, my self-confidence was rapidly decaying under a fast unwinding altimeter, a confusing kaleidoscope of blue sky, increasingly definable ground objects, and D.K. shouting, "Eject! Eject!" With all options fading fast, I tried different combinations of control inputs until one, I have no idea which, worked. I pulled out at 5,000 feet with a tight butt and bathed in sweat.

My heart was still pounding when D.K. pulled up along side and said, "Fer-cryin-out-loud Hank, didn't you hear me hollerin' at you to eject?"

"No," I lied.

"Well, why didn't you anyway?"

"Pure dumb pride, D.K. All the way down I kept thinking, what will people think if I eject because I couldn't get a little ole T-33 out of a spin?"

D.K. replied, "Humph! You're always on my ass for gambling. What the hell do you think that is?"

The Line Chief was waiting for us when we landed and I said to him, "Sergeant, let me see the results of the weight-and-balance check you completed on this bird."

He replied, "We didn't do it, Sir. It isn't necessary. It's not like the bombers you're used to where you have to check every plane. In these, the instructions say that you only have to check one fighter per block number."

I said, "Sarge, have the plane towed into the hangar, I want to check it."

"Oh, that's all right, Sir, if you really want it done, I'll get my people right on it."

"Sergeant, do it."

"Yes, Sir."

The problem surfaced when I opened the gun-bay doors. The basic equipment in a T-33 included two loaded machine guns. When they were removed, lead weights were installed in their place for ballast. The weights were missing from the aircraft. The result was that the center of gravity (CG) was moved aft, creating the tail-heavy condition that caused the erratic spin characteristic.

I felt betrayed; the bond of trust and respect that I had always shared with aircraft maintenance men had been shattered. I left the doors open, spun on my heels and wordlessly left the hangar. Angry and disappointed, I wanted to lash out at the crew chief who had certified the aircraft as being air-worthy and at the line chief for "willful disobedience of a lawful order." Instead, I took a different track.

When preparing to fly a T-33, I would ask him, "Is it ready to fly, Sergeant?" "Yes, Sir!" "Thank you." Then while he stood by embarrassed to the point of tears and shuffling from one foot to another, I performed a painstaking preflight inspection. I loved him like a brother, but we all learn our lessons in different ways.

Julie

I was window-shopping at Wichita's only department store when someone slapped my shoulder, and a feminine voice said, "Hey, what are you doing here?" I turned to find two stylishly dressed women smiling at me. Marla Schuster was a friend of a friend, and the other was a gorgeous Latina in a casual outfit more suited for shopping in New York than Wichita. Momentarily stunned by her beauty, I mumbled some inane thing.

Marla said, "Julie, meet a friend of mine, Hank Cervantes, he's a test pilot out at the base. Hank, this is Julie Johnson."

Julie adjusted the sunglasses anchoring her hair and with that lilting kind of laughter women only use when attracting a man said, "Oh, hi, Hank. My husband's a Boeing test pilot, too. He's in Renton, Washington, on a special project."

"Great," I said, "in that case you won't mind if I tag along and play the part of a bored husband." Feigning anger, they each took an arm and marched me into the store. I waited until Julie and I had a moment alone then pulled her close to me, said, "Later," and left.

The phone book listed Julie's address, so around midnight I drove by her darkened house and parked nearby. A lone man in a car late at night is cause for concern in an upscale neighborhood and I could feel wary eyes peering at me from behind shaded windows. Nevertheless, I waited until the last house light was turned off, checked for any midnight strollers, got out and clicked the car door shut.

Shivering with cold and sexual excitement, I hurried across a wide expanse of lawn and as I tiptoed up the back steps, I thought, Now that I'm here, what do I do? As if by magic, the door opened and there stood Julie in a softly wafting diaphanous white negligee.

She eased the door shut, holding an index finger to her lips. As we were tiptoeing toward an atrium she stopped and whispered, "Why are you shaking so?"

I wanted to say, "Because I don't know if you're husband's standing behind the door with a shotgun." Instead, I replied, "Because I'm so excited."

"Calm down, calm down, we have all night."

"I can't, you're all I can think about."

"Oh my."

I reached for her.

"No," she pushed against my chest with both hands and backed away. "Promise not to hurt me or leave any marks."

"I promise, I promise."

"All right, come here."

Julie and I were perfect together. Witty and beautiful, she had a ready laugh, our coloring matched, and her high breasts and smooth hips drove me wild. Everything seemed to be moving toward my asking her to get a divorce and marry me. Only one obstacle remained and it needed to be aired out.

I called her, "Hi, sweetheart can I see you tonight? I need to tell you something."

"What is it? Tell me now."

"No I can't. It's something personal that I haven't told you about me and I want to say it to you face to face."

"Oh, I know. You want to tell me that you like Eileen more than me."

"Huh, what are you talking about?"

"Eileen told me that she saw you at the Starlight last night after you left me and that you got fresh with her."

"I did not. She was alone so I bought her a drink and sat with her for a minute because she's your friend."

"That's not what she said. She said you to put your hand on her leg."

I swallowed hard, "Look, honey, she went to cross her legs and I put my hand out to keep her from bumping my drink. That's all that happened. Boy, I'm in big trouble here."

"Yes, you are."

"Honey, forget all that. I want us to get married."

"Whaat? Are you crazy? You know I can't do that."

"Why not? You know I love you. I want us to be together."

"Oh, Hank, you don't want get married, you're just saying that. You're a playboy, you'll never change. Besides, Paul's coming home soon."

"Good. That'll make it easier for you to get a divorce."

"Don't be silly," she laughed, "you know I'm Catholic. I've got to go."

"Will I still see you?"

"No."

"Why?"

"Because."

"Don't say that, Julie. I love you."

Click.

I can still see Julie breezing down Douglas Avenue in her yellow Caddy convertible. Top down, dazzling smile, over-size sun glasses, black mane flowing, men's heads swiveling, and wives looking in the opposite direction for a plate glass window to see just how long the fools would stand there gawking.

California, Here I Come

Once when I was in his office, General Carter's phone rang and he said to me, "Whenever that instrument rings, I know that someone wants to hand me a problem." Then one day, my phone rang: "Hank, this is Colonel Moffett. Colonel Coddington is here in my office. We want to talk to you. Can you come over?"

"Yes, Sir, I'll be right there," I replied, immediately reminded of General Carter's observation.

Colonel Moffett was my boss and Colonel Coddington had replaced Colonel Spicer as wing commander. I entered, saluted, and Colonel Moffett said, "Hank, You're a good nuts-and-bolts guy and good with people. We want you to take over as aircraft maintenance supervisor. You'll manage 700 civilian and GI mechanics in the Field Maintenance Squadron. The shops are a mess and it's a big job but we think you can handle it."

"Thank you for the compliment, Sir," I said. "But you know that I've applied for the test pilot school at Edwards (AFB) and I think they'll take me."

"Oh, yes, I recall the application," he said. "I gave you a good endorsement but had to add that I need a suitable replacement before I can let you go." No one had bothered to inform me of that and we both knew that it would be difficult to find a pilot with my qualifications in the Training Command. The news scorched my shorts and he saw the defiance in my eyes. "Hank," he said, "I'm sorry that we had to do that. But you'll retain your test pilot status and should the opportunity arise, we'll resubmit the paperwork. Further, the job should help you at promotion time." That convinced me; I accepted the job.

We toured the aircraft maintenance shops then Colonel Coddington asked, "Captain, how long will it take you to clean this place up and make it look like a real outfit?"

1955, McConnell AFB, Kansas. Irrepressible Kathy Nutter

"Sir," I said, "give me forty-five days."

"Good, I'll be back to see you then."

They departed and I rushed back to my new office. Colonel Moffett had not mentioned what I considered the only reward that came with the position—my new secretary. Kathy Nutter was about twenty, outgoing, stacked, and blessed with that innocent kind of wide-eyed beauty big-town girls do not have.

I have never believed that leadership is a function of technical expertise. I knew little about heavy aircraft maintenance and wondered if the troops had accepted me. I learned the answer on the day before the re-inspection. I asked that the GIs clean the outside areas and the senior civilian foreman said to me, "Sir, I want to know why you're discriminating against your civilian employees?"

That hit a tender spot and I replied, "I'm surprised to hear you say that, Fred. What did I do?"

He said, "It's unfair of you not to ask your civilian employees to pull their load. We helped litter the grounds, we should help clean them." I knew I had it made.

The two colonels seemed satisfied with the re-inspection until Colonel Coddington headed toward our last stop, the jet engine repair shop. I held out my hand to stop him and said, "Sir, that shop isn't ready for inspection."

His gimlet eyes narrowed and he said, "Captain, you told me these shops would be ready today."

"Yes, Sir, but that one isn't and I'm not going to show it to you. It will be ready in a month." Thirty days later, a shop that once looked like a shade tree mechanic's greasy garage had been scrubbed, painted, and converted into an assembly-line operation. The facility became the colonel's showplace. Vice President Hubert H. Humphrey sent me a nice "atta boy" letter after his visit there.

* * * *

One afternoon we received word that (now) Major General Spicer was due to make a fuel-stop at the base early that evening and my senior sergeant and I decided to stay over to assure all went well for him. He landed, taxied in much too fast, and rocked to a stop before us. High rank had not changed our former commander's swashbuckling style—his helmet and the F-86 Saberjet fighter had a customized paint job that rivaled that of any stock-car race driver. His ever-present pipe was already in place when he flashed us a trademark smile and shouted, *"Como estas, Kiki? Que pasa? Todavia no the has casado?"*

I laughed, "No I haven't gotten married yet."

He shook his head and addressed the sergeant, "Bill, how's Betty? And little Jeannie, did you take her to get her teeth fixed where I told you? And Timmie, did his arm heal OK?" Amazing, here was a two-star general that had been away for more than two years, yet he knew more about my assistant's personal concerns than I did; I vowed to be a better supervisor. "Russ" Spicer was renowned for his flying skill and fantastic recall of names. I will best remember him, however, as a superb leader, mentor, and friend. Unfortunately, he died at an early age of lung cancer.

* * * *

"Hank, this is Colonel Moffett, one of our men just committed suicide. I want you to run the 'Line of Duty' investigation on the case. Please go see the legal officer for the details."

"Yes, Sir, I replied. "I'll leave in a minute."

The assignment required that I determine if the staff sergeant had died due to his personal misconduct. If so, the government would withhold payment of the free $10,000 GI life insurance policy that covered all enlisted men.

My investigation revealed that the sergeant and his wife had purchased a small table radio "on credit" at a sleazy store. They fell behind in the payments and the merchant wrote to his commanding officer demanding the money. On the morning the sergeant was scheduled to face the captain, his wife found him polishing their revolver. She asked why, and he said that he was preparing to sell it. She dismissed the thought and returned to her chores. Two hours later a state trooper found him parked beside a country road with a bullet in his head.

Upon learning of my role in the matter, one of his sisters called from another state and asked that I come to see them. We met in the airport lounge. They were in mourning clothes, extremely polite, and had my sympathy until they got on the subject of his wife. Almost in unison, they castigated her for having borne a son out of wedlock prior to the marriage and demanded that this disqualify her from receiving the insurance money.

"She and her little bastard son don't deserve a dime of it," the sister said. "It's Mother's!"

My findings stated that when he enlisted, the sergeant received a thorough physical and psychological examination and was judged sane. Accordingly, his suicide resulted from a "service-related injury," and I recommended that his wife be awarded the money. When informed of the decision, one of his sisters called to let me know what she thought of "all you goddamn Mexicans."

* * * *

By late 1956, Wichita had been my home for more than five years and the time had come to find a new assignment. Most of the B-47 pilots who started with me were now in SAC under tough-minded General Curtis E. LeMay and I, along with many others, wanted no part of him.

The Air Force acceptance test pilots at the Tulsa-Douglas plant heard of my dilemma and invited me to join them. It was a flattering offer, somewhat dimmed by the fact that my piloting skills had not prompted the bid. Their operations officer kept a little black book crammed with local girls' telephone numbers, each rated from one to five stars. He readily shared the treasure with favored visiting pilots; all he asked in return was that after a date, the book be updated as appropriate. My entries had been of such a high caliber that they sent a "by name" request for me to Air Training Command Headquarters.

A few days after receiving the offer, a major in the Directorate of Military Personnel at SAC Headquarters called and said, "Captain Cervantes, this is a 'heads-up.' I'm cutting orders transferring you and Major Charles Bell to McDill Air Force Base, Tampa, Florida."

"Sorry, Major," I replied, "I'm waiting for orders reassigning me to the Douglas plant in Tulsa. How did you get my name?"

"Captain, whenever any pilot with B-47 experience is transferred anywhere in the Air Force, I get a copy of the orders. We received an information copy of yours, and you, my friend, are going to McDill. I've already talked to them down there. They remember you well and are looking forward to your arrival."

"I don't want to go to McDill, I'd rather go to California."

"That's odd. I heard that you and Major Bell are good buddies and go everywhere together."

"I like Charlie but not that much. If I have to go to SAC, I want to go to California."

He warmed to the idea. "Do you have a compassionate reason?"

"No, I don't. But California's my home and all my family is there."

"Well, let me see what I can do and I'll get back to you."

Orders came through transferring Charlie to Florida and me to March Field near Riverside, California. Charlie's wife refused to accompany him. A week later the Base Chaplain at McDill called me; Charlie had committed suicide with a .45.

A note he left behind confirmed earlier suspicions that his collision with a tree had been his first attempt to kill himself. I lost a dear friend and the Air Force lost an excellent pilot.

Chapter 6

Strategic Air Command
(1956–1960)

Peace Is Our Profession

In September 1945, the Strategic Air Command (SAC) was created to be the first intercontinental strategic bombing force. The ground rule for development of the command was the recognition that the United States would not always have a monopoly on the atomic bomb, and that other countries would be developing a delivery system as well. Secondly, it had been determined that the heavy bomber would be the delivery system for the next ten years and that the next war would begin by surprise attack, allowing little time for mobilization. Thus, the people in charge concluded that the Air Force must be ready to fight at the beginning of hostilities, and that strategic deterrence was our best line of defense against surprise attack.

In 1948, General LeMay was appointed to head the fledgling organization. As he wrote in his memoirs: "My determination was to put everyone in SAC into this frame of mind: We are at war now!" His first action was to clean house of non-performers and replace them with the best men he could find anywhere in the Air Force. He then upgraded everything in sight and assigned every combat flight crew an enemy target. If a crew was assigned the Kremlin in Moscow, as closely as possible, it flew practice missions that simulated the actual sortie; including high-and-low level navigation problems, aerial refueling and simulated bomb drops. Further, actual cities in the United States that appeared similar to the target on radar were "bombed" day and night, good weather or bad. And if that weren't enough, the crew also practiced with scale models of Moscow as training aids. Perfection in all aspects of mission performance was the goal, and excuses were seldom tolerated.

General LeMay ruthlessly set the tone. Every SAC bomb wing would maintain a third of its bombers and inflight refuelers together with their flight crews constantly "on alert," cocked and ready to go to war on a 15-minute notice. Moreover, all the remaining bombers and refuelers, other than those stripped down for heavy maintenance, had to be repaired as necessary, uploaded, and launched in compliance with an exacting takeoff schedule. To remain ready to accomplish this demanding task, all military personnel and key civilians workers were required to provide their whereabouts to a central point 24 hours a day, including weekends and holidays. Everything and everyone was evaluated. If a man or woman could not deliver, regardless of rank or position, they were quickly shipped out and replaced with someone who could.

SAC became the elite organization in the Air Force if not in the Department of Defense. Headquartered at Offutt Air Force Base, Omaha, Nebraska, it had three major sub-commands—the 2nd, 8th, and 15th Air Forces. The 15th was headquartered at March along with two bomb wings, the 22nd and the 320th. Each wing had three squadrons of B-47s and one squadron of KC-97s, Boeing's air refueler version of its bulbous double-deck transport.

My brother, his wife Lupe and their kids, Irene (Cookie), Susan, Kathy, and Michael, were only sixty miles away in Montebello. I spent a few days getting reacquainted with them and feeling very comfortable with having them nearby, I moved into an apartment near Riverside College and reported to work. I was assigned to the 320th as a B-47 air crew commander and aircraft maintenance supervisor.

Never Ride Shotgun for a Hothead

My first day began with a tour of a gigantic aircraft hangar that housed my offices. A 320th B-47 was in the hangar due to a malfunction of the critical flight control system and my guide introduced me to the repairman, Technical Sergeant Kenneth Chasie. We chatted for a bit, then I left.

Early the next morning, I entered the hangar and Sergeant Chasie waved to me from atop the bomber. He shouted, "Good morning, Sir."

"Morning, Sergeant," I said. "You're here early, aren't you?"

"No, Sir, I've been here all night. I'm the only one in the wing qualified to adjust the flight control system and this one is giving me fits."

"Don't tell me you've been here all night alone. Isn't anyone helping you?"

"No, Sir. Do you think someone could bring me a cup of coffee?"

Surprised, I said, "Sergeant, come down from there."

Reluctant to comply, he said, "Sir, this plane is scheduled to fly at noon, and if I don't finish the job, the mission will be canceled."

"Sergeant," I said, "I'm sure you're a good mechanic. But I'd be afraid to fly this plane in a heavily loaded condition knowing the flight controls had been adjusted by a man who worked on them all night, alone. You go home, I'll deal with the mission cancellation."

"Thank you, Sir. But you're going to get in trouble."

"Thank you for your concern, we'll see."

The mission canceled "Due to Maintenance," and within a minute the Chief of Maintenance, Major Bill (William R.) Hayes, called. "Captain Cervantes, meet me at the wing commander's office on the double."

"Yes, Sir, I'll be right there."

Without any form of preamble, Colonel (Robert B.) Miller read me the riot act. "Who are you? Where'd you come from? Who do you think you are? This isn't the Training Command. This is the Strategic Air Command! You don't have any say here. This is my wing. I run it. I make all decisions here. "You're dismissed! Get out of here before I lose my temper."

We retreated to the hallway where we were met by a tall, handsome, slightly balding lieutenant colonel. His blue eyes crinkled and he said, "Hi, William, is this our new flight scheduler?"

Bill laughed. "Well yes and no, Colonel Crumm. Hank just had a 'Come to Jesus' meeting with Colonel Miller for canceling the mission. Hank, meet Bill (William J.) Crumm, our director of operations."

Colonel Crumm pumped my hand and said, "Welcome to SAC, Hank."

"Colonel," I replied, "if it weren't for the honor of the occasion, I'd rather be somewhere else right now."

He laughed, "Don't let it bother you. He'll get over it."

I returned to the hangar but remained in the car. No one had ever spoken to me that way before and I wanted to regain my composure before facing the office staff. I did not regret having canceled the mission. This was not Wichita, however, where everyone accepted my decisions just because "Hank said so." These people were serious. This was their ballpark, their game, their rules, and I had to adapt to them, not them to me. Nevertheless, I could not picture myself standing before a crash investigation board and forced to say, "Yes, Sir, in retrospect, I know better and should have, but ...."

The story made the rounds, however, I refused to let it die. Once my feet were on the ground, I gathered the shop supervisors, reviewed the incident, and asked, "What can we do to fix the problem?"

Sergeant Chasie spoke up, "We need to dust off the on-the-job training programs that we've never put into action. Everyone should be held responsible for training with at least one man under him into the next higher skill level." Whip-smart and energetic, Chasie led the project. I am proud to have played a small part in Kenneth Chasie's career. He went on to become (at the time) the youngest chief master sergeant in the United States Air Force.

Within days, 15th Air Force Headquarters converted my air crew commander's job to a paper assignment and attached me to headquarters for flying duty. They needed T-33 pilots to fly colonels and generals around the countryside.

* * * *

Bill Hayes had prematurely graying blond hair, a twinkle in his blue eyes, and an uncommon knack for being able to find a smooth handle to problems he faced. Stocky and easy-going, my nickname for him was "Chubb," the result of his need for a leg-up in order to climb on the wing of the T-33. Bill's assistant, Major Mark McClain was his exact opposite. The lean, muscular six-footer wore a burr haircut and his face looked like he had lost a round or two in the ring. Along with his aggressive appearance, Mark had a serious deficiency in impulse control. One day, we were in his office when word came of an emergency on the flight line. Sirens were wailing everywhere as we ran to his jeep and took-off.

Access to the flight line was restricted and controlled at checkpoints where badges were checked by Air Police (APs) to insure that the face on the badge matched the bearer. Upon arrival at our customary checkpoint, a friendly-faced AP un-slung his carbine, drew it up to "port-arms," and casually stepped in front of the jeep to check our badges. I flipped mine up, but instead of exhibiting his, Mark threw him an impatient mini-salute and allowed the jeep to inch forward. The sentry knew us well but he upped the weapon a notch and ordered, "Halt! Show me your badge."

Mark's was still attached to his blouse back at the office but he pretended to search for it then said, "Hey, you know me, airman. I have to go. We've got an emergency."

The guard said, "Yes, Sir, I do. But you cannot enter the flight line without a security badge."

Mark's cork popped. He shouted, "Goddamn it! Get the hell out of my way. I don't have time for your nonsense." The sentry stomped his boots like a diminutive Japanese Sumo wrestler and stood his ground. Mark's eyes dilated, tendons stood in his neck, and his face turned purple. He jumped out and slugged the guard on the jaw. The rifle clattered on the sidewalk and the man went to his knees. Appalled, I began to clamber out but Mark was already grinding gears. He bellowed, "Damn dumb APs, they've got crap for brains!"

We had not gone 200 yards when a dozen jeeps, pickups, trucks, and an armored vehicle I had never seen before, came racing at us from all directions. Carbines were aimed at us and a hard-boiled sergeant ordered, "Get out. Now! Spread-eagle. Now!" Down we went. Aircraft mechanics came from near and far to stand out of our line of sight and watch our chins carve dents in the sizzling macadam. Twenty minutes later, Bill sauntered over at half-throttle to identify us and provide the missing badge. Mark shipped out, and I was advised, "Never ride shotgun for a hothead."

Going Hollywood

"Hank, this is Captain Wicks at 15th flight operations. General (Archie J.) Old has a friend that he wants us to take up for a T-33 ride. Can you get away for a couple of hours to do it?"

"Sure, Dave," I told him.

He continued, "His name is Joe Kirkwood, Jr. He's a pro-golfer and just finished touring the new golf course with the general. Oh, yeah. He was also in the movies. You may remember him, they tell me that he used to play the fighter Joe Palooka."

We met at base operations. Joe had the build of a heavy-weight boxer but his handsome, blond, blue-eyed, features did not appear to have suffered from anything more than a makeup artist's powder-puff. He seemed at ease in the aviation setting. I asked why. He pointed at a shiny twin-engine Cessna huddled between two olive-drab monsters and said, "That's mine."

He enjoyed the flight and invited me to visit him at his home in Studio City. On the weekend that I dropped by, he had just taken delivery of a new Caddy convertible and said, "I know a guy who lives up in Laurel Canyon. Let's go show him my new car." The housekeeper, Mary, led us to the swimming pool where sat John Bash and his daughter, Jeffri (or Jeffi as we called her), from a long-forgotten marriage. As we were leaving, John invited us to come over any Sunday afternoon for drinks around the pool.

1956, Beverly Hills, California. (L–R) John Bash, Mr. and Mrs. Russell Arms, Gloria Bash. Russell was a vocalist on radio's long running "Lucky Strike Hit Parade." After John died in 1992, Gloria married former Los Angeles Mayor Sam Yorty

As I was preparing to leave Joe's house for Riverside, he handed me a paper sack full of golf balls and said, "Here, Hank, give these to General Old as a token of my appreciation for the jet ride."

Early the next morning I went to the general's office, placed the gift on his secretary's desk, and said, "These golf balls are for the general. They're from Mr. Kirkwood in appreciation for the jet ride." I turned to leave but she said, "Oh, no, don't leave, go right in and give them to him yourself."

Reluctantly, I picked up the package and tiptoed down a short hallway to the vestibule of a large paneled office. Impeccably groomed and with ribbons up to here, the gray-haired officer was about to pour himself a cup of coffee. Just then, one of several telephones rang. He picked it up and listened as he continued to pour. I had never been in the presence of a three-star general before and could not decide whether to enter the room or retreat. The caller made the decision for me. Whatever his message, General Old reacted violently, "Goddamn it!" He slung the silver carafe across the room where it ricocheted off an elaborate SAC insignia, fell, and shattered a glass credenza. I spun around and as I rushed by the startled secretary, dropped the sack on her desk and continued out the door. I could hear balls clacking on the floor as I hurried away.

* * * *

John Bash and I became close friends. The tall, ruddy-faced extrovert had produced movies at the old Republic Pictures studio when Herbert Yates owned it. John knew tons of stars and his kitchen walls were lined with black-and-white stills of him with Phil Harris, Bing Crosby, Ava Gardner, Forrest Tucker, Vera Hruba Ralston, and so on. On Sunday afternoons, the house overflowed with movie people all spouting industry jargon. Out of my element, I usually wandered from one group to another like a lost puppy wanting a handout. One day, John asked Jeffi to fix drinks for several of us. She took our orders then went to the poolside bar to make them. Embarrassed to have a child prepare me a drink, I got up to help her but John objected. That was the first action that would eventually drive us apart.

One of my favorite women I met there, perhaps because she was also a neophyte in the movie business, was a vivacious twenty year-old brunette named Majel Barrett. Majel and I became friends and kept in touch for several years until she married Gene Rodenberry, another former B-17 pilot. She and Gene went on to produce the long-running TV series "Star Trek."

Diving was my shtick at those affairs. On one occasion, I went to the pool intent on putting on a show. A Hispanic-looking girl was sunbathing on the diving board and I stopped to admire her. She had the profile of a Greek goddess, a curvaceous body, and long black hair that cascaded practically to the water. I approached her and said, "*Yo me llamo Hank Cervantes. Como te llamas tu?*" (My name is .... What is your name?)

Her reply was heavily coated with British pronunciation. "I don't understand you," she replied, "I'm Hungarian. My name is Lita Milan, won't you join me?"

Lita had just finished co-starring with Paul Newman in *The Left Handed Gun*. The first-run movie was her big break and she was hoping that the role would catapult her career to a new level. As our day continued into evening, her accent faded, and it was but a memory by the time we said goodnight. Lita exhibited an unusual interest in the details of military life. I interpreted her curiosity as an indication that she wanted an enduring relationship. Wrong! The dictator of the Dominican Republic, Rafael Trujillo, had sent his son, Rafael (Rafi), to attend the Army Staff College at

Fort Leavenworth, Kansas. But rather than study, the international playboy spent his time in Hollywood making headlines by getting into fights and romancing the likes of Kim Novak, Zsa Zsa Gabor, and others. The school course ended, and Rafi's yacht sailed into Long Beach harbor to return him home in style. On the eve of his departure, a newspaper photographer snapped Lita boarding the yacht laden with luggage. Rafi died in a revolution and Lita disappeared, but it must have been great while it lasted.

* * * *

A handsome young actor named Krekor Ohanian changed his name to Mike Connors, and the studio threw him a "coming out" party. The event was held in a million-dollar house on stilts on Tiger Tail Road above Sunset Boulevard, and the building was rocking when Joe, John, and I arrived. Women descended on John and Joe, and I was out on the deck admiring the view when Joe came looking for me. I asked him, "Hey, pal, what does it take for me to get a little attention here?"

Joe said, "Tell them you're an actor, that your name is Steve Flick, and that, due to your background, you've been cast in a new film about flying. Trust me, they'll believe you." The "action" improved immediately; a couple of girls even complimented me on how well my career was going.

About this time, Joe became interested in building a golf course in Palm Springs and he got a house near the tract. It became my second home and that of a former All-America halfback at University of Maryland, Ron Waller. While a collegian, Ron was in Miami for a game when he met a tall attractive student named Margie. They eventually married and moved to Los Angeles when the Rams football team drafted him.

One Sunday morning, Joe, Ron, Margie, and I were in the living room talking football with the President of the University of Notre Dame, Reverend Ted (Theodore M.) Hesburgh, and Sid Gilman, the Rams' coach. Ron said, "Someone ought to buy the Baltimore Colts franchise and move it to Miami." (This was in the pre-Johnny Unitas days.)

I snorted at the suggestion. "Ron," I said, "Miami's so hot and humid that those old retired people aren't going to pay good money to broil while they watch a football game." Everyone nodded in agreement except Margie who was sitting in a corner knitting booties. She glanced up and in a low voice said, "How much do you think it would cost, Ron?"

"Oh, about a million, I guess," Ron said.

Margie replied, "Well, if you think it's a good idea, let's do it."

I whispered to Joe, "Yeah sure, football players don't make that kind of money."

Joe stood up and motioned me into the dining room. "Hank," he said, "you may not know it but Margie's grandmother is Marjorie Merriweather Post, the heiress to the Post Toasties fortune. I'd be careful what you say to Ron in front of her." I was thankful for the warning because whenever Margie was away, Ron and I played the field. Our favorite hangout was The Ranch Club, a normally serene and indifferent riding stable on the edge of town. There, on Sunday afternoons, a young standup comedian hosted an informal "amateur hour." He drew all levels of talent, from Hollywood stars in town for the weekend to gifted unknowns struggling to be heard. Harry Morgan went on to star in the TV series "M.A.S.H.," but I appreciated him more back in those days. His introductions enabled Ron and me to cavort with shop girls, who lived in one-room apartments, to movie queens in mansions where one could swim into the living room. Unfortunately, Ron never followed up on Margie's suggestion; she divorced him, the Rams cut him, and Joe Robbe put the Dolphins in Miami.

* * * *

Charlie Farrell's private Racquet Club was the center of Hollywood high life in Palm Springs. One Sunday morning, I drove by to admire its fabled green and white entrance then, on a whim, turned down the next side street. The grounds had a back entrance and I stopped at the gate to view the cottages and swimming pool where the stars came to play. I was reveling in the feeling of being so close to fame when the guard opened the gate and waved me in. I entered and made my way to the Bamboo Lounge. The bartender was preparing to open for business. Nevertheless, I expected him to challenge my right to be there and invite me to leave. Instead, he served me in an offhanded manner. I had frequented bars long enough, however, to know that a twenty-dollar bill will improve the attitude of most bartenders, so Tex and I had a nice chat. On my way out, I also tipped the gate guard and thanked him in Spanish. From that day on, and even after they dismantled the gate, Arnulfo never failed to welcome me to the most exclusive club in town.

The club's publicity director, Marge Pohl, and I became friends and one day, out of curiosity, I asked if the March Field Officer Wives Club could hold a luncheon there. Marge arranged the event and my stock soared with the ladies on the base. Now colonels who were once aloof (read Colonel Miller) had to endure being dragged over by the Mrs. to kiss-up to the nice captain who arranged for her "to rub elbows with movie stars and watch Dinah Shore play tennis."

* * * *

The date remains imprinted in my mind—November 30, 1957. It was a Sunday afternoon, few people were in the club, and Tex was entertaining me with white-haired knock-knock jokes. Laughing uproariously at them was a small price to pay for unending refills of his incomparable Ramos Fizzes. Suddenly he got serious, rolled his eyes toward the entrance and whispered, "Look at that." There stood a radiant Venus in a plum-colored dress, coal-black hair, and big dark violet eyes. Elizabeth Taylor waved at Tex and together with husband Mike Todd and her two little boys, sat at a table immediately behind me. The kids were dressed in cowboy outfits, and I asked four-year-old Michael, "Are you Hopalong Cassidy?"

"Oh no," his mother replied, "he's Wyatt Earp."

I lowered my voice and growled, "Well I'm the Cimarron Kid." Michael clutched his holstered guns; wrinkled his brow with thought then looked at his mother questioningly. She asked him, "Is he a good guy or a bad guy?"

He hunched his shoulders and I said, "I'm a good guy. Loan me one of your guns and I'll show you a trick." He handed me one. I twirled the trigger guard on my forefinger, flung it high, and caught it one-handed. I was as surprised as the boys were impressed, because it was my first attempt ever at it. They insisted that I repeat it but rather than press my luck, I played with them for the privilege of occasional glances at her.

After a while Mike Todd invited me over and said, "We were noticing how good you are with kids. You must have children of your own?"

"No, Mike," I replied, "I'm not married."

"Well you should be."

"I don't know about that, Mike. I'm a pilot in the Air Force and travel a lot."

He laughed, "That explains it." Then casting a mischievous glance at her he said, "If I were a pilot I wouldn't be married either."

Elizabeth grabbed a handful of his curly hair, shook hard and said, "And if you were a pilot I wouldn't have married you. See what you would have missed?" They kissed lovingly and we continued to chat. Four months later, Mike Todd's plane, *The Lucky Liz*, crashed, killing him and the others aboard.

* * * *

A week prior to Memorial Day, Marge Pohl called me at the office, "Hi Hank, next Saturday night is our annual Bailing Out party. It's the final event of the season before we close for the summer. Since it's a holiday, I thought you might be able to get away from those airplanes and come as my guest. We clean out the refrigerators, put on an unbelievable buffet, and have a great show and dancing. Please come."

"Gosh, Marge. I'd love to go. Thank you for the invitation."

"Don't think anything of it," she said. "Just remember, everything's on me, and it's a bailing out party." We hung up and I began to wonder what to wear and why she had invited me. I should have called back and asked. But being a man, I assumed it was to be an informal affair with a theme that related the club's closing to bailing out of a plane. It made sense to me. Hey, I thought, I'll knock 'em dead.

I timed my arrival to be fashionably late. The parking attendant took one look at me, coughed up his sleeve, and turned away. I thought, You don't bother me, pal, I'm Marge Pohl's guest. Proud to finally be entering the club through the front door, I nonchalantly stepped inside and nearly had a heart attack. A chic crowd of the rich and famous all in sequins and white dinner jackets was having cocktails. Meanwhile I was dressed in a green flying suit, a baseball cap, combat boots and a parachute slung over my shoulder. I felt like Bozo the clown; all I needed was a red ball on my nose and a flower that squirts water on my lapel. I backed out and was anxiously waiting for my car when Marge appeared. Red-faced I said, "Please forgive me Marge, I completely misunderstood the theme of the party. I'll be out of your hair in a minute."

She took my hand and said, "Don't go Hank. Please don't disappoint me. Come on, you'll be fine." Her pleading eyes were beyond resistance so I gave in and joined her. I suspected that when Marge extended the invitation, she pictured herself being escorted by a be-ribboned pilot in a formal uniform. To her credit, she made the best she could out of a disappointing situation. She led me to a prime ringside table where I hid the parachute beneath it.

We had a lavish dinner, after which Marge ran off to arrange the entertainment. This gave me a welcomed opportunity to stargaze. My head was swinging back and forth like a lawn sprinkler when the glamorous Gabor sisters, Magda, Zaza, and Eva, and their mother, Jolie, flounced by. They were preening and looking for a place to sit but the room was packed—except for our large table, and I was alone. I motioned them to join me.

Doubtful, they eyed me, held a whispered conversation then accepted. Intimidated by their beauty and flair, I stammered through our introductions and the small talk that followed. Famed comedian Jack Benny opened the show and as if on cue, their decorum flew out the window. They conversed, complained about the service, and stepped on Jack's lines at will. Jack's efforts to quiet them only added fuel to the fire and some of the old-money elite behind us began hissing at them to "Stop it!"

Mortified to be at the center of unwelcome attention, I was deciding on a graceful way to extricate myself from the situation when a balled-up napkin landed on my lap. The last thing I needed was visible contempt. I yanked the parachute out from under the table, popped it open and as the four women gazed in openmouthed bewilderment, enveloped them with the canopy. Jack went into his trademark pause. Sputtering and writhing like four cats in a sack, they jumped up frantically grasping handfuls of nylon desperately trying to find a fringe to the billowing tent. They were still cursing and untangling the risers from each other's coiffures when I bowed to the cheering crowd and sprinted to the door. The Air Force charged me $200.00 for the parachute, and Marge received a ton of compliments from guests who thought the stunt had been staged.

Sad to say, but Marge contracted polio as a little girl and was still a beautiful young woman when she died from complications brought on by the disease.

* * * *

Back in Los Angeles, a long palm-lined drive led to Alla Nazimova's Garden of Allah. Once the center of Hollywood life, the famed Moorish inn stood at the intersection of Crescent Heights and Sunset Boulevard. Embedded in the wall behind the front desk of the tiny lobby was an incongruous, bank-size safe, the type with gold script on the door. In addition to whatever else was kept there, the vault held several volumes of the hotel's earliest guest registration ledgers. A room over the lobby was my home away from home, and I was very friendly with one desk clerk. Occasionally she would dust off a ledger and bring it upstairs where we would lie in bed and scan it. Everything was documented in neat hand-written script including what Robert Benchley, Gilbert Roland, John Barrymore, and a dozen others were charged for liquor, torn bed sheets, broken mirrors, and destroyed furniture fished out of the pool. One entry remains etched in my mind: Robert Benchley once ordered a hundred dollars worth of booze delivered to his cabana. In 1938, that was a load.

The hotel remained a popular watering hole long after its glitter had faded. One Sunday afternoon, I was with Marilyn Morrison, whose dad owned the nearby Mocambo, and Anita Loos, a screenwriter who authored the hilarious novel *Gentlemen Prefer Blondes*. We wanted to drum up a party but couldn't think of an innocuous date for Marilyn who was having problems with her husband, singer Johnny Ray. I suggested Ralph Meeker, the handsome, six-foot, 200-pound hunk I met in Acapulco. Ralph usually played lead and character parts, typically cocky, and often with a mean or yellow streak. In real life, however, he was mild and easygoing. They liked the idea, so I called Ralph and we met in the foyer. We were entering the lounge when he suddenly rushed across the room, pulled a fellow off a barstool, and punched him. The fellow fell back into Jack Costanzo's felt-draped drum set. After untangling himself from the congas, bongos, and timbales and checking his jaw, he wheezed, "That's not much, you don't impress me."

Furious, Ralph shook off his jacket and challenged him to stand up for more. But the guy was no hero; he stayed down. As several of us struggled to get the incensed Ralph out of the room I asked him, "Hey, pal, what set you off?" He caught his breath and said, "I've been looking for that bastard a long time. He cut my best scenes when he edited *A Woman's Devotion*. I hope Ralph decked the right guy because someone certainly deserved it. The movie is among the most forgettable I have ever watched.

Marilyn and Anita skipped out when the fracas started, so Ralph and I spent the evening at Musso & Frank's drinking classic martinis with Barbara Nichols and a friend of hers. Barbara was a zany blond movie star who made a career out of playing broads and floozies. True to her persona, she drank me under the table.

* * * *

Jesse White had a long background in vaudeville before he made it in Hollywood. Later, he became the Maytag repairman on TV. But during this time, he along with other unemployed actors, practically lived across the street at the soda counter in Schawb's Drug Store. Jesse had a voice that rivaled a foghorn in zero-zero weather, loved showing me off, and would periodically blast his friends with the tired news that his pal was a jet pilot. Playing the modest hero got old in a hurry, so I switched to frequenting the back of the store where wheedling juicy gossip items out of Hollywood columnist Sidney Sokolsky was much more fun and enlightening.

* * * *

1967, Los Angeles Air Force Base, California. Greeting veteran actor and retired USAF Col. Gene Raymond

Gene Raymond had been a handsome leading man but is best remembered as the husband of Jeanette McDonald, a singing star at MGM in the late 30's. Gene held the rank of colonel in the reserves and along with other stars, maintained his flight credentials at March Field. We were friends and it became a late Saturday night ritual for us to meet at a Denny's on Palm Canyon Drive in Palm Springs. Whenever I arrived, rather than search the parking lot for his Studebaker Hawk, I simply looked through the plate glass window. Mrs. Raymond customarily wore large picture hats swathed with veils and in that setting stood out like a dowager queen at a barbecue.

Gene had not flown with us for a while and Dave Wicks asked me to check-ride him before releasing him to fly solo in a T-33. During the flight, I tested his knowledge of the "critical" emergency procedures; those steps that must be performed immediately and instinctively without reference to written checklists. I noted several deficiencies, so we practiced them for a while, then landed. As we were walking back to Operations, I said, "Colonel, you need to do some homework."

He replied, "Yeah, I know Hank, but you're going to release me aren't you?"

Our friendship had never been tested before but I said, "No I'm not. You really need to know the emergency procedures better than you do." He became closed-mouth, and later a sergeant called to advise me that hereafter, the colonel would fly with another instructor.

Saturday night came and I joined the Raymond's at Denny's. He seemed surprised to see me and ignored my attempts at lighthearted conversation with him. Mrs. Raymond noticed his attitude and asked, "What's the matter with you?" Before he could reply, I said, "Mrs. Raymond, Gene and I had a difference of opinion on something and he's upset with me."

She reached over, smoothed his hair back and replied, "Yes, I know, he told me about it." Then she said to him, "Don't be angry, dear. I know you won't listen to me but Henry is your instructor and you really do need to mind him." He grumbled under his breath and continued to stir at his coffee.

I said, "Gene, the pilot of the B-47 that went down the other day was my student back in Wichita. He was the weakest pupil I ever passed, and I should have never signed him off. I can't change that now. But I'll never make that mistake again, regardless of what you or anyone else thinks of me." I got up to leave but she took my hand, coaxed me down again and said, "Henry, thank you so much for being concerned about him. I pray every time he puts on that uniform and goes out to the base. He's getting too old for that."

She continued to hold my hand, smiled and said, "Let's change the subject. When are you going to bring a lady friend and visit us in Los Angeles? We'd love to have you. If you don't have a friend, there are a dozen young ladies at our church who are dying to meet you."

I said, "Thank you Mrs. Raymond, I promise you I'll do it soon." Although our friendship continued, I never did. They were so close and devoted to each other that it seemed an imposition to barge in on them.

* * * *

The day I completed two years at March Field, a major in the military personnel office called, "Captain Cervantes, you have less overseas time than any other company grade officer in the command. You're highly regarded here but we cannot defer sending you overseas any longer. You have three options: a one-year 'hardship' tour in Korea, or Greenland, or a regular three-year tour in Europe. Regardless of which you pick, we guarantee that you'll return to March when it's completed. What do you say, want some time to think about it?"

"No," I replied, "I'll take Greenland. That way I can come home on leave to visit my family and stop by here to assure I get a good job when I return."

"It all counts toward twenty," he said. "I'll get your orders ready."

Help Keep Greenland Green

Beside a brain-rattling gravel road that leads from Thule Air Base to the 1,500-mile long, two-mile thick ice cap, the U.S. Corps of Engineers erected a sign:

Use Your Ash Tray. Help Keep Greenland Green.

The screwball request is the only official attempt at humor I saw at the northern-most air base in the world.

Situated more than 700 miles north of the Arctic Circle, the inhospitable outpost clings to the barren edge of the west coast of Greenland. You've heard of the middle of nowhere? It's a 1,000 miles north of that.

No one who has ever been to the land of the midnight sun forgets the weather or the seasons. The early days of spring are the most normal. Gradually, they lengthen into a three-month summer during which the sun circles overhead with a dazzling brilliancy that hurts the eyes. Day by day, it inches down until the dimming light ushers in three months of unrelenting darkness. It is at this time that Thule is subjected to violent storms of mythical proportions.

1957, Thule Air Base, Greenland. Headquarters of the northernmost air base in the world

The airfield once served as a refueling stop for planes flying between the States and Denmark. However, jets and the Soviet missile threat changed that and the Danes allowed us to build a huge Distant Early Warning Line radar installation there. A squadron of F-102 supersonic delta-wing fighters and several batteries of Nike ground-to-air missiles served as deterrents to an air raid. If barracks defense experts are to be believed, our only protection from ground attack was the backscatter from the super powerful electronic signals emitted by the antennas. They would sterilize a man in a second.

From a distance the base looked like an Air Stream house-trailer club that took a wrong turn and got lost. Perched on wood stilts to keep them from sinking into the encroaching permafrost, the unpainted aluminum buildings had refrigerator-like double walls and doors to keep the cold air out, not in.

Despite the proximity of the world's largest glacier, water was a priceless commodity and conservation was strictly enforced. Three installed water tanks provided each building an independent water supply system. Weekly, a tanker truck replenished one tank with potable water. We used it sparingly to drink and bathe, and the residue drained into another tank. From there we hand-pumped it to flush the toilets and the waste went to a third tank from where a (different) truck siphoned it for disposal. We lived in spartan rooms that were about the size of an average walk-in closet. Each was equipped with a small double-paned window, a bunk, a clothes bar, and an unpainted table and chair. A tiny latrine at the end seemed to have been designed to enable a man to shower, shave, and urinate all at the same time. Prisoners lived better than we did.

Some 2,000 men and eleven nurses staffed the base. We seldom saw the women. On the rare occasions when one came into the officers club, all activity stopped and from the padre to the dishwasher, we mentally undressed her. They never lingered.

During summer, several scientific projects operated from the base. For example, the Army Corps of Engineers brought in large boring machines to dig long horizontal tunnels into the towering mass of ice. The caverns were wide enough to drive a trailer truck through and were rigged with strain gauges to measure their movement. Each was crammed with acres of crates, cartons, and pallets crammed with home and office equipment foodstuff, and all manner of military equipment. The government was testing the feasibility of using the caverns as last-resort relocation facilities in case of nuclear war.

Centuries of layer upon layer of snowfall packed into ice provided a unique test tube of ancient climactic and geological data, and scientists criss-crossed the cap testing them. The men lived in Army BARC-5s; monstrous, diesel-powered amphibious vehicles that they often hitched together to form snow-trains.

Primarily, the men extracted mile-long ice cores that provided them ancient climactic and geological data that read like pages of a book. Occasionally, cores were brought to the base for further study and when discarded, the officers club bartenders amused us by chilling our drinks with the bits and pieces. Having been formed under crushing pressure, the melting ice snapped, crackled, and popped with amazing energy. (Some people watch grass grow for amusement, we watched ice melt.) More recently, scientists have been able to discern live 250 million-year-old microorganisms in similar ice cores. This causes me to wonder if all the germs I drank in Thule might not resurrect one dark night and turn me into some kind of Jurassic-like creature.

1957, Thule Air Base, Greenland. A huge U.S. Army BARC-5 on parade. Note the soldier standing at the rear

Greenland is a place where no one truly belongs and errors, no matter how slight, extract a price. Once when a snow-train was about 200 miles out on the cap, the commander radioed a request for an emergency airdrop of diesel oil. While the steel drums were being loaded into a ski-equipped, four-engine C-54 transport, the pilot invited six friends to go along for the ride.

Barometric pressure readings needed for a basic altimeter to operate accurately were not available in the drop area. Accordingly, upon his arrival, the pilot, a Captain Johnson planned to use the installed radio-altimeter for altitude indications. He took-off, checked the accuracy of the radio-altimeter while over the field, and went on his way.

The C-54 arrived over the snow train in the flat light of a whiteout. No sky, horizon, or landmarks, only a soft, cotton-like sea of white in which all sense of scale, perspective, and distance is lost. Johnson slowed, letdown to what he considered a safe altitude, and prepared to make the first drop. The train commander chastised him over the radio, "Get down damn it! We have to dig those barrels out of the ice. Get down!" Johnson aborted the run and relying on the radio-altimeter, letdown to 75 feet "Above Ground Level" (AGL). He began the second run and the "kickers" in the back were about to drop the first drum when *zip, zip, zip, zip!* All four propellers sheared from the engines and the C-54 slid to a stop before the astonished scientists. No need for picks and shovels; the oil had been delivered to their doorstep along with five crewmen and six inadequately dressed looky-loos, including two nurses. Everyone adjourned to the snow train, and Johnson reported the accident to Thule.

A large helicopter was dispatched to return the C-54 people to the base. Halfway there, the chopper's engine quit and the pilot made a safe emergency landing. A second helicopter went out to fetch the stranded crew. It crashed and the two pilots were killed. A third chopper retrieved the bodies and the C-54 people. With that, Eighth Air Force Headquarters grounded all aircraft in the area.

As flight test and quality assurance officer, the accident investigation board assigned me to examine the engineering aspect of the C-54 crash. Based on crew interviews and the aircraft maintenance records, I developed the following finding:

Radio-altimeters emit radio signals that travel downward until they encounter a solid substance then reverse course to the system receiver. The receiver converts the time-delays into altitude readings. In this case, the radio signals traversed 75 feet of the cap before reaching a propagation of ice solid enough to deflect the signal back to the antenna. Accordingly, when the altimeter indicated 75 feet AGL, the C-54 was actually at or very near "ground level." The four propellers contacted the ice simultaneously and flight terminated with an unscheduled wheels-up landing.

The Air Force Flight Safety Office accepted the finding and the pilot handbooks for all radio-altimeter-equipped aircraft were amended to include a warning to this effect.

* * * *

Occasionally when flying our ski-equipped C-47Es over the northern reaches of the Arctic expanse, we would sight a solitary sled track leading from one distant Inuit settlement to another. More often than not, a woman was carving the trail. Although a few Inuit families lived in well-built homes, most lived in stone and turf huts, and all were deprived of basic dental care. To help alleviate the condition, a Danish dentist devoted his life to this endeavor. He died, and although his wife lacked formal training, she continued his labor of love. On one occasion, bad weather and her need for medical supplies forced her to come into the base. She moved into the nurses' quarters and apparently without consulting her, the base commander directed that she be honored with a banquet. Cheered by the break in boredom, we preened and practiced our dance steps certain that the eleven nurses would attend the event. One desperate major even checked-out a Danish-English Dictionary to learn Danish sweet-talk to impress the lonely dentist.

Meanwhile, the officers club was cleaned fore and aft, national and military flags were arrayed behind the head table, and a seating chart was posted. As expected, it reflected that the nurses would sit among the "brass." On the night of the event, we shed the polar gear, donned our best uniforms, and with heads down like wolves slavering for prey, went to the club. Only six nurses showed up and during the cocktail hour they stood butt-back in a circle, like covered wagons holding off the Indians. We were so intent on breaking them up that hardly anyone noticed the guest of honor when she appeared. Tall and angular with windblown hair and a weathered face, she had discarded her polar-bear breeches and sealskin boots in favor of a parka, a frazzled fisherman's sweater, heavy GI wool trousers, and mukluks. She struck a just-out-of-the-trenches stance in the center of the room and scanned us with a critical eye. Aided by a Danish cook as an interpreter, she thanked the colonel for the fancy spread but noted that no one had asked her opinion on the matter. She sorted through a stack of gifts that included the requisite plaque, selected a few items, and asked that the remainder be donated to a nearby Inuit settlement. She and the nurses trooped out, and we were left staring at the door like lost five-year-olds.

* * * *

To prepare us for an emergency, all flyers were required to attend a local Arctic survival school. There, seasoned instructors taught survival techniques using typically available supplies and equipment. The emergency procedure for killing a polar bear for food never failed to capture students' attention. It went like this:

1. Stick your hunting knife hilt down in the ice and urinate on it.

2. An arctic fox will come by and lick the frozen blade for the salt. Due to the cold, he will not feel his tongue being cut.
3. Follow the trail of blood.
4. When the fox dies, skin it.
5. If very hungry, eat it. If not, eviscerate the carcass. Compress your parachute spring and using a shroud line, wrap the carcass and entrails around it.
6. Place the packet in a prominent spot.
7. Hide and wait. A polar bear will eventually come by and swallow the packet. When he digests the meat, the spring will extend and cause him to bleed internally.
8. Follow the trail until he dies.
9. Should the bear's mate come calling and you survive the visit, revert to rule number 1.

As a final test, students were required to spend three nights on the ice cap. Everyone in my nine-man class received a provisioned emergency vest, a three-day supply of K-rations, a parachute, and two polar-rated sleeping bags. We greased our faces as insulation against frostbite, bundled in heavy cold weather gear, climbed aboard an open-door helicopter, and took off.

1957, Thule Air Base, Greenland. An instructor demonstrates how to call for help during a survival school exercise on the ice cap

As we skimmed along, the pale sun cast a soft pastel light giving the glacier a friendly appearance. The instructor dispelled that idea by pointing at a thermometer that read –65° F.

We landed about two miles from the aircraft control tower. The instructor handed me two red flares along with some explicit face-to-face instructions. "You're the senior officer," he said. "The lives of these men are in your hands. Use these flares in case of emergency. If you fire them, the tower operators will send a chopper out to get you. But you'd better have a good reason or you'll all come right back out again. Good luck. Oh yeah, keep an eye out for polar bears." He may have meant it as a joke but we took the remark seriously. As the winter ice melts away, the bears head for land where food is scarce and they can smell a meal from miles away.

The chopper's *thump-thump-thump* had hardly faded when a crew chief opened a box of rations and said, "I'm hungry, I'm gonna eat."

I said, "Stop that Sergeant, you had breakfast two hours ago. You will be our supply officer. It's your job to assure that our food lasts a full three days. Collect all the rations and any other food items anyone brought with them. Keep them sealed so as not to attract animals, develop a chow schedule, and make sure we stick to it." The order cost me several candy bars.

Although we were surrounded by ice, it is possible to die of thirst on the cap and the sergeant's scruffy assistant became our all-important "water officer." He filled a canteen cup with ice, lit a can of Sterno and by varying the distance between the cup and the flame allowed it to melt rather than steam away. Once our canteens were full, we relied on body heat to keep the water from freezing.

Shelter was our next concern. Two fighter pilots decided to go on their own and build a para-igloo. They erected a center-post, draped their parachute-canopies over it, spread the skirts, anchored them with blocks of ice and went inside their tent to relax and have a smoke.

For the rest of us, I proposed that we build an igloo complete with a cute little tunnel-entrance and a chimney hole—much like the ones in children's books. Bad decision; the blocks of packed ice were heavy, broke apart, had to be shaped, and refused to stay erect. We shelved the idea and feverishly began digging a cave. Three hours later, we were drained of energy, plumes of steam were streaming from our fur-lined parka hoods like car exhaust on a cold day, and we were soaked with sweat. The shelter only measured eight feet wide and four feet high but darkness was approaching, the wind-chill had lowered the temperature even further, and we had no

1957, Thule Air Base. A failed attempt to build an igloo. They dug a cave instead

time to waste. Quickly, everyone put one sleeping bag inside the other and the two men who were to occupy the edges of the cave went in. They twisted and squirmed out of their clothes and socks, then the next two, two more, then me. We placed our socks on top of the bags, allowed the sweat to freeze, then slapped it off and completed the drying process under our armpits. We were packed like sardines in a can, nursing our little sufferings, when the first man in whispered, "I gotta go." A collective groan arose and I began trying to think like a leader. Scruffy bailed me out; he extracted an old, yellowed condom from his wallet and said, "Here, use this." The fellow turned on his belly, urinated into the tube, tied a knot in it and put it atop his bag. When it froze, I tossed it out. Fortunately, the problem did not recur because Scruffy only came prepared for one emergency of another kind.

Morning came and to our surprise, body heat had enlarged the cave considerably. I dressed and went to check on the two fighter pilots. They looked like a pair of frosted mummies. The moisture in their breath had risen, crystallized, and rained on them. Their faces were ashen and their Cheshire cat grins were long-gone. We helped them into the cave and took turns massaging them until they recovered complete feeling in faces, fingers, and toes.

A fox appeared and soon several white, blue, and black scavengers were nearby, nervously pacing back and forth hoping for a free meal. Rather

1957. Wild foxes with Thule Air Base in background

than dwell on the amount of money their pelts would bring back home, we prepared to have a fox steak. Scruffy inventoried his supplies, developed a menu, shaped a low ice-table, centered it with a can of Sterno, and prepared place settings; he was ready. Before turning-in, everyone found a good spot, stuck his knife in the ice, and peed on it; if anyone ran short, others helped. High-pitched barking and yelps kept us awake half the night and when daylight came, we rushed out to count the bodies. There were none, zero, nada. Disgruntled by the disappointing turn of events, Scruffy took his sweet time melting the extra ice needed to wash our knives; my breakfast tasted salty. Our diplomas declared us: "Certified Arctic Fliers of the Northern Most Air Base in the World.

Back at the office, I sent an official suggestion to the Air Force Flight Safety Office in which I described the condom incident. For a recommended corrective action I proposed that the item be added to the equipment list for Arctic survival vests. A curtly worded reply rejected the proposal and requested that any further discussion of the subject be conducted over the radio-telephone. Although un-stated, their concern came through loud and clear; how dare I subject their innocent secretaries to such coarseness. I dropped the matter, however, our instructors did not. They had the PX officer order a gross of Trojans for distribution to future classes sent to the cap. PX officials in the States must have wondered about the level of "TLC" the eleven nurses were providing us.

Dusk turned to night and an oppressive air of isolation and deprivation settled over the base. Low energy and mental depression were the most common symptoms. My neighbor, the all-important base postal officer, failed to appear for breakfast one morning and I went to check on him. The once happy-go-lucky lieutenant was in bed curled up in the fetal position crying like a baby. He, along with the other two percent who lacked the mettle to cope, were returned to the States for medical discharge or reassignment elsewhere.

During this period of darkness, the 40th Air Refueling Squadron arrived from Schilling AFB, Kansas, for a ninety-day stay. On one occasion, my work shift had ended and I took a ride around the aircraft parking area to assure all was in order before turning in. Off in the distance I noticed a light and went to investigate. Alone and out in the open, a youthful C-97 crew chief was changing the spark plugs on one of his plane's engines. I had never witnessed that level of dedication and close to tears, I got him down and drove him to the hospital. He was trembling so hard I thought we had a flat tire. Whenever I hear people lament that the younger generation is going to hell in a hand basket, I think of that young man and know that they are wrong. I am proud to have been afforded the opportunity to work with so many extraordinary young men. However, heroics such as his were insufficient to overcome his supervisors' lack of preparation to perform aircraft maintenance in polar conditions. The squadron was unable to meet its mission commitments and its wing commander, my former student Colonel Jumper, was summoned to correct the problems. He had to do some serious head knocking to develop an effective plan of corrective action. Before his departure, we had time to renew our friendship and he praised my assistance.

Major Sally Carpenter, a girl-friend during my days at Lowry, transferred in as chief nurse and I became a fixture in the nurses' dayroom. So much so, that one day a fighter pilot approached me in the officers club and said, "Sir, next Saturday night is the grand opening of our new squadron dayroom. Would you mind if we invite the USO girls that are staying in the nurses' quarters to come over and cut the ribbon? It would really mean a lot to us."

"Why are you asking me, Lieutenant?"

"Well, Sir, you're the special services (recreational activities) officer, so I thought you'd be the one to ask."

"I assure you I'm not. But I'll help you because I'd like to meet the girls myself."

A week later, "Hey, Hank, this is Bob."

"Who?"

"Bob. Bob Benedetti, the F-102 operations officer. We met at the party Saturday night. Thanks for bringing the USO girls over. The guys really appreciated it. Now I want to return the favor."

"Oh, how so?"

"I recall you saying that you're current in the T-bird. Is that true?"

"Yes. I've told everyone over there that I don't want to let my currency lapse."

"I know. Bring me a copy of your Form 5 that shows the date of your last flight in the bird, and if everything looks okay, I'll put you up tonight. I need someone to fly target. Do you want to do it?"

"Does an accordion player wear a ring?"

"What? What are you talking about?"

"Never mind Bob, sure I will. When do you want me there?"

"You'll have to be here by 1400 for a 1700 takeoff."

"What the hell for?"

"Well, Hank, this isn't like flying one of your old gooney birds, we need to fit your survival equipment."

"OK," I replied, "I'll be there at 1400."

"Come a little earlier if you can. It'll take a while." He hung up.

The flight briefing was short: "Go up to 20,000 feet. Take up an easterly heading until you're about seventy-five miles out, then fly a race-track pattern."

I arrived at the personal equipment room wearing an arctic uniform over heavy longjohns. A specialist brought out a one-piece, rubberized, anti-exposure "poopie suit" that smelled like a pair of waders on a hot summer day. I held my breath, inserted myself into its narrow umbilical tube, then wriggled and writhed until my extremities reached their destinations (picture Harry Houdini trying to wriggle out of a straight jacket). He then rolled-up the tube, zippered it into place across my chest, and adjusted the suit skintight. Next came a helmet, oxygen mask, an emergency supply vest, and a parachute.

As each item was added, it occurred to me that I was about to do something dangerous. The cold clammy hands of fear took over, and I suffered an attack of the Puckers (a medical condition that causes pilots to count the number of seat cushions before they sit in the ejection seat). I marched out like a frightened robot being led to the electric chair.

Two crew chiefs practically lifted me into the T-33, strapped me in, set the radios, hooked-up all the gizmos, and started the engine. I found the stick and throttle by-feel and took-off. The blue runway lights slipped under the wing and it was as if I had entered outer space: no lights, no horizon, no stars, only cave-like blackness. I felt minuscule and isolated in a cocoon formed by the red glow of the instrument lights. Beneath me lay an uncharted glacier and civilization was 5,000 miles away. My eyes locked on the critical engine instruments and my butt monitored the steady whine of the powerful J-33 engine compressor behind me.

I longed to hear the sound of a human voice assuring me that someone knew and cared that I was here. My machismo ebbed, deep loneliness took over, and I imagined the most unlikely emergencies. *Kablooom!* A powerful shock wave jolted the T-33 as if hit by a gigantic sledgehammer. My helmet rattled off the canopy, and I held on to the stick with both hands. Guided by his fire control system, an F-102 fighter pilot had just completed a practice attack. He acquired my T-33 as a target and guided by a blip in his radarscope, thundered in at supersonic speed. At the proper instant, the system automatically fired air-to-air missiles (if he had them aboard), and he turned away. God help us if the system should malfunction. These runs

Convair F-102 Delta Dagger. A single seat all-weather interceptor capable of 825 mph (Mach 1.25) Courtesy of USAF Museum

continued for an hour. Several flights would pass before I stopped counting seat cushions.

* * * *

In December, Sally and I took a thirty-day leave, spent a few days in Palm Springs, and then went our separate ways to check on our next assignments. At March Field, a personnel officer did his best to sugar coat the bad news. He said, "You're next station is only ninety miles north of your old stomping grounds, Wichita. The wing commander there, Colonel Jumper really likes you and asked that you be assigned to his unit. General Old always approves 'by name' requests from his commanders so your next address is 40th Bomb Wing, Schilling Air Force Base, Salina, Kansas."

Depressed by the unexpected change, I went to nearby Montebello to spend the holidays with Gus and his family. He met me at the door with a telegram in hand. Oh, oh, I thought, more bad news. It read:

TO MAJOR CERVANTES: I AM PLEASED TO ANNOUNCE YOUR PROMOTION TO MAJOR EFFECTIVE 17 FEBRUARY 1959. CONGRATULATIONS AND BEST WISHES FOR A MERRY CHRISTMAS AND A PROSPEROUS NEW YEAR. COLONEL VAUGHN COMMANDER 4083RD STRATEGIC WING.

I could now wear "scrambled eggs" on my cap. Sally stayed over; and I returned to McGuire AFB, New Jersey, to board a creaky old C-54 that made a weekly run to Thule.

Two messages were awaiting me when I landed. One was a telegram that read:

HANK: I WILL NOT RETURN TO THULE. AM GETTING MARRIED AND HAVE TRANSFERRED TO HANSCOM AFB. BE HAPPY FOR ME. SALLY.

The second was an invitation to a party. Eleven other officers, including two nurses, had also been promoted, and the hospital staff wanted to celebrate.

Most of us went to the affair armed with untouched holiday gift bottles of wine, champagne, and liqueurs. But we had badly underestimated the power and resourcefulness of women. The nurses had decorated their dayroom with red, white, and blue streamers. A makeshift bar was loaded with all types of booze and beer. Two tables groaned under an array of assorted breads, sliced beef, ribs, hot dogs, finger sandwiches, and chips and dips. Another table featured rich, buttery pastries sent over by the Danish baker at the officers club. If that were not enough, they had coaxed the disc jockey at KOOL radio to play dance music instead of opera. This alone was reason to celebrate.

Everyone seemed to be enjoying the festivities except a nurse clad in whites, curled up in the corner of a distraught green leather divan. The tiny, new second lieutenant had short blond hair, a strawberry and cream complexion, a button nose, and deep blue eyes highly magnified by a pair of thick-rimmed librarian's glasses. She and I had come in on the C-54 but other passengers had constantly competed for her attention so I held back. During a fuel stop at Goose Bay, Labrador, we were in the passenger terminal when I noticed her kneeling before a large wall map vainly trying to pinpoint Thule. The room was unbearably hot and we were all in parkas preparing to return to the plane. I joined her and while explaining the chart, noted that her shirt was undone far enough for me to ogle the top of her pale, perfect little breasts.

She caught me at it and while buttoning-up said, "You're bad. Don't you know it's not nice to do that? I ought to report you to someone."

"You'd better not," I replied. "If you do, you're going to have a tough year at Thule. I happen to be the special services officer up there."

"Humph, you must not be doing a good job. They tell me there's nothing to do."

"There isn't. That's why we selected you to come and liven things up."

"That's not true, I volunteered to go because I need time to study. I'm going to be an M.D. and that seems like a good place to take care of some core subjects."

"Well OK. But just remember, what little there is to do up there, I know where to do it."

"You must be the tenth guy who's said that to me." She went to board the plane.

Now here she was at the party, seemingly disinterested, taking it all in. Firm refusals had driven other men away but, if nothing more, I am a patient man. Determined to break through her defenses, I approached her and said, "Talk to me. What have you learned about Thule since I last saw you?"

"I've learned that I don't like it here. I can't believe that I volunteered to spend a year of my life in this sorry place."

"Oh, it's not so bad. It grows on you," I said.

"You can say that. They tell me that you get to travel a lot."

"Yeah, I fly our planes down to St. John's, Newfoundland, when they need heavy maintenance."

"Can I go?"

"Well, you can on some flights but not on others. What else did they tell you about me?"

"That you're not the special services officer and that you were Major Carpenter's boyfriend."

"Oh, you know about that too?"

"Sure, everyone does. We were wondering if you would show up tonight?"

"Hey, I wouldn't miss a party for anything. Besides that's water over the dam."

"What's that you're drinking?" she asked.

"It's a shot of aquavit. Want some?"

She held the glass up to her nose, let the fumes waft upward and said, "No, but I'll tell you what. Why don't you have another while I go change."

"Great, maybe then you'll dance with me."

"OK, but it's going to take me a while."

She returned wearing a white angora sweater, blue wool pants and a parka that she immediately put aside. I expected her to come to me. Instead, other than an occasional smile and possibly a sly wink, it was hard to tell with the glasses, she seemed to have forgotten our conversation.

Finally, it was decision time. I caught her eye from across the room, held up my forefinger, and pointed outside. She smiled her assent and I left the party. An hour later we were in a beat-up, old maintenance pickup truck, careening over the rutty road to the ice cap, when she smiled at me, placed her hands over mine, and gently guided us to the side of the road. I stopped and turned the heater switch to high. That night, we upgraded our tour category from "hardship" to "not bad."

* * * *

Ever since the tenth century, when Eric the Red arrived in Greenland, until a relatively short while ago, time stood still for the Inuits there. Seal hunting provided for all of their needs—food, clothes, lighting, and heat. They lived lives of independent people, and differences were settled with a drum dance to the accompaniment of lampooning songs about one another's wrongdoings; the one made to appear the most ridiculous lost.

However, the introduction of European civilization and firearms changed all that, initiating the transition from a primitive economy to a modern one. In addition, the influx of the white man introduced influenza, tuberculosis, and venereal disease.

It was soon discovered that beneath long successions of great floating icebergs that suggest the beginning of time, lay the world's richest fishing grounds. Those who profit from the fur trade found rich populations of seals, musk oxen, bear, and fox. And concealed beneath the ice cap were minerals such as gold, silver, nickel, lead, graphite, coal, oil, iron, and much more. In the course of a few decades, native Greenlanders had to adapt as the Missile Age brought with it many of the negative trappings of the modern world.

I will always remember my time spent in that wondrous frozen land and am thankful that I was able to experience it before the arrival of cruise ships, ski resorts, and McDonald's.

Miss Kansas

Salina was the kind of town where John Deere tractors used the fast lane on Main Street and the bowling alley was the place to be seen on Saturday night. I moved into a small two-bedroom clapboard house, then went out to see the sights. One pass up the '40s-era main drag and the park where they filmed *Picnic*, and I had seen it all.

The 310th and 40th Bomb Wings were stationed at the base. The two units mirrored one another. Both were equipped with B-47's and KC-97 tankers and their men worked, flew, and lived side-by-side. The one significant difference was their standings in the ferocious competition for top honors as the best unit in SAC. The 310th perennially ranked among the leaders and the 40th endured among the also-rans.

My arrival triggered a familiar question. Should I be assigned to a B-47 air crew or as an aircraft maintenance supervisor? After six years of manhandling B-47s, that thrill had worn thin and I asked for the maintenance job and flying T-33s.

No one who has ever lived there forgets the hot, humid, Midwest small-town summer evenings. On one occasion, the streets were dead, moths bouncing off the screen door drummed the passage of time, midget wrestling was on prime time TV, and I just had to get out of the house or go ape. A lone bartender at the officers club fixed us both a cool drink, waved away my attempt to pay, and we settled down to watch the main event. Suddenly he ducked his glass and began making work-like motions as Base Commander Colonel Julius "Zeke" Summers, his wife Marion, and Millie Saunders made their way to a far table. Once before when I had ogled the striking former Miss Kansas, one of the wives sidled up to me and half-whispered, "Back off Hank, Millie's only twenty three and much too young for you." The remark made me sorry that I wasn't ten years younger, and I mentally cut Millie from my wish list of prospects.

Men are slaves to beauty, however, and never stop shopping for that subtle smile or flashing eye that signal interest, so I perked up. Millie was stylishly dressed in a white sheer silk blouse, wine skirt, and silver jewelry. Her shoulder-length black hair glistened under the peanut lights as her sandals clacked across the parquet dance floor.

The sergeant served them cocktails and we returned to watching the wrestling match. Mrs. Summers must have noticed my glances in their direction because she came over and invited me to join them. We introduced ourselves then Marion said, "We want to know why you ignore us and won't speak to Millie?"

I replied, "You're so high up on the totem pole and Millie is so beautiful that I'm intimidated by all of you." Millie smiled in that special way a woman who is used to being complimented smiles.

I had heard that Colonel Summers was a Doolittle Raider and asked him to tell me about the mission. They were a legendary group of B-25 pilots revered for having flown from the deck of an aircraft carrier to bomb Japan. Marion rolled her eyes, heaved a sigh and said, "He can tell you about that some other time, we hear that you know Patrice Wymore. I'd rather hear about her." Patrice was a local girl who began as a singer and dancer before becoming a movie star and marrying Errol Flynn. Those days were over, however, and I had met her while she was in town visiting family. The colonel got with the program and said, "Yeah, tell us if all those things we hear about you and Hollywood are true?"

My stories were nearing an end when a Frank Sinatra record came up on the jukebox and Millie asked me, "Do you dance?" It seemed more a question than an invitation; nevertheless, I stood up and in an undertone said, "For you, I'll do anything." She eyed me and shook her head as if she had made a bad decision. Afraid that she might reconsider, I quickly led her through a set of sliding glass doors to a small outdoor patio made intimate with flowering plants and dim Japanese lanterns.

As we began to dance, she said, "I'm sorry I asked you. You're so trim."

I had previously admired her sleek cinnamon body at the swimming pool, and to ease her moment of uncertainty said, "Millie, for me, the crickets just stopped chirping on Main Street."

"What?"

I extended my arms and chuckled, "Millie, it's raining angels!"

She giggled, "I still don't know what you're talking about."

She knew.

Her breasts were straining the silky smoothness of her blouse, and I tried to draw her close. She gently resisted so I closed my eyes, breathed in the scent of her hair, and allowed the haunting music to carry me away:

In the wee small hours of the morning, when the whole wide world is fast asleep.
You lie awake and think about the girl and never ever think of counting sheep.
When your lonely heart has learned its lesson. You'd be hurt if only she would call . . . .

She jabbed my back, "Wake up, am I boring you?" My reaction caused her lips to brush my jaw and I scolded her, "Don't change the subject. That's no kiss. If you're going to kiss me, do it right."

Millie stopped, took my face in her hands gave me a velvety kiss on the cheek and in a childlike voice said, "That's a butterfly kiss." I wanted to crush her to me but calmed the urge and resumed dancing.

The song ended but I continued to hold her close and love-dance. Again, she dug a sharp nail into my ribs and said, "Hey, silly, the music stopped."

"Yeah, I know. Do you have a quarter for another song?"

"No."

"It's just as well 'cause my dance card is filled for the rest of the evening."

"Oh, yeah, that's what you think." She straightened her blouse, laced our fingers together and led me back to the table. The Summers had been watching us and were beaming like contented cats. I drove home dizzy with the excitement of new love.

Our thirteen-year age difference seemed not to bother Millie. Her lingering glances and unmasked hand holding at the club dances made it clear that she was a one-man woman. Yet, she was so drop-dead stunning that I could not believe that of all people she truly wanted me. Whenever the telephone rang at home, I would feel a twinge—it might be her about to say, "You're a nice guy but I'm sorry, I don't think things are going to work out."

* * * *

My former boss at the 320th Bomb Wing called. Lieutenant Colonel Bill Hayes now headed the Aircraft Branch, Weapons Maintenance Division at Headquarters SAC. He said, "Hank, I have the Inspector General's (IG) Report on the Schilling ORI on my desk. I'm impressed with the comments he made about the test cell and the engine calibration program you installed there. I'd like to stop by and see it. Would you mind?"

"Hell, no, Bill. It would be great to see you again, come on over anytime. I'll be looking for you." He hung up and I called the noncommissioned officer (NCO) at the cell, "Sergeant, You're going to be inspected by a SAC colonel who knows all about maintenance and wants to see if what the IG said about your operation is true. Don't let me down."

"Don't worry, Sir, we'll take care of it."

Bill landed and after checking in with the wing commander, I drove him to the isolated concrete bunker. Bill appeared distracted during the tour and that bothered me. He had always been cordial with enlisted men and although he generously complimented the sergeant when it was over, I remained annoyed and thought, The sooner you leave the better. We departed for the base and had not gone far when he asked that we pull over. I thought that he wanted to take a pee and stopped behind a grove of poplar trees.

Bill leaned back, lit a Marlboro, took a drag and said, "Relax, Hank, I'm not here to inspect you. I just needed an excuse to see you without causing suspicion."

Still bent out of shape, I thought, What the hell could a colonel from SAC Headquarters and I possibly talk about that might invite comment. He's so high up that I wonder why he is here at all, every base has a test cell.

Bill looked into the distance and said, "Hank, as you know the B-47 and the B-52 are our fastest big planes, however they're power-limited and subsonic. SAC is getting a new top-secret bomber, the B-58 Hustler. It will be the first supersonic bomber in the world and they've already started rolling off the production line at the plant in Fort Worth. We're going to get over a hundred of them and, you'll appreciate this, it goes 1,300 miles an hour, and it climbs at 17,000 feet a minute loaded, 46,000 feet a minute unloaded." He took another drag, looked sideways at me and said, "How'd you like to come work for me as the B-58 Project Officer?"

One of Bill's most engaging qualities was his inclination to joke regardless of the occasion and I said, "Bill, you know I like fast planes. You don't mean that. Don't kid me that way."

In an agitated voice he replied, "Certainly I do, Major. I don't have all day. What do you say?"

I knew colonels and West Pointers who would give their eyeteeth for such an assignment. Yet, here he was inviting a guy with a 12th grade education to lead SAC's maintainability and reliability program for the most sophisticated bomber in the world. I was astounded! To serve at the headquarters was the ultimate testimonial to a SAC officer's professionalism. I would have gladly pumped gas at the PX service station just for the privilege of being able to say, "I'm stationed at Offutt." But to be assigned there and be associated with a Mach-2 aircraft far exceeded my wildest dreams.

Millie called me at the office the next day. "One of the wives just told me that you're being transferred. Why didn't you tell me?"

I fumbled, "I'm sorry, honey. I was going to tell you tonight."

"Oh?"

"Millie, I'm so afraid of losing you that I'm worried sick about what you might say or do."

With impatience ringing in her voice she said, "Listen, what is it going to take for you to understand that I'm not going anywhere, I love you?"

"I love you, too, honey but I'm so excited. Can you believe it? They're sending me to Fort Worth for a couple of months then to SAC headquarters permanently. You can come to Texas with me if you want and Omaha isn't that far away. We'll still be together on weekends."

The silence was deafening.

Two sets of orders arrived on the same day. One directed that I attend the B-58 course at Carswell AFB, Texas. The other awarded me the coveted Command Pilot rating. The badge topped by a star surrounded by a wreath is my proudest achievement in or out of the service. When I was a young lieutenant flying with old warriors Colonels Umstead and Killer Kane, their gleaming Command Pilot wings seemed a vaguely ludicrous and utterly unattainable goal. But the struggle, the bigots, the humiliation, and the pain were all worth it, for they had motivated a Mexican-American who once groveled in the dirt to value himself and endowed him with the perseverance to earn the master-level rating as a thirty-five year old major.

Chapter 7

The B-58 Hustler
(1961–1965)

Willing, Able, Ready

In his book, *Mission With LeMay*, General Curtis E. LeMay is quoted as having once described the lethality of the B-58 in the following manner: "The B-58 carries all the conventional bomb explosive force of World War II and everything which came before. A single B-58 can do that. It lugs the flame and misery of attacks on London ... [the] rubble of Coventry and [the] rubble of Plymouth ... [it can] blow or burn up fifty-three percent of Hamburg's buildings, and sixty percent of the port installations, and kill fifty thousand people in the bargain. Mutilate and lay waste the Polish cities and the Dutch cities, the Warsaws and the Rotterdams. Shatter and fry Essen and Dortmund and Gelsen-kirchen, and every other town in the Ruhr. Shatter the city of Berlin. Do what the Japanese did to us at Pearl, and what we did to the Japanese at Osaka and Yokohama and Nagoya. And explode Japanese industry with a flash of magnesium, and make the canals boil around bloated bodies of the people. Do Tokyo over again. The force of these in a single pod. One B-58 can load that comprehensive concentrated firepower, and convey it to any place on the globe, and let it sink down, and let go off, and bruise the stars and planets and satellites listening in. Every petard, every culverin, every old Long Tom or mortar of a naval ship in the eighteenth or nineteenth centuries, every turret full of smoky cannon at Jutland—Big Bertha bombarding Paris—musketry of the American Revolutionary battles or the Napoleonic ones, Spotsylvania and Shiloh and the battles for Atlanta. All the paper cartridges torn with the teeth, and all the crude metallic cartridges forced in new hot chambers . . . . Firepower. All the firepower ever heard or experienced upon this earth. All in one bomb, all in one B-58."

His fearsome description of the B-58's destructive capability may have been overblown. However, the general also once described the bomber as "a beautifully packaged nest of intertwined snakes." No question about the accuracy of this observation, for from its inception, the B-58 was a troubled weapon system.

At the outset, the announced objective of the B-58 program was to build thirteen aircraft to provide "high-speed, high altitude aircraft for investigating aerodynamic problems of sustained supersonic flight and for use as the test vehicles in the development of sub-systems and components for future weapon systems." With the foot in the door, and after several fits and starts, the contractor and the Air Force (together with a bit of pressure from Congress), forced the aircraft on SAC and the initial buy was eventually parleyed into a contract for 116 planes. Severely hampered by lack of an orderly and economical development, and production and operational programs, the bomber entered the SAC inventory with a host of unresolved problems. Among them were minimal spare parts support, a less than nominal unrefueled range, limited low altitude capability, a questionable safety record, and the public's adverse reaction to sonic booms caused by the B-58 and other supersonic aircraft. The last item eventually led to elimination of supersonic flights over much of the United States.

From cradle to grave, however, the prime problem was money. Opinionated political and technological decisions coupled with the attendant lags and spurts in the production schedule eventually drove the price much higher. But in 1960, the program unit cost of a B-58 was $14 million, making it, at the time, the most expensive production aircraft in the world and almost three times as expensive as a production Boeing B-52G. However, the B-58 was the only new bomber in the hardware stage and the B-47 was rapidly becoming obsolete. Although the small number of B-58s could hardly replace the huge B-47 fleet, SAC felt that the Hustler's speed and flexibility, coupled with its innovative electronic counter measures, would complicate and magnify the Soviet's defense and funding problems. Therefore, despite the deficiencies associated with the aircraft, in August 1960, The Air Force Systems Command (charged with acquisition, development, and testing) relinquished to SAC the executive management responsibility for the bomber.

Shortly thereafter, I airily arrived at the headquarters to fill the new position Bill Hayes had created in his office: B-58 Project Officer. As such, I was the using command's single point of contact for aircraft systems maintainability and reliability issues. Other officers in my area had similar responsibility for the B-58's engines, electronics, ground support equipment, and supply problems. Collectively our duties required that we assure the reliability of our respective aircraft systems, assure that the bomb wings had the wherewithal to maintain those systems in an optimum condition, and where necessary, expeditiously obtain fixes for problems limiting the fleet from performing the SAC mission. Realistically, I was usually involved to one degree or another in most mechanical problems including the all-important maintenance technical data. Given the weapon system's problems, I quickly learned that I was up to my hips in alligators. I dropped the swagger and hit the floor running.

"Two moves are worth one fire," is how one old soldier described the effect multiple re-locations have on personal belongings. I rented a nice house on Omaha's Westside and because my mismatched furniture had made too many moves, I pitched it and asked Millie to come up and refurnish the place. She went about it like a wren building a nest in springtime. With unconcealed joy, she was in and out of stores, trying this here, and that there, returning it, and trying again. The end product tended toward deep leather and briarwood, except for a corner of the bedroom. There she placed a tiny vanity table with a cascade of handmade ruffles, a three-view mirror and my favorite snapshot of her by a fountain. Being a generous man, I set aside two dresser drawers for her things.

At work, (now) Colonel Bill Hayes introduced me to my direct supervisor Lieutenant Colonel John F. Kelly. A tall brown-eyed Irishman, John had a ready smile, a bit of a paunch, and spoke with a wee touch of brogue. He echoed Bill's easy supervisory style and I knew we would work well together. John walked me around the large office and introduced me to my peers: the B-47, B-52, KC-135, and KC-97 project officers and one other person.

"Easy, this is Hank Cervantes. He's our new B-58 Project Officer. I'm looking to you to take care of him. Hank, this is Easy Parham. His real name is Ezequiel but I wouldn't call him that. Easy used to play basketball for good ole' Texas U. but he's now a GD (General Dynamics Corporation) employee and is here as the B-58 technical representative. He'll assist with any problems you might have with the aircraft systems and help you contact the right people at the plant, which is co-located with Carswell Air Force Base. I'll leave, so you two can get better acquainted."

Pleased to have the unexpected assistance, I kicked-in a big smile, stuck my hand out and said, "Hi, Easy glad to know you." The doughy, six-foot-five, 240-pounder remained silent. Instead, a limp handshake and a pained expression on his once handsome face informed me in a language we both understood of his contempt for Mexicans. My grin faded and neither of us made any attempt at the small talk that normally follows such a meeting. He returned to his desk, and I retrieved a stack of paperwork that John had saved for me.

There might have been a time when I would have remembered "my place" and adjusted to Easy's attitude but those days were long-gone. I thought, Try me pal, just try me. If you think I'm some kind of ditty-bump who will let you jack him around, you've bent one too many basketball hoops with your head. It was not long before Easy tried.

I left a "Please See Me" note on his desk and he came over. Rather than say anything, he gave me a little "What do you want?" upward bob of the head. We both knew it was a test. I looked him in the eye. In return he flicked the ashes off his stogie, glanced at the mess on the floor, and gave me an insolent grin. Determined to face him down, and rather than discuss the matter there, I said, "We need to go see General Crumm" (my friend from our days in the 320th Bomb Wing), and headed for the door. He shuffled out behind me and once away from the office I stopped him and said, "Easy, when I call you, I don't expect you to come over and kiss my ring finger but on the other hand that head-bob won't cut it. I don't give a rat's fanny what you think of me personally but this is a military business office and I expect you to conduct yourself accordingly. If you don't, I'll guarantee you one of us is leaving this place. OK?" He grunted, turned away, and spit on the floor. The exchange was the baseline for our relationship during the four years we worked together. Neither of us gave an inch, it was hard-knuckles all the way.

* * * *

The Cold War was on. Accelerated production of the radically designed bomber had peaked, and my desk was the mail-drop for all manner of problems. High among them was the staff's push to declare the two B-58 units—the 43rd Bomb Wing at Carswell and the 305th Bomb Wing at Bunker Hill AFB, Indiana—combat ready. On the other hand, the wings were resisting the action due to a host of technical difficulties including bombing-navigation system failures, flight control malfunctions, engine problems, and tire failures due to the bombers' fast landing speed, to name a few.

A mountain of paper in my "IN" basket was growing on a daily basis and, after struggling with it for three months I went to John Kelly and said, "John, I don't think I'm doing the job you have a right to expect from a guy in this position. I can't seem to keep up with the paperwork. You might be better off replacing me."

He laughed, "Hank, every newcomer to this puzzle palace has the same problem. I did. Bill did. Stick with it, you'll catch on."

Thirty days later, I returned and voiced the same concern. John said, "Go back and separate the 'Priority' and 'Classified' correspondence from the stack, then call me." I did. He gathered the unclassified stack and threw it in the wastebasket. "There, you're now current," he said. "If anyone calls about their letter, apologize, ask them to re-transmit and answer it." When he left I retrieved the papers and hid them in the lowest drawer of my filing cabinet. No one called. It was a practical lesson in one bureaucratic method for the correction of problems.

The SAC Director of Materiel, Major General Michael J. "Iron Mike" Vinson, was our big boss. Six feet tall and well built, he had carefully dyed black hair, the face of an overage altar boy, and the charm and grace of a prince. But exhibit weakness or incompetence and all the niceties disappeared, and his features transformed into a baleful mask. Precision-driven, demanding, and unforgiving, when he said, "Take off is at six o'clock," he did not mean, "We'll meet at base operations at six." He meant, "Wheels-up at six." He often loaded a VC-97 (a passenger model of the tanker) with project officers and went on multiple-day jaunts to several bases looking for developing problems to nip at the bud.

On one occasion, we stayed overnight at Altus AFB, Oklahoma. The next morning we boarded the plane at 0430, and at 0435 the passenger door closed for a 0500 takeoff. The plane hadn't moved when a car came screeching to the door with three late arrivals. The flight engineer ran forward and informed Vinson, but Iron Mike disregarded him, released the brakes, and began to taxi. Frantically, the men ran along side with their luggage in hand waving for him to stop. Without so much as a glance in their direction, he took off, leaving the exasperated men standing on the taxi strip.

The general tracked significant aircraft maintenance and materiel problems by means of an Action Item system. For example, if a B-58 aircraft system problem came to his attention, he assigned me an action item and I used flip charts to keep him current on the "get-well" program. Every project officer maintained status on twenty or more problems and God help the man who was not prepared to brief on a moment's notice; or worse yet, was less informed than Iron Mike.

He normally communicated with us through three layers of supervision, so his first direct call to me came as a surprise. "Hank, this is General Vinson, be ready for take off to Fort Worth in one hour. We will RON at the Westward Ho Hotel. Please make side-by-side room reservations for us." Click.

Quickly, I made the reservations, grabbed my overnighter and Action Item briefing charts, and hurried to base operations. A seven-passenger North American T-39 Saberliner was idling on the ramp waiting for us. He arrived, I saluted, he gave me a curt "Hi" and we boarded. Filled with apprehension because I did not know the reason for the trip, I carefully watched him out of the corner of my eye hoping for a clue. He did paperwork until we reached flight altitude then put it away, lit a cigar, leaned back, and closed his eyes. Pursed lips and a furrowed forehead gave him a crisis look that I had not seen before and I worried, What kind of major disaster occurred at Carswell or General Dynamics that requires his and my presence? Did I do something wrong? The pilots had begun their descent into Carswell when he sat up, resolutely stubbed out the cigar as if punctuating an important decision, and leaned across the aisle toward me. Oh, oh, here comes the bad news, I thought.

In a conspiratorial tone of voice he said, "Hank, you don't have any problem with going on a blind date do you?"

All expression drained from my face, "No, Sir."

Animated by my response, he unsnapped his safety belt, got a hammerlock on my shoulders, pulled me half-way across the aisle and said, "A couple of days ago, I met a couple of good looking girls at the Sheppard Field PX. They're both married, but I know you don't care. They're driving down from Wichita Falls to meet us and I expect that they'll arrive shortly after we land. OK?"

"Great," was all I could manage.

"You're a good man, Hank," he said as he released me. I fell back into my chair.

Several senior officers and a flag-flying honor guard were lined-up in front of the terminal when we taxied in. A blue staff car with a two-star license plate came to the plane and Vinson said, "Don't pay any attention to them. Just go over and get in the car." I ran down the stairs and jumped in. He remained inside until our luggage was transferred then stepped down as if walking on eggs. The welcoming party drew up to attention and saluted. He glanced in their direction, gave them a half-ass wave, hopped in the car and commanded, "Let's go." The driver sped by the startled officers at fifty miles an hour.

At the Westward Ho he said, "Hank, let's make dinner reservations in the dining room for the four of us and if the brand is OK with you, get us a bottle of Jack Daniels." I took care of the chore and we drank and chatted through the two sets of open double-doors as we freshened up and changed into civilian clothes.

The women called from the lobby and he invited them up. I would not have gone across town to see either of them much less five hundred miles but I do not turn down gifts. I served them drinks and the chitchat had hardly gotten started when he invited my date, Viola, and me to leave and locked both sets of doors behind us.

Viola had a nice body, brown wind-blown hair, a raw-boned face, and stood a head taller than me. For openers I asked, "Where are you from, Viola?" Using words like "ass" for ice, "core" for car, and "wan" for wine, Viola launched into a travel agent's description of the splendors of dusty Burkeburnett, Texas. Her words were cascading out at an astonishing rate when we heard a loud crash in Vinson's room. Their doors opened and while pounding on our doors, his date Wanda shouted, "Open the doah, open this goddamn doah!"

We did nothing.

"Damn you, Viola. I said open this goddamn doah!"

Vinson said, "Open the door, Hank."

"OK," I replied, "but please wait a couple of minutes then come in through the front door. It'll be open." I unlocked the front door then ran to the bed, pulled the covers back and said, "Come on, Viola, jump in. Hurry."

Viola glared at me, "Have yew lost yoah mine? I certainly will not."

"Look," I said. "We're going to have some fun. Keep your clothes on, but do it, hurry."

Realizing my intentions, she got under the covers, I followed and we snuggled together as the door opened. Vinson got wide-eyed, rushed to the foot of the bed and in a voice filled with admiration said, "Hank, I heard you were good. But I didn't know you were that good!"

Rather than respond, I scrunched my head under the covers as if I had unfinished business to tend to. He apologized, "I'm sorry. We'll wait for you in the bar."

Wanda said, "Not me, I'll wait in the hallway and yew two hurry with whatevah yewre doin."

Viola and Wanda left and were not mentioned again. Vinson and I dined alone and were back in our offices by 0730.

Not long thereafter, I received a phone call. "Hank, this is General Vinson. Be ready for take off to Bunker Hill in one hour." I grabbed my bag and dashed to base operations. The B-58 Supply Project Officer, Major Alioto, was already there waiting to board the T-39. He greeted me and asked, "Where's your Action Item briefing?"

"Geez, I forgot the damn thing. Do you think I've got time to go back and get it?"

"Nah, you'll be better off getting wire-brushed for being absent-minded than for missing take off." I agreed. The general boarded and motioned me to sit across the aisle from him.

We leveled off at altitude and Vinson motioned with his cigar for Alioto to brief his action items. The major propped the charts on a seat back and began his review. Meanwhile, I sat ramrod straight, eyes forward, dreading his request for my briefing.

Alioto was in mid-sentence, when Vinson leaned toward me and said, "Go get on the radio, raise the base commander at Bunker Hill, and tell Colonel Boyle to get a couple of good looking nurses to have dinner with us at seven o'clock tonight at the officers club."

Relieved that his thoughts were far from the B-58, I went forward, asked the copilot for his headset, and called. "Colonel," I said, "this is Colonel Cervantes, (I made lieutenant colonel in July 1963.) General Vinson, Major Alioto, and I are inbound to your base and ..."

He interrupted, "Yes, I know. What can I do for you?"

"Colonel, General Vinson asked me to give you this message: 'Please have two good looking nurses meet us for dinner at the officers club tonight at seven.'"

A long silence followed then, "Goddamn it!"

He hung up and I returned to my seat.

Vinson leaned over and asked, "What did he say?"

"Sir, he said he would look into it."

Vinson's gaze never wavered, "Go back and tell him I want to know if he is going to do it."

I hated what he was making me do, but anything to forestall discussing the charts. I went up, yanked the headset off the copilot's head and again called the hapless Boyle. I said, "Colonel, this is Hank again. He wants to know if you're going to do it."

A very long silence followed. Meanwhile the pilot motioned that he needed to use the radio, "Sir, I repeat, he wants to know if you are going to do it?"

"Yes, goddamn it, tell him yes," he hung up.

I returned and whispered in Vinson's ear, "He's going to do it."

He smiled, lit a cigar, and waved at Alioto to sit down.

We landed, checked into our quarters, and he and I met at the club. We were chatting over drinks when two young women dressed in civvies approached. I stepped forward, met Lieutenants Janice Brock and Nancy Sadler, then introduced the general. After a pleasant dinner and a nightcap, I walked Nancy to her quarters.

Early the next morning, I was preparing to leave her apartment when I noticed some packed boxes. "Nancy," I asked, "where are you going?"

"I'm going back to the University of Tennessee. I don't like it here. I asked for a transfer to any one of five SAC bases and the personnel officer turned me down, so I'm getting out."

"Which bases did you request, Nancy?"

She named five, one of which was Carswell.

"If you were transferred to Carswell, would you stay in?"

She laughed, "Yes, but it's too late, I already have my orders."

Quietly, I opened the door to leave, stuck my head back inside and whispered, "Don't pack your sombrero. You're going to Texas."

Alioto and I followed Vinson aboard the plane. Dapper as ever, he settled back in his seat and asked, "How'd it go last night, Hank?"

"Great, General. Nancy's a lot of fun. But I want to apologize for my bleary-eyed appearance. I only got about an hour's sleep last night."

He rolled his eyes, gave me a delighted clap on the shoulder, and reached for a cigar. He did not seem willing to share details about his date and to keep the conversation going I said, "Nancy is about to leave the Air Force. She asked for a transfer to Carswell but the personnel officer turned her down. Considering the shortage of nurses in SAC, that doesn't seem like a good move to me."

Vinson reacted, "Oh, we'll see about that. When we land, go see General Knapp (Major General James B. Knapp, SAC Director of Personnel.) Tell him to transfer Nancy to Carswell. Mention that I am personally interested in this matter."

I related Nancy's story to General Knapp and added Vinson's comment. A broad smile crossed his face, "What's that name again?" He wrote it down and said, "Tell him I'll take care of it."

I relayed the message to General Vinson and three hours later I received a call on the autovon line. "Hey, this is Nancy Sadler. The personnel officer just called me. He said that my separation orders are canceled and that I'm going to Carswell. Boy, you sure have a lot of power."

"That's great, Nancy. When will I see you again?"

"Anytime you want."

Nancy transferred to Carswell and their flight operations office soon developed a standard operating procedure to notify Nancy whenever they had a flight departing for Offutt Air Force Base. Thus began a relationship that would last for several years.

1961, Bunker Hill Air Force Base, Indiana. Lt. Nancy Sadler

* * * *

Colonel Everett "Stinky" Davis was the chief of maintenance at the San Antonio Air Logistics Center, Kelly AFB, Texas. Stinky and I were in his office having a heated discussion over the specifications in a B-58 modification contract. I was losing and to regain lost ground, I invited him to verify the SAC position by calling General Vinson on the speakerphone. Vinson listened to his side of the argument. Then asked, "What did Hank say?" Stinky stated my position and Vinson hung up in his ear. The contract was written to our specifications and I immediately returned to the headquarters. A Vinson "See Me" note was on my desk when I arrived. Eager to crow over our victory, I rushed into his office, saluted and burst out, "We got it ...."

He interrupted me, "Colonel, you are supposed to be 'at attention.' When I send you out to represent this headquarters, don't you ever invite anyone to call me to back you up. When you're out there, you are wearing these two stars and don't you forget it. You're dismissed." On another occasion he advised, "When dealing with the bomb wings, if you're going to approve a request, do it on paper that way you can take credit for it. If you intend to deny it, tell them over the telephone, that way you can change your mind." General Vinson did not teach me much about women, but more than anyone, he helped me to grow professionally and I am deeply grateful to him for it

* * * *

I was coming up on three years at the headquarters when my office telephone rang and the caller asked, "How would you like to go to Ecuador?" I assumed that someone in the building wanted me to take a flight there and replied, "I don't know. It sounds good. How long would we be gone?"

"A minimum of two years."

"What, who is this?"

"It doesn't matter. You speak Spanish and we'd like to have you in Quito as a member of the Air Force Legation. You'll be working closely with the ambassador and his staff."

The existing regulation limited legation assignments to married officers and required that their wives accompany them. The purpose was to decrease the likelihood of an embarrassing problem with a local member of the opposite sex. Aware of the restriction, I said, "You may not know it, but I'm single."

"Oh, we know all about you and have no problem on that score."

"Well, give me your number. Let me look into it and I'll call you back."

"No, that's OK, I'll call you." He hung up.

The implications were clear; they considered me over the hill and no threat to the intent of the regulation. That hurt. Nevertheless, I put the word out and an officer who had been in Quito for three days called me. He advised, "Don't go Hank. You like jets and the only planes our people down there have to fly are a couple of old museum-age transports. Worse yet, all the women are Indian and nowhere near as beautiful as Millie. Turn it down."

A week later, the unidentified caller was back on the line. "Hi, Colonel, what did you decide about Ecuador?"

"I don't think I care to go."

He hung up.

Soon thereafter, a beauteous "Miss Ecuador" won the "Miss Universe" pageant and it was not long before I spotted the ill-informed major coming down the hall. He let out a giant whoop and took off running in the opposite direction.

* * * *

Anyone who has ever purchased a computer, or a VCR for that matter, knows how important it is to have detailed, clearly-written instructions in the owner's manual. Nothing is more irritating or difficult to deal with than to discover that the manual applies to more than one model of the product, or that several "slip-sheets" provide directions that supersede or augment the original data.

This was the situation with the B-58. The aircraft had more than thirty classified and unclassified maintenance manuals while the flight crew had several also. General Dynamics was contractually bound to issue concurrent technical data with each change introduced into a weapons system. Instead, the contractor had "slip-sheeted" the manuals so extensively that it was impossible to find a book that was not crammed with dog-eared pieces of paper of various colors, each hue representing a different generation of changes. It is not difficult to imagine a young mechanic flipping back and forth between loose pages in a thick binder in order to find the instructions necessary to do his job. This was a critical deficiency and it prompted my first major confrontation with the contractor. I wrote a letter reminding them of the contractual requirement and in response, they sent a Latino engineer who could hardly speak English and was unfamiliar with the problem to discuss the matter with me. I suspected Easy Parham of having engineered the insult but said nothing to him. Instead, I chased the fellow home and fired off a General Vinson wire to General Dynamics giving them forty-five days to issue updated technical data or we would stop accepting new aircraft. Contractors rely heavily on this programmed flow of funds, and a hail of telegrams and letters arrived from people ranging from congressional representatives to generals of other commands pleading that we not do that. This escalated the issue to the General Power level, but he backed us all the way and the upgraded data was produced.

There would be many such confrontations, but that put an end to the overt bigotry. A few years after I retired, the former B-58 Program Manager and I met at a cocktail party. I reminded him of the incident and he offered me a Martini to soothe my feelings. I accepted it and while looking him in the eye, poured the drink into a wastebasket.

Greased Lightning!

The needle-nosed B-58 ushered bombers into the supersonic age. The 1,325-mile-an-hour speedster had four after-burner-equipped engines suspended beneath thin dart-shaped wings, a tall tail, and a spindly landing gear. A thin fuselage prevented the internal carriage of bombs, so an external 75-foot releasable pod (called the MB-1) was mounted beneath the fuselage to carry extra fuel and a beer-barrel shaped nuclear weapon. Later, General Dynamics developed a two-component (TCP) version of the huge tank. The lower section contained the fuel and could be jettisoned after it was empty to extend the range of the aircraft, and the upper component carried the weapon.

Years ahead of its time, the Hustler demanded the full attention of its crew, each of whom were seated in separate cockpits (pilot, bombardier/navigator, and defense systems operator). All this aside, this spectacular

A SAC TB-58 (training model) Hustler. Maximum speed: 1,325 mph. Service ceiling: 60,000 feet. The free world's first Mach-2 bomber set 19 world speed and altitude records during 1961–69

performer will undoubtedly be best remembered for winning the Bleriot, Bendix, Thompson, Mackay, and Harmon trophies while setting nineteen world speed and altitude records. To visualize how this singular achievement came about, one needs only look behind the scenes surrounding one record-setting event.

Following a military speed dash, press releases will usually imply that a plane just happened to be flying from here to there and upon landing, low and behold, to everyone's surprise, a new record was set.

Not true. Speed record attempts are finely tuned affairs usually driven by a contractor seeking headlines that will enable him to sell more planes. For example, our most prestigious speed record has long been the west-to-east cross-country flight. The attempt is usually made in spring due to good weather and the proximity of a strong jet stream.

On March 5, 1962, SAC and General Dynamics launched a well-calculated effort to capture both transcontinental speed records—Los Angeles to New York in 2:47, set by an F-4H Phantom; and New York to Los Angeles in 3:36, set by an F-101 Voodoo.

The planners envisioned that a B-58 could obliterate the records by flying the west-east leg in less than two hours, and "beat the sun" (traverse the country faster than the rotational speed of the earth) on the return leg to Los Angeles. Capt. Robert G. Sowers, Navigator Capt. Robert MacDonald, and Defensive Systems Operator Capt. John T. Walton of the 43rd Bomb Wing, were selected to make the attempt. They took-off and before leaving the Fort Worth area, carefully checked their "tweaked-up" B-58, *Greased Lightning*. All systems were "Go." Had they not been, a backup B-58 was also aloft ready to replace them.

Sowers flew to Los Angeles, continued out over the Pacific, made a 180 degree turn and while flying on an easterly heading, hooked-up with a KC-135 Stratotanker to top-off the fuel tanks. He disconnected, advanced the engines to maximum-afterburner, and accelerated in the climb to altitude.

As they passed over the Los Angeles checkpoint, National Aeronautics Administration (NAA) representatives aboard another KC-135 recorded their exact time, visually and by radar. Sixteen minutes later the B-58 arrived over the Grand Canyon still in maximum afterburner and doing Mach 2 at 50,000 feet. Afterburner triples the fuel consumption rate, therefore the Hustler's engines would deplete the entire fuel supply in about 45 minutes. Over Kirksville, Missouri, Sowers descended to 30,000 feet, slowed to 400-miles-an-hour, and hooked-up with a third KC-135.

Ten minutes later he had returned to altitude and resumed top speed. A NAA timer aboard a fourth KC-135 verified their time over the New York checkpoint as 2 hours, 0 minutes, 56.8 seconds.

Greased Lightning continued over the Atlantic Ocean, made a 180, hooked-up with a fifth KC-135, then began the east-to-west run. Again, it accelerated to twice the speed of sound, hit a sixth tanker over Kansas City, and continued into Los Angeles. Time: 2 hours, 15 minutes, 48.6 seconds. It had beaten the sun's arc across the country by 45 minutes and in the process won the Bendix Transcontinental Speed Trophy. The award is on display at the entrance to Washington's Air & Space Museum.

By late 1962, the two bomb wings had eclipsed every major speed, altitude, and payload record in the books. Rather than leave it there, they dusted-off musty old ledgers to search for more obscure records to erase. Having done that, their representatives arrived at the headquarters to brief the staff on fresh ideas aimed at keeping the B-58 in the news. They were bucking the odds because their operational readiness (combat ready) date had already been deferred once and many hard-liners in the building held the opinion that they were more interested in setting records than being governed by SAC's stringent alert system.

A head-on view of a B-58 without the dropable pod that carried a portion of the aircraft's fuel supply in addition to an A-bomb. When loaded, the plane climbed at 17,000 feet-per-minute, unloaded at 46,000 feet-per-minute

The Commander In Chief (CINC), General Thomas S. Power, presided over the meeting. The first proposal called for a speed run from Hawaii to London and they even had a motto for it: "Leis to the Queen." General Power promptly shot it down and the briefing deteriorated into a bull session.

Following the meeting, Colonel "Skip" (Barnett B.) Young and I were in his office and still laughing about an incident that occurred during the briefing. General John C. Meyer had shot down 39 enemy planes in two wars and later commanded SAC but he was then the two-star deputy director of operations. We had partied with the B-58 troops the night before and minutes into the meeting John's head began rocking like one of those bobble-headed dolls motorists put in their back windows. General Power saw him, raised his arm high and slammed the flat of his hand against the conference table. John must have thought a MIG had just blown him away. Head oscillating, eyelids half-open and eyes rolled back, John jumped to his feet, struggled to get everything working right and stammered an apology. No one heard it; we were all laughing too hard.

* * * *

Generals love beautiful airplanes just like the rest of us. In my opinion, they have only approved two ugly airplanes for mass production: Fairchild's C-119, an aluminum box to which they attached wings and two elongated tail booms, calling it a "Flying Boxcar"; and the A-10, a twin engine, close-air support killer armed with a Gatling gun, aptly called the "Warthog."

But looks can be deceiving. The B-58 was no exception. The first B-58s came equipped with standard ejection seats that provided a capability to emergency-eject from above 50,000 feet at Mach 2, down to 120 miles per hour at 100 feet above ground level. Early on, however, several accidents established that the open seats did not protect the occupants from supersonic windblasts during high-speed bailouts. This harsh reality was clearly demonstrated during a practice mission over Texas when a crew was forced to bail out at 1,300 miles per hour. One man died and the other two sustained severe injuries. The tragic event provided justification to upgrade a requirement for encapsulated seats to "safety of flight" status, generally defined as "a flight-related condition that if not expeditiously corrected will result in fatalities."

After several fits and starts, testing began on a first-of-its-type encapsulated ejection seat. The system operated in a two-step process. When the occupant raised either armrest, the following occurred in quick sequence:

1. The seat harness locked and a leg retraction mechanism tucked his shins back.
2. Telescoping clamshell doors stowed above the occupant's head, rotated down to enclose him.
3. An independent oxygen system pressurized the capsule.

When he actuated a trigger on the armrest:
1. The canopy jettisoned and the capsule ejected from the plane.
2. As the capsule emerged, two finned booms and a small parachute deployed to stabilize it and keep it from tumbling in flight.
3. If the occupant ejected at high altitude and high speed, the enclosed capsule free-fell, slowing down in the process, until at about 15,000 feet, a barometer sensed the thicker air and automatically opened a 42-foot recovery parachute to slow the capsule to touchdown speed. If he ejected below 15,000, the recovery parachute opened immediately. Shock absorbers eased the landing and in case of a water landing, flotation bags automatically inflated to convert the capsule into a life raft. Either way, the capsule could be used as a shelter from heat or cold and was stocked with food, water, a radio, a rifle, and survival clothing.

Labeled the Rolls Royce of escape systems, the new technology would enable the crews to fly in a "shirt sleeve environment," or free of a parachute, partial-pressure suit, Mae West water flotation gear, exposure suit, and other items of personal equipment.

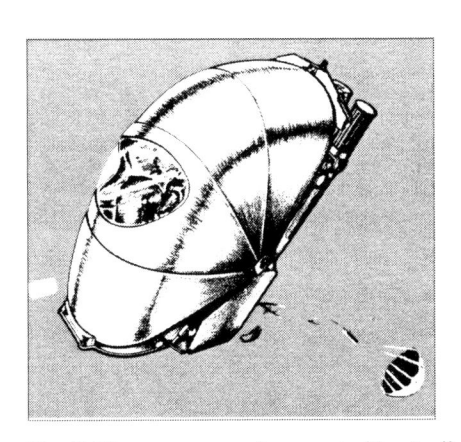

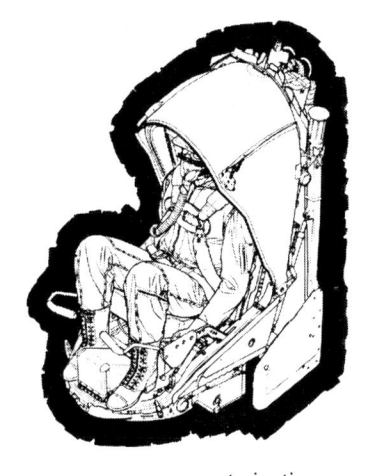

The B-58 escape capsule operated basically the same as an open seat ejection system with one major difference: telescoping clam-shell doors formed an airtight, pressurized compartment around the crew member prior to his ejection

Rather than a control wheel as most bombers have, the B-58 had a flight control stick located within the confines of the capsule. In an emergency, buttons on the stick-grip provided the pilot the capability to disconnect the autopilot, retard the throttles, and shift the center of gravity (CG) by transferring fuel. The pilot's compartment differed from the two other crew stations in that it had a window in the doors that enabled the occupant to see out after encapsulation. Some critics regarded the system as "gingerbread," until the day a malfunction caused a pilot to be encapsulated inflight. Fortunately, he was not ejected and, thanks to the buttons on the control stick, was able to safely land the plane.

Early in the capsule test program, human factor engineers found that when seated, a brown bear's weight, internal organs, spinal column, and CG approximates that of most men. Thus, bears were the first subjects to be ejected. During these tests, powerful explosive devices shot the capsules up well enough, however, they accelerated so violently that the bears suffered spinal compression fractures. The problem remained unresolved until the advent of better solid propellants and shaped charges. This allowed the development of a dual manifold rocket system and research advanced to a new plateau.

The new devices enabled the capsule's upward progress to begin slowly (speaking in milliseconds), allowing the seat cushions and occupant's butt to compress. Acceleration then increased rapidly to catapult the capsule high enough for a safe bailout at 100 knots while on the runway, and fast enough for the three capsules to clear the 14-foot vertical tail in sequence at Mach-2.

Late one night several of us were in the office anxiously awaiting the results of a bear test that would signal engineering approval of the capsules. At last, the message came in from the General Dynamics flight test group at Edwards AFB, California. As expected, it cited several pages of engineering details, then declared the test "highly successful." Our whoops of approval abruptly ended when we read the last paragraph. Almost as an afterthought it stated, "Unfortunately, the bear died shortly after landing. Preliminary examination attributes the cause of death to a brain tumor." It was too coincidental; the engineers were sent back to the drawing boards.

After additional engineering, a chimpanzee survived a successful ejection at Mach 1.6 at 45,000 feet. Soon thereafter, a brave warrant officer successfully ejected at 565 mph at 20,000 feet. With that, the capsules were approved for installation. The unwieldy seats exacerbated the already limited crew accommodations. Consequently, a strict physical limitation was placed on crew members' height and weight, and the star-crossed program continued on. Because the requirement to retrofit the fleet with the capsules was "the long pole in the tent," a modification program known as Project Hustle-Up was developed to concurrently install other required fixes as well as changes that would bring the fleet up to a standard configuration. A sampling of the twenty-one major problems we addressed provides insight into some little-known features of the B-58:

1. Although at cruise altitude the outside air temperature normally hovered around −50 degrees Fahrenheit, air friction caused the B-58's metal skin to heat up to 260 degrees Fahrenheit. The fuel and hydraulic oil absorbed the heat and this degraded their efficiency. To offset the problem, the fluids were piped through water tanks installed in the wings. The water acted as a heat exchanger much like a car radiator. It seemed like a great idea when the system was designed, but there are no free lunches in aerodynamics. As the water in the tanks sloshed around in flight, it became electrolytic and corroded the least noble of several types of metal that formed the two tanks. The corrosion needed to be repaired, and a new sealant invented and applied.

2. War planners loved the eight-engine B-52 bomber because it provided them various options through its ability to carry warheads, multiple iron bombs, and Hound Dog missiles. The B-58 had no optional attack capabilities beyond the weapon in the bomb/fuel pod and this limited its role as a strategic weapon system. A modification would enable it to carry various smaller thermonuclear weapons on external racks mounted on either side of the pod. Here again the enhancement extracted a penalty. The increase in aerodynamic drag would decrease the B-58's already limited range.

3. The pod was so aerodynamically clean that after release, it continued to "fly" below the fuselage rather than follow a predicted path to the target. A pogo stick device was needed to help it separate cleanly.

4. Each main landing gear assembly had four split wheels with eight, 22-inch, high pressure, nitrogen-filled tires, two per wheel. Thin, solid steel wheels were needed between each set of two tires to decrease the possibility of a blowout causing the spindly nine-foot landing gear struts to fail and allow the fuselage to fall, catastrophically crushing the bomb/fuel pod.

5. The plane had warning lights to visually warn the pilot of malfunctions. This was insufficient; an auditory warning was needed to augment the primary system. For example, if a fire developed in the number one engine, in addition to a red light, a recorded voice warned, "Fire, engine number one." If more than one malfunction occurred, the system would tell him the most important problem and continue repeating the statement until something was done about it. Although everyone agreed with its necessity, several meetings were required to approve this modification. The unsettled question was which would be more apt to capture a pilot's immediate attention, a dominant male or a female voice? A woman's voice won. Pilots promptly dubbed the system, "the old bitch."
6. To minimize disruption of the crew from its in-flight duties, a fix was borrowed from the space program. Each cockpit canopy hatch was modified to hold plastic containers with tubes to enable the crew to suck water and soft food upon demand.

Time came to fund the $46 million project and I made an appointment for my boss, Colonel Ernie (Ernest B.) Wilson, and me to go to the Pentagon to brief the Air Force Director of Operational Requirements, General Jack Catton, and the Air Force Comptroller, Lieutenant General Charles B. Stone. They held the purse strings.

We were preparing to go in a T-33 when we learned that a gleaming blue-and-white C-21 Learjet belonging to the Special Air Mission (SAM) unit in Washington was about to leave on a flight home. Quickly, we obtained special dispensation to hitch a ride with them and changed into dress uniform. Feeling very self-important, we swaggered up the steps and into the door bearing the presidential seal. A steward in a white waiter's jacket deflated us in a hurry. He said, "Sit in the last two seats and don't bother anybody." Soon, the Advisor to the President on Atomic Policy, Paul Nitze, and the British Minister of Defense came aboard and also ignored us. All the way there, the steward plied them with a steady stream of martinis, snacks, and fruit. We didn't even rate the leftovers or a "have a nice day" when we deplaned.

When General Catton greeted us in his reception area, I thought that we had accidentally wandered into a Hollywood film set. The general exemplified command presence. He was tall and slim, with aquiline features, movie-star looks, wavy salt and pepper hair, an impeccable uniform, brilliant stars, command pilot wings, and an impressive clutch of ribbons.

Early in his career, the general gained renown when, as a SAC commander, he said to his troops, "There are just three things you have to remember in SAC: the mission, the mission, the mission."

Other major command representatives also in the hunt for money were already in his office and we found seats on either side of an old fellow in a rumpled gray civilian suit. Several well-crafted requests for funds were made during which General Catton remained non-committal. Meanwhile, Ernie and I had a constant flow of notes between us using the old fellow as a go-between. Then it was SAC's turn. In quick order, I reviewed the major modifications, costs, and intended benefits. General Catton asked a few questions then leaned back and said, "Well, let's see how we're going to fund this program. Let's hear from General Stone." Surprise. Our rumpled friend went to a blackboard, listed all the Air Force's foremost modification programs along with their funding levels, then lapsed into a series of, "We'll take so much from this one and so much from that one. No problem, we can fund it."

The meeting ended and I rushed to General Stone and apologized for using him as a messenger boy. He chuckled, placed a fatherly arm on my shoulder and said, "That was a good briefing, son. Take care of that B-58."

* * * *

"Hank, this is General Vinson. Write a little billet doux from General Power to David Lewis, the CEO of General Dynamics, thanking him for the good job his people did on Project Hustle-Up."

"Yes, sir, I'll get right on it" He hung up and I thought, Billet doux. What the hell's a billet doux? No problem, I'll ask one of the West Pointers in the office; they learn all those highfalutin' words at the Academy. Not one of them had a clue. I called our busty base librarian and sometimes girlfriend, Marilyn Lucero. Coyly she said, "It's French for 'love letter,' Hank. Why do you want to know?"

"Thanks, Marilyn," I replied, "you wouldn't believe it if I told you." Next question: How do four-star generals and high-powered CEO's address one another—Tommy and Dave? I wrote a three-page letter, synthesized it into six sentences, and took it to General Power's steel-spectacled ghost-writer, Colonel Albert Arnhym. He checked it word-for-word, initialed it, and then gave me a gratuitous kick in the pants with, "He'll never sign that." Filled with trepidation, I sucked up my courage and marched into the general's office. He signed it without a blink. As I floated by Arnhym's desk, I waved the letter under his nose and wished him a nice day. He didn't even bother to look up.

The incident may seem trivial to a Harvard graduate with a Ph.D. in Letters, but to a guy who had to be held back in the third grade to learn the language and only got a "B" in Miss Hansen's Liberty High English class, it was a victory I still savor.

Cats and Dogs

Aoooo-gah! Aoooo-gah! An ear-shattering Klaxon horn erupted and a coded message blared from hidden loudspeakers. Quickly, everyone in the SAC underground command post sprang into action and the IMAX-high projection screen changed from the SAC shield to a worldwide display depicting the locations of the bomber fleet, missile silos, and attack submarines. The scene was overwhelming, and my thought was, we must be going to war.

The colonel in charge saw my mouth hanging open and motioned to one of the big, brown, over-stuffed chairs at the commanders' table. "Want to see something Hank? Have a seat," he said. I had hardly settled down when up came a live picture of two missiles lifting off from Vandenberg AFB, California. Their contrails disappeared into infinity, and a disembodied voice over a loudspeaker tracked the dummy warheads as they over-flew Hawaii and impacted Kwajalein. I had just witnessed the birth of a new age of intercontinental warfare. At the time, ground-to-air missiles were viewed as the death knell for the future of bomber aircraft. Time proved otherwise. However, the new weapons severely complicated the war planners' task of timing the arrival of missiles and bombers, with their vastly different speeds, over a target area and generated new requirements for deployment of SAC's bombers to overseas locations.

John Kelly said to me, "Hank, Major Pete Hillman is being reassigned to us from the B-58 Operational Engineering Section at Carswell. You'll be his supervisor, but on the technical level he'll report to Bill Hayes. That's because Pete's an aeronautical engineer and we're not, so we can't supervise his professional performance. Pete will be responsible for all the 'cats and dogs'—except the TFX. It will be added to your responsibilities." (The last B-58 came off the production line in March 1962, and was followed by an airframe dubbed the "TFX" (Tactical Fighter Experimental) and later the F-111. Secretary of Defense Robert McNamara envisioned the F-111 as an all-service fighter. However, General Power accurately predicted that both the Tactical Air Command (TAC) and the Navy would reject it and SAC would inherit it by default.)

I laughed, "John, cats and dogs? What's that?"

"The B-36 atomic propulsion test, North American's B-70 Valkyrie, the U-2s, and the SR-71 project," he answered.

I said, "There go my weekend trips to Salina."

"Why don't you marry Millie and quit fooling around? You keep it up and you're going to lose her. Alma really likes her and she's never wrong about these things."

"I'm thinking about it," I said.

People who knew him, described Pete as mild-mannered, partially balding, average height, and all Texan. Upon meeting him, my assessment leaned more toward "Pete knows a lot about how airplanes fly but is as naive about staff work as I once was." Soon after Pete arrived, General Vinson came into the office for an Action Item briefing on his cats and dogs. Pete circumvented mentioning a highly classified detail on one of the projects and Iron Mike asked why. Pete replied, "Sir, your security clearance doesn't allow you to access that level of information."

Vinson lunged from the chair, loomed over Pete and using his cigar to punctuate every word, scowled, "Major, I'm cleared to know everything you know and don't you ever forget it. If you ever say that to me again, I'll throw you out the window." Pete didn't know whether to scratch his watch or wind his butt. He sidled away from the third story window, assumed the stance of a relay runner awaiting the baton, and in a warbled voice disclosed the data.

In September 1962, the Cuban Missile Crisis came along and overnight the CINC placed the B-58 fleet on SAC alert. Shortly thereafter, our cute little secretary, Rose, called out over her shoulder, "Hank, report to General Power's office on the double." All the movers and shakers were already there when I arrived. Among them were General Vinson, Major General Keith Compton (director of operations), Major General Bill Crumm (director of operational plans), and several others.

General Power said, "I don't like having to ask TAC for anything that we can provide ourselves. Within ninety days I want us to have a photo-reconnaissance capability installed in a dozen or so B-58s. Let's get it done." He dismissed everyone but General Vinson and me, and said, "Hank, I think a vertically-mounted KA-56 camera will fit in the nose cone of an

MB-1 bomb pod. Photo interpretation and measurements over the target will be more precise with the camera on that axis rather than if mounted on a 45-degree angle. Take a look at it with the Intelligence people." I said, "Yes, Sir." As we were leaving the command section, General Vinson said, "Take care of it," and walked away. (The panoramic camera provided horizon-to-horizon coverage with a capability for high-resolution photography of tiny objects from an altitude of 500 feet at speeds approaching Mach 1. The camera did not have a shutter. Instead, the system froze the image on the film by driving it at the correct speed to synchronize with the image motion. Coincidentally, we also established requirements to enlarge the film's temperature parameters and for thinner film to increase the camera's capacity.)

A warrant officer in an obscure office in the Pentagon dubbed the program a "Big Safari" Project and funded it on the spot. That done, I rounded up Colonel Frank Petersen, an Intelligence officer, and we departed for Carswell. Along the way, I reiterated the general's comments regarding the camera type and its positioning but Frank never said a word. The General Dynamics engineers briefed us on the mechanical problems associated with the installation and as the meeting was nearing conclusion, Frank said, "We want the camera installed on a 45-degree angle." Surprised, I asked him to join me outside where I repeated General Power's instructions. Without a word, Frank returned to the meeting. The session ended and I waited until Frank went off somewhere before persuading the engineers to produce plans with the camera mounted in both positions

A month later, General Power asked for a progress report on the project. I put together a briefing and invited Frank to review it but he was too busy. The same cast of high-ranking officers attended this meeting. All went well until I displayed the chart that depicted the camera mounted on a 45-degree angle. I was listing the advantages of this position when in a stern voice General Power said, "Hank, those were not my instructions."

"General Power," I replied, "that's the way the Intelligence people say they want it." From behind a large globe-map that trademarked the office, Petersen was vigorously nodding his head. This was in violation of a cardinal rule that Iron Mike taught me: never to visibly agree or disagree with a briefer.

General Power's face reddened, he reached for a sheaf of papers, flung them toward Petersen and said, "You think you're so damn smart? Here, read this. Those gangsters (he always called the Russians gangsters) are way ahead of you!" The papers scattered on the floor in front of the globe and Petersen hesitated to retrieve them. The general's face got redder and he shouted, "Pick them up, goddamn it! Pick them up, get out of here and read them."

Big drops of sweat were trickling down the back of my legs as Petersen gathered the papers and headed for the door. Quickly, I flipped to the chart with the camera on a vertical axis. General Power saw it, took a big puff of his cigar and leaned back. When I finished, he asked me to wait. Everyone cleared the room except Captain Jerome F. "Jerry" O'Malley, the aide-de-camp to Vice CINC General Hunter Harris. General Power twiddled his ring and while examining it closely said, "Hank, I understand that Colonel Petersen hasn't done much to help you?" Not knowing what to say, I hesitated. He cast a sly look at Jerry and added, "I'll bet he improves." Jerry's cheeks puffed out and his face turned bright red as he struggled to keep from laughing aloud. Jerry had reported what I had said to him in confidence. (Jerry went on to become a four-star general. Tragically, in 1985 while still on active duty, he and Mrs. O'Malley died in the crash of a T-39 Saberliner.)

* * * *

The General Dynamics project manager and I were standing by the Carswell runway when the first modified B-58 took off to test the camera system. The pilot flew east, made a 180-degree turn, and activated the camera. As he neared Carswell, on his way to a high-resolution target in New Mexico, my partner placed a cardboard matchbook on the hood of our GI station wagon. I returned to Omaha immediately and the following day, a classified photo arrived. Clearly visible on the matchbook were the words, "Close Cover Before Striking." I sent it to General Power.

Thirty days later, this secret capability was declassified. On Good Friday of 1964, the most violent earthquake to ever hit North America badly damaged Anchorage, Alaska. Near Valdez, a massive tsunami had hardly subsided when the Pentagon dispatched two B-58s to photograph the damage. Fortunately, the camera systems worked as predicted and within a week, the images appeared on the cover of *Life* magazine.

* * * *

John Kelly called me on the phone. "Hank," he said, "go down and get on General Power's VC-97. The B-58 troops are unhappy and he's going down to Carswell to speak to them." On my way to the plane I worried that the crews might be upset by something I had done, or worse yet, not done. The fireguard was already in position for "start engines" when I boarded the plane. In the cabin, other officers with B-58 responsibilities were speculating about reasons for the meeting.

The air crews were in the base theater when we arrived. MP's locked the doors and the session began. The men were upset because our operations planners had changed their combat mission profiles. In the future, B-58s would no longer take off from the States and fly the entire mission at altitude. The new plan called for them to letdown as they neared their targets and attack from 500 feet at 700 miles an hour. The change severely compromised the already limited range of the B-58s and the crews were questioning the order. One intrepid spokesman said, "We can outperform anything in the air. The Russian fighters might catch-up but they can't keep-up. With our speed, small size, and minimal radar reflectivity, the Russian fighters will have a hell of a time finding us, let alone attacking. Furthermore, we don't like a bunch of headquarters 'weenies' changing our plans without consulting us first."

General Power let them rant and rave for a while then stood up and said, "The most significant changes in air power since the Wright brothers are the jet engine, air refueling, and ground-to-air missiles. In the past you have depended on high speed and advanced electronics to accomplish your mission. But the Soviets have improved their high altitude defense systems and at Mach 2 it's impossible to evade the new SAMs (Soviet Air Missiles). SAMs don't chase B-58s; they come up and meet them. You must now rely on stealth and low-level penetration under their radar nets to evade this new and constantly evolving threat. The plans will not be changed." The meeting ended and for all intent and purposes so did the B-58's abbreviated role as a first-line SAC weapon system. Almost immediately pilots began applying for entry into the SR-71 program, which was still very tightly under wraps.

Salud, Dinero Y Amor (Health, Money, Love)

The B-58s were too "short-legged" to be stationed in the States and perform their new low-altitude mission profiles over the vast expanse that is Eastern Europe. To keep them a viable weapon system until the B-1 bomber came aboard, elements of the Hustler strike force would have to be stationed in Europe.

A two-star general at Barksdale AFB, Louisiana, assembled a team to go evaluate two air bases in Spain, Torrejon near Madrid and Zaragoza, 100 miles east. Major Jack Thompson, an operations officer, and I went along. Equipment and modifications required for B-58 operations at the two bases were developed, first at Torrejon then Zaragoza. On the eve of our return to Torrejon and return to the States, the Spanish base commander honored us with a farewell dinner. We arrived to find a long table perfectly set with shimmering silverware, assorted wines, and an elaborate centerpiece. Only one detail had been overlooked. Without an interpreter, conversation between our general and the Spanish general ranged somewhere between sign language and lip reading. No one asked if I spoke Spanish and ever cautious in that area, I did not volunteer.

El General opened the affair with a toast. He lifted a wineglass high and said, *"Bienvenidos a nuestro lindo paiz, la gran Espana. Espero que todo les fue bien en su visita, y que tengan un buen vuelo de regreso a Los Estados Unidos."* Everyone took a sip and he sat down. An awkward silence followed and to fill the void I stood up and said, *"Muchas gracias mi general, y a usted le deseamos, salud, dinero, y amor, y mucho tiempo para gastarlos."* In reply to his toast, "Welcome to grand Spain. I trust that all went well during your visit and that you will have a safe flight back to the United States," I offered an old Mexican toast: "Thank you general and we wish you health, money, love, and a long life to enjoy them." Given the circumstances, it may not have been the most appropriate toast, but it was all that came to mind. My place immediately improved from the far end of the table to a hastily arranged setting between the two generals. As we were leaving the affair our general whispered, "Thanks for bailing me out, Hank. Next time we attend one of these things, you sit where I was and I'll go down where you were."

We returned to Torrejon. Take off for the Azores had been set for 0900 the following morning so Jack and I hired a driver to show us Madrid. Our first stop was La Plaza de Espana where I paid my respects to the monument of the author Miguel de Cervantes. We then criss-crossed the city seeing the sights until sunset, the hour for *tapas* (Spanish appetizers). The guide dropped us off at what he said was the *numero uno* Castilian restaurant, El San Fermin. In the lobby, a hostess proudly pointed out Manolete and other heroes from among a mass of bullfight photos plastered on the walls, then led us to a large central patio.

The area was crowded with Andalusian horse aficionados. The men were in tight, gray-striped, flannel pants with red sashes at the waist and wide-brimmed black Cordovan hats set at a rakish angle. The women had slicked-back hair, bright lipstick, shoulder-duster earrings, and flamenco dresses. Dryly, Jack said, "They look like a TGIF (Thank God, It's Friday) Happy Hour crowd on Halloween night. I'm going to see what else is going on in this dump." He left and I made a beeline to a tiled table loaded with *tapas* and sliced *jamon serrano*, a tasty cured ham. At the bar, I asked the bartender to recommend a good local wine. In response, he set up an impromptu wine tasting. A crowd gathered, some to offer recommendations and others to marvel at the Americano's Spanish.

By midnight, they had me clapping hands and clicking my heels to fast strumming guitars. A couple was trying to teach me the "La Sevillana" when a waiter invited me off the floor and said, "Senor, please come with me. Your friend is making a problem." He led me to a room where Jack and four women were at a table. Empty champagne bottles were everywhere along with the remains of a *tapa* feast. From the waiters, I determined that despite a posted price list, Jack was aggressively arguing that he was being overcharged.

I good-naturedly offered to pay the tab to avoid a problem but Jack snapped, "Stay out of my business," and emphasized "my business" by draining his glass dry. The women disappeared and tempers were running short. I got close to Jack and whispered, "Jack, we're about to get in trouble here. You have one more chance. Either you pay or I'll pay, but either way, I'm leaving." He refused on both counts, so I left.

The next morning everyone but Jack was aboard the plane waiting for the general to join us. At the last minute, an unmarked car appeared at the foot of the stairs and two huge *Guardias Civiles* (Spanish police) in three-cornered hats got out. They yanked Jack out from the back seat, shoved him toward the plane, and drove away. Drunk and disheveled, Jack staggered aboard in a sour cloud of alcohol. The flight engineer helped him to the rear of the cabin, buckled him into a seat, and instructed him to stay there. Upon landing at Barksdale, a legal officer recorded my account of the incident and within days, Jack departed the headquarters for places unknown.

* * * *

By late 1963, the record setting days of the two B-58 wings were over. They went on alert and began deploying to Zaragoza, Spain, and later to England, Guam, and Okinawa. This not withstanding, an endless flow of operational and maintenance problems continued to plague the fleet. Not the least among them was higher than anticipated modification, maintenance,

December 8, 1964; Bunker Hill AFB, Indiana. A landing gear collapsed during taxi. Pilot, Capt. Leary J. Johnson, and Defensive Systems Officer, Capt. Roger L. Hall, survived the ensuing fire. Navigator Bombardier, Capt. Manuel Cervantes, Jr. (no relation to author) ejected in his encapsulated seat. The capsule parachute did not have time to fully open, and he perished

and support costs, and a high accident rate. Of the 116 aircraft built, 26 were destroyed; several during the test and evaluation phase, some due to loss of control in flight, landing accidents, and various other reasons.

By now my duties had enabled me to know most of the heavy-hitters in SAC headquarters, including the officers who paraded through the Vice CINC's chair. There was General John McConnell with his dry humor and grandfatherly twang of his suspenders when he made a point; General Joe Nazzaro, who also appreciated a well-turned ankle; and of course General Hunter Harris.

I would like to believe that those fine men and others I worked with considered me a good officer. However, Millie's beauty may have contributed more toward my status than I care to admit. Conversations stopped and heads turned when she entered a room. All too often colonels and generals aloof elsewhere, became my arm-over-the-shoulder pals in her presence.

Shove in Your Clutch

A call summoned me to Major General A. J. Beck's office. He replaced Iron Mike who had been promoted and sent to the Pentagon. Instinctively I knew the subject of the meeting; I was approaching twenty-two years in the Air Force and four years at headquarters. The general said, "Hank, as you know we have no professional headquarters types in SAC. Four years is the maximum any of us can stay in the building before we must return to a field unit for at least two years. You're nearing the four-year limit. Have you given any thought as to what you would like to do next?"

"Not really, sir."

"Well, that doesn't surprise me. Time has a habit of creeping up on all of us. I asked Personnel to look into your options. At this point, it looks like you can 'shove in your clutch' and retire. Or you can go to either B-58 unit as deputy chief of maintenance."

The 43rd Bomb Wing was still at Fort Worth, Texas, while the 305th had relocated to Little Rock, Arkansas. Both were nice towns but with little to offer me. More significantly, Air Force Headquarters had issued an order grounding field grade officers not in full-time flying jobs. We would continue to receive flying pay, but not have to fly to get it. That sealed the decision: May 1, 1965, would be my retirement date.

General Crumm called me to his office, "What's this I hear about you retiring, Hank?"

"Yes, Sir, I've got four months to go."

"I suppose you'll go back out to Hollywood and take up where you left off when we were at March Field."

"Well, in a way, yes. I'm thinking of living in Playa del Rey and trying to get on with one of the airlines."

He laughed, "I know why you're going there. That's where they have a beach colony called 'The Jungle,' and it's chock-full of airline stewardesses."

"I didn't know about that. But I'm thinking about asking Millie to marry me."

"You should have done that long ago. Millie's a beautiful girl and a fine lady. Don't press your luck. Whenever Tenney sees you two together, she wonders how much longer Millie will put up with your mischief. Invite us to the wedding, but forget the airlines, you don't need that. I have a friend at the McDonnell Douglas plant at Long Beach whose looking for guys like you. Give me a resume of your flying experience and I'll see what I can do."

"Thanks, General Crumm. That would be great."

(General Crumm got me the job-offer. Two years later, as Commander of SAC's 3rd Air Division, he was leading a flight of B-52s to a night target in Viet Nam when two bombers ran together. His name is sculpted in stone at the entrance to Hawaii's Punch Bowl Cemetery.)

A few days later a friend from our days in the 100th, Colonel Mark Wilson, called from his flight scheduling office. "Hey ole' buddy, I've got a T-bird ready to fly if you want it. Today's the last day you can take one up cause tomorrow we'll start closing out your Form 5 flight records."

"Thanks, Mark," I said, "but I can't come down till after work. Is it OK if I take it up at six?"

"Well, you're stretching it. But because it's you, we'll make an exception."

"Thanks, pal."

Flying a jet fighter is more fun than any human being should be allowed to have. The power, maneuverability, and freedom it offers transcend that inherent in all other types of ground, water, air, or stratospheric vehicles. Fighter pilots are not restricted to making dizzying circles as racecars do at Indy and motorcycles do on Motocross tracks. Nor must they hold to a black line as they do at Bonneville, find smooth water as they do in speed boats, or wait for someone to "light the candle" as in space capsules. A fighter pilot is king in the world of locomotion and has the freedom of a bird. He can fly upright or inverted, climb, dive, turn, roll, loop, buzz, or go in any direction in-between. It's a big sky and freeways, turnpikes, car lanes, stoplights, road signs, speed bumps, and cops don't exist. The pilot is the master of his universe and the exhilaration is incomparable.

I climbed to altitude, leveled-off, leaned back, and admired my surroundings. Off to the west the sky was a vast panorama of purple and reds, while down below, city lights were blooming like white flowers on a black landscape. Twilight was always my favorite time to fly.

Mindful that this would be my last flight as an Air Force pilot, I had but one purpose, to imprint my mind and body with the gut-wrenching sensations of high G-forces. The awesome power of gravity is indescribable to anyone who has not experienced it. A roller coaster ride is about as close as one can come but that doesn't touch it. Sustained high-Gs can force a pilot to his limits of consciousness, induce tunnel vision, punch his helmeted head into his body, convert his shoulders into barbells, hunch his back under the weight of a back-pack parachute, painfully press his butt into the seat, and make sweat gush from every pore like water from a faucet.

I went into a steep dive and held it past the airspeed red line. When the controls began to shiver and the wing-tip tanks fluttered, I pulled up into a loop then repeated it. Half way into the third one, I retarded the throttle, allowed the bird to stop flying and kicked it into an inverted spin. The engine quit and the spin wound up. I restarted, pulled out hard, and did it again. Any maneuver that came to mind I did or tried to do—Chandelles, Immelmanns, Split-Ss, Cuban Eights-8s, and Clover Leafs.

All the red low-fuel lights were glowing as I coasted home to the 1,001st landing of my career. I taxied in. The hour was late and everyone had gone home, I was glad. Ever so slowly, I reluctantly stop-cocked the throttle. The engine wound down and from force of habit, I patted the instrument panel and thanked her for a good ride. But a gesture that had evolved into a routine, now seemed empty and phony. I was a used-to-be-lover who had been given an unemotional last ride for old time's sake. I could almost feel her coyly peeking over my shoulder looking for a young buck to replace me. All that remained were the embarrassing formalities of parting. I chocked the wheels, shut the canopy, then stood back and tearfully admired her sleek lines. The moment defined my conscious retirement from the Air Force.

* * * *

Except for my infrequent flights to Salina, Millie had all but worn out a four-door Chevy making weekly trips to Omaha. One day she called and said, "I won't be coming up for a while. My mother's not feeling well and I'm going to move back home until she gets better."

"Gosh, I'm sorry to hear that honey," I said. "Is there anything I can do to help?"

"No," she replied. "I've already quit my job and my brother is going to help me move. I'll call you when I get to Cheyenne, OK?"

"Fine, I'll miss you. I hope she feels better soon and please don't hesitate to call if I can be of help."

All in one breath she said, "Gotta go goodbye," and hung up.

I waited until Millie settled in, then arranged a long weekend for us in Las Vegas. She had not been there and I hoped the visit would help convince her to move with me to Los Angeles. I caught a United flight, she came aboard in Cheyenne, and we were off. In Vegas, I got a rental car and on our way to the Tropicana Hotel, drove the length of the Strip then said, "Honey, why don't we plan to get away together at least once a month. We can come here or go anywhere else you might want to go. Don't you think it would be fun?" She nodded, blinked, and continued looking out the window.

The next morning I awoke to find Millie quietly donning her nightie. "Hey, not yet," I fussed, and began romping around the room after her. She was fending me off from behind a chair when I stopped, held up my hands and said, "Don't move honey. You look terrific." Behind her, defused desert sunlight was streaming in through the window, accentuating her hair, exquisite facial structure, and the soft curvatures of her body. I had never seen her look so beautiful.

"Let me take your picture," I said. She ran by me like a scared rabbit, jumped into the bed, covered herself with the sheet, and demanded, "Put the camera away. I won't move until you put it away." I complied but her refusal troubled me. She had often posed for me in bathing suits as tight as cling wrap. Why the problem now? We had a great time, but I deferred asking the Los Angeles question.

Our plane was on the approach for landing at Cheyenne when Millie said, "There's something I need to tell you."

I looked up from a magazine and said, "Sure honey, what is it?"

"I'm not going to see you anymore. I'm thinking of marrying a guy who's stationed at Fort Warren."

Our eyes locked and in a strained voice I said, "I knew something was wrong when you wouldn't let me take the picture. Don't even think of it honey. I'm going to retire in May and McDonnell-Douglas offered me a job testing fighters in Long Beach. We'll have a great time. I plan for us to live by the water. Wouldn't you like that?"

Millie heaved a sigh and leaned toward me, "You just don't get it do you? I don't want to shack-up with you on the beach. I want to get married."

"All right then, we'll get married. I was going to ask you in Vegas until that happened. Marry me."

Her eyes welled with tears, "Damn you. Why are you asking me now? Everybody said you wouldn't marry me. I've wasted four years of my life. Four years and you haven't mentioned marriage one time. Not once! I've found a guy who loves me and I'm going to marry him."

Unable to find words to change her mind, I could only beg, "I love you with all my heart honey, please don't do that."

She looked away and whispered, "Keep your voice down, people are looking."

A kaleidoscope of memories flashed through my mind; my hazy forecasts when others asked, "When are you two going to do it?" Her joy when she decorated the house. How she snuggled close when other men approached us. The soft pulse and throb of her body when she slept and her animal earthiness when we made love. I took her hand to plead but she pulled away, "No, let go. I know you know a lot of women, you won't miss me one bit." She looked out the window. I wanted to hold her close and ask for forgiveness but I knew that she had already withdrawn mentally and physically. She had inherited a stubborn streak from her Puerto Rican mother and once her mind was made up, it was useless to argue. She turned back, "There's another thing. Tell all those colonels and generals you think are such good friends of yours to stop calling me at all hours of the day and night. Some friends."

I swallowed hard, only one came to mind, Iron Mike. We didn't say more but the cloud of friction and resentment enveloped us until the plane shuddered to a stop at the gate. Aware that my time was fast disappearing, I gathered my things and followed her out. At the terminal door, I held it closed and groaned, "Millie, please, please don't go, honey. I'll do anything you say."

"Stop begging, it's not like you. You knew this day would come."

In the baggage area, I picked out her suitcase from the carousel and held it back. But with a determined tug, she yanked it away, patted my cheek, gave me a butterfly kiss, and disappeared into the departing crowd. I collapsed into a chair and spent the next three hours fantasizing that at any moment she would be back pleading to continue where we'd left off. The terminal had all but emptied when a ticket agent came by and reminded me that the last plane to Omaha was about to depart.

With Millie gone, the job and my late-night games lost their attraction. Everyone in the office knew my problem. Occasionally an outsider would come by and ask, "Hey Hank, where's Millie? We haven't seen her lately." I'd turn away. No one likes to see a grown man cry.

I had not noticed it before, but at home her fragrance was everywhere. One night I walked in and was so sure that she'd come back that I called out her name, "Millie, Millie honey, where are you? Come out here." Cold, dead silence. A bowling ball of hurt and pain dropped to the pit of my stomach and I cried. The next morning, I arranged for a moving company to pack everything she had bought for the house and deliver it to her address in Cheyenne. If she refused it, they were to drop the load at the nearest Salvation Army outlet. I saved my favorite photograph of her and moved to the base. A small crowd attended my retirement ceremony. I returned to my desk, worked until five, then went to the officers club for my farewell dinner. I left the dinner early; why beat a dead horse?

* * * *

Evening, May 1st, 1965: A long day of driving had taken me across Kansas and Oklahoma. In the distance shone the outpost lights of Amarillo, Texas. I planned to stay there overnight, have a weekend in Las Vegas, then go on to Long Beach for the job interview.

The time had come to end the flashback into my life. Only one facet remained unexplored, the reason for my being a forty-one-year-old bachelor. It was insecurity brought about by the Great Depression, the absence of my biological father, an emotionally distant stepfather, the loss of Mother to illness, and of Gus' going to war. The feeling of abandonment cast me adrift and the military became my home. No other alliance guaranteed me so solid an anchor. The emotional lock-down also induced the painful separations from Mary, Millie, Nancy, and one other woman I cherished, Gayle. In return, I avoided the prospect of transmitting a genetic disorder to an offspring, had an unfettered military career, and evaded the specter of Father's never-ending struggle to pay the rent, buy a tank of gas, a bag of groceries, or another pair of shoes.

Epilogue

The B-58 fleet closely followed me into retirement. Despite their spectacular record-breaking entry into SAC in 1960, on December 8, 1965, seven months after I retired, Secretary of Defense Robert McNamara announced the phaseout of the B-58s. (Although the two events may seem related, they were completely coincidental.) In November 1969, the command began sending Hustlers to the bone-yard. By January 1970, every one of the truly magnificent aircraft were gone. Their fate was sealed when auditors found that the costs associated with maintaining and operating the two B-58 wings equaled that of six B-52 wings. Today, only eight B-58s remain on display in museums and military bases.

At Nellis AFB, a doctor hospitalized me for a couple of days due to a severe case of Menieres disease—vertigo. The cause was unknown but thought to result from stress. He warned against taking the flight test job at McDonnell-Douglas, at least for the time being. Given that the offer was tendered based on friendship, I canceled the interview.

I settled in Marina del Rey, California. Every morning, driven by habit, I bolted from the bed ready to go to work, except there was no place to go. After years of slavery to deadlines and timetables, I had nothing to do but go to the clubhouse at nearby Westchester golf course and drink dispenser coffee until the course opened. The links were not well lit for evening play and being the first off the tee, it was not unusual to find assorted clubs and balls, as well as women's underwear in poorly lighted areas of the course.

Conveying misplaced falsies and two-way stretch panties to the Lost & Found desk, however, hardly qualified as "responsibility," and I went into a yearlong post-military funk.

Nancy Sadler left the service to join me, but when I failed to exhibit traces of recovery, she moved on to a successful career in medical research. Her departure was my wake-up call. I qualified for a commercial flying license and got a job at Northrop writing the pilot flight handbook for the F-5 Freedom Fighter.

After having worked for so many years on the other side of the fence, I felt uncomfortable in the contractor environment; but a chance meeting with my old friend, Colonel Zeke Summers, resolved the problem. Zeke was base commander at Los Angeles AFB, home of the Space and Missile Systems Organization (SAMSO), and he was in dire need of someone to manage its large, long-neglected officers club. I took the job. That eventually led to the position of Director of Policy and Plans in the Los Angeles Area Office of the Defense Contract Administration Service. Forty-one years after entering the Army, I retired from the Defense Department. The next day, Los Angeles Mayor Tom Bradley invited me to serve him as a staff advisor. To this day, I continue to head personnel boards for the city.

1976, Pittsburg, California. With siblings and stepfather at a family gathering. (L–R) Henry, Steve, Evelyn, Gus, Father, Jennie, Aurora, and Ruben

Away from the desk, I am a nationally-rated U.S.A. Track & Field official (I officiated in the 1984 Los Angeles Olympic Games), work with the California Special Olympics, give motivational talks at schools, and am a member of the Los Angeles Single Ski Club. Some say that I cannot stop trying to prove myself worthy of being called an American, they may be right. Perhaps this is also why I have written this book; to help find myself.

* * * *

Better medicines enabled Mother to spend increasingly longer periods at home. However, our joy was short lived, for in 1968 she died under the wheels of a speeding auto. Losing her caused the most intense pain I have suffered and, not having her share a part of my success, my greatest disappointment. Twenty years later, almost to the day, Father passed away from an acute case of shingles. As I held his pain-wracked body in my arms on our last night together, he kissed me and whispered, *"Te voy a dejar mijo. Voy a ver a mi mama."* (I am going to leave you my son. I'm going to see my mother.) At long last he had uttered the words I yearned to hear him say, "My son."